# Testing Extreme
# Programming

Ke███████s Advisor

Extreme ███amming, familiarly known as XP, is a discipline of business and software development that focuses both parties on common, reachable goals. XP teams produce quality software at a sustainable pace. The practices that make up "book" XP are chosen for their dependence on human creativity and acceptance of human frailty.

Although XP is often presented as a list of practices, XP is not a finish line. You don't get better and better grades at doing XP until you finally receive the coveted gold star. XP is a starting line. It asks the question, "How little can we do and still build great software?"

The beginning of the answer is that, if we want to leave software development uncluttered, we must be prepared to completely embrace the few practices we adopt. Half measures leave problems unsolved to be addressed by further half measures. Eventually you are surrounded by so many half measures that you can no longer see that the heart of the value programmers create comes from programming.

I say, "The beginning of the answer …" because there is no final answer. The authors in the XP Series have been that and done there, and returned to tell their story. The books in this series are the signposts they have planted along the way: "Here lie dragons," "Scenic drive next 15 km," "Slippery when wet."

Excuse me, I gotta go program.

## Titles in the Series

For more information, check out the series Web site at http://www.awprofessional.com/series/XP/

# Testing Extreme Programming

## Lisa Crispin
## Tip House

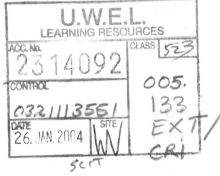
✦✦ Addison-Wesley

Boston • San Francisco • New York • Toronto • Montreal
London • Munich • Paris • Madrid
Capetown • Sydney • Tokyo • Singapore • Mexico City

The publisher offers discounts on this book when ordered in quantity for special sales. For more information, please contact:

U.S. Corporate and Government Sales
(800) 382-3419
corpsales@pearsontechgroup.com

For sales outside of the U.S., please contact:

International Sales
(317) 581-3793
international@pearsontechgroup.com

Visit Addison-Wesley on the Web at www.awprofessional.com

*Library of Congress Cataloging-in-Publication Data*

Crispin, Lisa.
    Testing Extreme Programming / Lisa Crispin, Tip House.
        p. cm.
    Includes bibliographical references and index.
    ISBN 0-321-11355-1 (alk. paper)
    1. Computer software—Development.   2. Extreme programming.   3. Computer software—testing.   I. House, Tip.   II. Title.

QA76.76.D47  C75  2003
005.1'1—dc21

                                                                    2002026083

ISBN 0-321-11355-1
Text printed on recycled paper
1 2 3 4 5 6 7 8 9 10—MA—0605040302
First printing, October 2002

*To my husband, Bob, light of my life*
—Lisa

*To my wife, Barbara, and my children:*
*Christopher, Sarah, and Joshua*

*And to Scott Alexander—I miss you, buddy*
—Tip

# Contents

- - - - - - - - - - - - - - - - - - - - - - - - - - - - - - - - - - - - - - - - - - - - - - - - - -

# Foreword

As I see it, I have two jobs to do in this foreword. The first is to persuade you that it's worth your time to keep reading this book. The second is to place the book in context—what does it say about the world of testing and about how that world is changing?

My first job is easy. The reason is that the book you're holding is both skimmable and eloquent. Stop reading this foreword. Go to Part II. Browse some chapters. Do you see tidbits you can put to immediate, practical use on an XP or agile project? That's a sign Lisa and Tip are writing from experience. Do the chapters seem to hang together into a coherent testing strategy? That's a sign they've thought about their experience. Is the tone flexible, avoiding dogmatism? That's a sign that you'll readily be able to adapt what you read to your local circumstances. These are the things that make the book worth reading. Don't believe me; check for yourself.

The second job is harder. How does this book fit in? As I write (May 2002), the world of testing seems stuck. We're all supposed to know certain fixed concepts: what the purpose of testing is, what the relationship of testers to programmers should be, what test planning means. When presented with a new project, it seems we're intended to take those concepts as givens, follow some methodology, and fill in the blanks through a process of top-down, stepwise refinement.

But that's not really what happens, at least not on good projects. The tester comes to a project equipped with a hodgepodge of resources: concepts, attitudes, habits, tools, and skills—some complementary, some contradictory. She begins by modeling her new situation after one she's experienced before. She applies her habits and skills. She keeps what works and changes what proves awkward. She fluidly adapts any of her resources to the situation. In her project, testing goes through what Andrew Pickering calls "the mangle of practice" (in his book of the same name).

All this is hidden, because it's disreputable in at least two ways. First, everything is up for grabs, including those seemingly fixed concepts we're all supposed to know. The practice of testing, when applied in specific contexts, changes the purpose of testing, the relations of people, what test planning means. There's precious little solid ground to stand on. Second, the trivial can be as important as the lofty. Knowing how to use 3 x 5 cards well may matter more than knowing test design techniques. Unthinking work habits may have more effect than reasoned decisions.

We need to make the mangle respectable. It's harmful when people feel vaguely ashamed of doing what has to be done. It's even worse when they don't do it because they think they must follow the rules to be "professional."

And *that* marks this book's significance beyond simply (!) helping XP testers. In it, you can see the traces of two people interactively adapting their practice of testing to a new sort of project, arriving at last at a point of stability: something that works well enough that they can gift it to others. It's an inspiring example. I mean that literally, in that I hope it inspires you to model your testing after it, run that model through the mangle of practice, and report back to us, saying, "Here. Here's what I do. Here's what I've seen. Here's what works for me. Try it."

Brian Marick
Champaign, Illinois
May 2002

# Preface

This is a book about being a tester on an Extreme Programming (XP) team. It plugs a gap in the currently available XP materials by defining how an XP tester can contribute to the project, including what testers should do, when they should do it, and how they should do it. We wrote it because we think XP is a better way to develop software and that more teams should use it. We believe an acknowledged place in XP teams for testing and quality assurance will help bring that about.

Our goals in this book are to

- ✧ Convince current XP practitioners that a tester has a valid role on the team
- ✧ Convince testing and quality assurance professionals that XP offers solutions to some of their worst problems
- ✧ Convince both groups that testers are needed just as much in an XP project as in a traditional development project
- ✧ Provide enough detail and practical example to allow you to either perform the XP tester role yourself or work productively with a tester on your team, whether you're an XP newbie or veteran, tester, programmer, guide, customer, or manager

We hope that if you're not currently using XP, you can influence your organization to try it. Even if your team uses some other process for software development, we think you can apply "extreme testing" practices to add value.

Because not everyone will be familiar with XP, we provide an overview of the basic concepts in the introduction and describe a few aspects in more detail as necessary throughout the text. But this will be a bare-bones summary, at best. We list several excellent books on the subject in the bibliography, and a wealth of information is available on the Web.

The book is divided into three major sections:

## Part I: The XP Tester Role

This is where we define what we think the tester role is (and is not), how a project will benefit from it, what's in it for the tester, and generally why XP needs a tester role.

## Part II: Test Drive through an XP Project

Here we navigate an XP project step by step and suggest what goals to shoot for, which activities to engage in, and helpful techniques to try as a tester on an XP project.

## Part III: Road Hazard Survival Kit

Finally, we provide some resources to help you cope when the real world doesn't conform to the ideal XP project: large projects, for instance, where an XP team is embedded in a larger, non-XP effort or when critical XP practices are modified or omitted.

We've tried to keep things as practical as possible and have provided real-life examples. We've also included exercises, so you can try the ideas out for yourself. The exercises are built around an XP project to develop a simple Web-based tracking application. We provide portions of the application at various stages for you to practice on.

We think you'll find this book helpful if you're already a member of an XP team, if you're a testing/quality assurance professional, or if you're in any software development role and are considering XP.

Lisa Crispin
Tip House
June 2002

# Acknowledgments

## Lisa

First of all, thanks for the people who got me into Extreme Programming to begin with, my first terrific XP team, at Tensegrent: John Sims, Steve Graese, Kevin Blankenship, Steve Strobel, Steve Collins, Natraj Kini, Peter Gumeson, Jason Kay, Bryan Uegawachi, John VanSant, Russ Heithoff, and Brock Norvell

Thanks to Kent Beck, Ron Jeffries, and Brian Marick, who encouraged me when I had the idea to write this book, helped us get started on it, and who (in the case of Ron and Kent) have never given up in trying to get me to really "get" XP. I never met a nicer, more accessible and helpful bunch of "gurus" than the Extremos, including Bob Martin, Ward Cunningham, and many others.

Gigantic thanks to the reviewers of our book, all through its life cycle, for their feedback and especially for their support and encouragement. Many of you are quoted or paraphrased in this book. Ron Jeffries, our muse, thank you for all the time and effort—I hope you think it paid off. Mike Clark and Janet Gregory, I didn't even know you when you started reviewing the early drafts, yet you spent so much time and gave us such great feedback and real-world examples, which we naturally stole for the book. Special thanks also to reviewers Rick Craig, David Gelperin, and Ron, and to Brian Marick, who wasn't an official reviewer but read both early and late drafts and gave invaluable input.

A thousand thanks as well to all who read early drafts and contributed to shaping the book: Bill Wake, Andy Tinkham, Anko Tijman, Willem van den

Ende, Darryl Fortunato, Marcus Makaiwi, Lynne Christensen, Jef Knutson, and all those I've forgotten to name. To all the folks posting on the agile-testing mailing list who made me think, such as Cem Kaner, Bret Pettichord, Stefan Steurs, and many others, your challenges and ideas made this a better book.

Thanks to my XP team coworkers, from whom I learned so much, at BoldTech Systems. My experiences there provided many of the helpful examples in this book.

Mike Hendrickson and Ross Venables of Addison-Wesley, I still can't believe you wanted to publish this book—thanks for this wonderful opportunity and your infinite patience.

Deborah Krinitzsky, thanks for your help with the road trip, thanks to you and Joan Dunn for your support! Thanks to Melody Soell for the great learning-to-drive story.

Tip is the real brains behind this book. There might have been a book without Tip, but it would have been pretty lame. All the cool ideas are his. He provided all the infrastructure, too, including www.xptester.org. He wrote all the hardest parts of the book and made it fun! Everything I know about test automation, I learned from Tip. I wish he could teach me to turn wood and play the banjo, too. I'm privileged to cowrite a book with one of the smartest and most talented people I know.

How can I even begin to thank my wonderful, smart, and multitalented mom, Beth Crispin, for all she's done for me? And my amazing dad, Andre Crispin, who is also always an inspiration. I'm so proud to be their kid, I hope I've made them proud too. I'm infamous for interrupting ceremonies to tell my whole family I love them, so here's to all the Crispins, Heffernans, Sankeys, Gaxiolas, Downings, Guinns, Hammons, Moores, McDonalds, and Williamsons. Thanks to my Aunt Dovie, one of my role models. Thanks to Elise, for helping me be strong.

Thanks to all my terrific friends and neighbors for support and understanding. I apologize for the times I ignored you because I was writing. Thanks for not saying, "You're *still* working on that book?" Anna Blake, I couldn't have gotten through this book-writing time without all those inspiring rides on Dodger and Spirit. Thanks to my book club, the Women Who Read Too Much and the Dogs Who Love Them, for thinking it was cool that I'm writing a book, even one we'll never read together! I can't name all my friends without forgetting and thus offending someone, so consider yourselves all appreciated and acknowledged. I wouldn't be who I am without you. You know who you are.

Most of all, infinite thanks to my wonderful husband, Bob Downing, for taking care of me, our beloved pets, and our homestead uncomplainingly, providing me such a beautiful place to work, loving me even when I was crabby and stressed out, gently encouraging me to work on the book every day, cooking such tasty *moules* (which he can't stand) for me during the crunch days and nights of winding up the book. For believing in me and for brewing all that delicious wheat beer just for me—thanks, honey! And—you were right, dear!

## Tip

I'd like to thank all the reviewers of the book, especially Ron Jeffries, David Gelperin, and Rick Craig. I'm grateful for all your excellent feedback, criticism, and advice (even the parts I foolishly didn't take).

Thanks to the management team and my many colleagues at OCLC, who have been supporters and users of the tools and systems I've written over the years—in particular Richard Hale, the absolute best boss I've ever had; Don Muccino, who made it possible to provide WebART outside OCLC; Gary Houk, who originally set me to the task of test automation in 1982; and Cindy Bean, Mike Veselenak, Geoff Curtis, and all the other testers, programmers, and analysts who contributed ideas, tried things out, suggested improvements, and occasionally became willing guinea pigs for experimental tools and techniques.

I'd like to acknowledge the influence of two excellent teachers from my school days: Lloyd Evans, my algebra and geometry teacher from Crestview Junior High School, who first got me started in mathematics, and Kevin Morrin, my English teacher and soccer coach at Columbus Academy, who gave me the idea I could write.

Thanks to Lisa, who got me interested in XP, then dragged me kicking and screaming in with her. Despite anything she might say, the best parts of this book exist as a result of her courage, keen insight, and just plain stubbornness about what's right and what works in both Extreme Programming and quality assurance.

Finally, thanks especially to my family for putting up with my extended absences, late nights, and the early morning trumpet practice while working on the book—which, I know, seemed to go on forever.

# Part I

## The XP Tester Role

# Chapter 1

# An Overview

## Introduction

Extreme Programming, or XP, was first introduced by Kent Beck in 1996. Since that time, programmers around the world have been embracing it with great enthusiasm. If you ask programmers on an XP team why, they will respond with answers like, "It's fun," "It just feels right," "It's the way code is supposed to be developed," and "It's all the good without any of the bad." In fact, Kent Beck has described XP as coming close to the practices programmers would follow "in the wild."

XP is not a throw-out-the-rulebook, anything-goes technique. It is actually a deliberate and disciplined approach to software development. And despite the name, XP practitioners are probably more concerned about following rules than developers using traditional methodologies. Rules do exist in XP, but only a few, and they lead to an entirely different type of development process.

In this book, we'll focus on how the rules of XP affect testing and quality assurance activities and illustrate how those activities can and should be carried out on an XP project. This may seem, at first glance, like arranging a date between oil and water. But testing and quality are at the core of XP, and XP offers solutions to some vexing testing and quality assurance problems that arise in traditional software development. All the parties stand to benefit from this seemingly unholy alliance.

We'll start with a brief overview of XP and describe what it has to offer in terms of solving testing and quality assurance problems. In the next chapter, we'll go on and make our case that testers have something to offer XP.

## Overview of XP

XP is best summed up by its set of *values* and *practices*:

> *Extreme Programming is a discipline of software development based on values of simplicity, communication, feedback, and courage. It works by bringing the whole team together in the presence of simple practices, with enough feedback to enable the team to see where they are and to tune the practices to their unique situation. (Ron Jeffries, "What is Extreme Programming?")*

The four values at the core of XP are communication, simplicity, feedback, and courage. These come from a realization by Kent Beck that much of what has plagued software development can be traced to failures in one of these four areas and, consequently, that improvements in these areas would lead to a significantly better development process. The four values lead to a set of 12 practices, which essentially form the rules of XP. It is worth noting that this fairly short list of things to remember is just about right to fit into the short-term memory of a pair of programmers, thus enabling XP practitioners to be so disciplined in following the rules. They can actually keep them in mind instead of having to check a 500-page manual!

Here's a description of the 12 practices, which we've grouped under the values from which they're primarily derived. This is mostly as an aid to memory, because several practices are driven by more than one of the values:

### Communication

✧ **Onsite customer.** The development team has continuous access to the customer or customer team, who actually functions as part of the project team. The customer describes the system functionality in user stories, negotiates the timing and scheduling of releases, and makes all decisions that affect business goals. He's always available to answer questions regarding the details of user stories during programming tasks. He helps with functional testing and makes the final decisions on whether to allow the system to continue into production or stop it.

- **Pair programming.** Teams of two programmers working together write all the production code. This means at least two people are always intimately familiar with every part of the system, and every line of code is reviewed as it's written.
- **Coding standards.** Everyone codes to the same set of standards, to keep the code consistent and devoid of idiosyncratic quirks that could complicate understanding and refactoring by the entire team.

## Simplicity

- **Metaphor.** Each project has an organizing metaphor from which the names of programming entities (e.g., classes and methods) are drawn, providing a simple way to remember the naming conventions.
- **Simple design.** XP developers always do the simplest thing that could possibly work. They never solve a more general problem than the specific problem at hand, and they never add functionality sooner than needed.
- **Refactoring.** Duplication and needless complexity are removed from the code during each coding session, even when this requires modifying components that are already "complete." Automated unit tests are used to verify every change.

## Feedback

- **Testing.** Unit tests are at the heart of XP. Every piece of code has a set of automated unit tests, which are released into the code repository along with the code. The programmers write the unit tests before they write the code, then add unit tests whenever one is found to be missing. No modification or refactoring of code is complete until 100% of the unit tests have run successfully. Acceptance tests validate larger blocks of system functionality, such as user stories. When all the acceptance tests pass for a given user story, that story is considered complete.
- **Continuous integration.** Additions and modifications to the code are integrated into the system on at least a daily basis, and the unit tests must run 100% successfully, both before and after each integration.
- **Small releases.** The smallest useful feature set is identified for the first release, and releases are performed as early and often as possible, with a few new features added each time.

**Courage**

- ✧ **Planning game.** The customers and developers cooperate in planning the order and timing of the features in system releases. The customer provides system specifications in the form of user stories, and developers provide the estimates of the time and effort required for each. The customer then makes the decision on which stories to implement and in what order. The developers and customer jointly negotiate a sequence of short iterations, each implementing a new set of stories, culminating in the final release, containing all the stories.

- ✧ **Collective code ownership.** No one person owns the modules. All programmers are expected to be able to work on any part of the system at any time and to refactor any part of the system as necessary, to remove duplication.

- ✧ **Sustainable pace.** Everyone works at a pace that can be sustained for the long term without sacrificing his or her sanity, health, family, or productivity. Occasional bouts of overtime may occur, but consecutive weeks of overtime are considered a sign that something is very wrong.

## How XP Solves Testing and Quality Assurance Problems

That's XP in a nutshell: a collection of simple practices, taken to an extreme. Perhaps the most extreme thing of all about XP teams is the discipline with which they follow the practices. For instance, a 100% pass rate on unit tests doesn't mean 90% when the project is behind schedule. It means 100%, all the time.

So how can something as seemingly simple as this solve testing and quality assurance problems? Well, if you look closely, you can see that some of these practices relate directly to themes that testing and quality assurance professionals have been preaching for years.

Take code inspections, for instance, which many QA departments have tried to get into general practice as a more cost-effective way to identify defects. On an XP project, pair programming of production code means that 100% of all code is inspected *when written*. Or take the idea of "test first"—reviewing the test cases before writing the code, which testing professionals have promoted for years as a way of avoiding defects in the first place. Programmers on XP teams *write their unit tests first*, before they write the code.

These ideas really work, just as the quality assurance and testing professionals said they would. Unlike most traditional software projects, XP projects actually apply these ideas diligently and consistently, instead of just paying lip service. Here are some specific problems the XP approach can solve:

## System and Acceptance Testing Resources Wasted on Unit- and Integration-Level Bugs

One common problem testers experience on traditional software projects arises when they try to run system-level tests on code that's never been tested at the unit or integration level. This is an expensive and inefficient way to locate unit- and integration-level bugs and can easily consume all the time allocated for system and acceptance testing. Either the software is delivered late or the system- and acceptance-level testing is never completed, and the software suffers significant quality problems in operation.

This is especially frustrating to testers, because they really can't do anything about it. No matter how thorough, efficient, and/or automated are the tests they develop, they can't put either functionality or quality into the system; they can only detect its presence or absence.

XP avoids this scenario completely through the practices of 100% unit-test automation and continuous integration. Programmer pairs detect and correct unit and integration bugs during the coding sessions. By the time the code gets to acceptance testing, it's doing what the programmers intend, and the acceptance tests can focus on determining how well that intent matches the customer's expectations.

## Missing and Out-of-Date Requirements

Moving upstream in the process, another common problem in developing tests occurs when requirements are missing or out of date. The heavyweight, detailed requirement documents favored by traditional software development are ideal for use in developing tests but frequently turn out to be too expensive to create and maintain, and they leave the tester with no alternative when they inevitably become obsolete.

Testers find this frustrating, because they know the tests developed from the out-of-date requirements are inaccurate, but they have nothing else to go on except nonbinding verbal communication. Even getting that can be difficult, because those in the know will resent having to spend more time on questions after having already spent way too much time on the heavyweight documents in the first place.

XP solves this problem by replacing the massive requirements document with lightweight user stories that are easily maintained, augmented by the onsite customer, who functions as the oracle for all details the stories don't cover.

### Huge Gaps between the System and User Expectations

Finally, one of the most painful things for a tester or quality assurance person to experience is when a significant gap develops between what a project is delivering and what the customer is expecting. This can easily happen in traditional software development, where the customer is out of the loop after the requirements phase, and months or even years can go by before any functioning code is delivered. Pointing out the gap can cause the tester to be viewed as having a negative attitude, not being a team player, and, eventually, as "the enemy." Not pointing it out leads to a significantly unhappy customer and also reflects badly on the tester (e.g., "Why wasn't this caught in testing?").

XP eliminates this scenario by producing frequent, small releases that provide exactly those features the customer has most recently prioritized as the most important. If a gap starts to develop, it naturally becomes visible within the space of an iteration (two to three weeks at the most) and is dealt with by the entire team.

These three problems—lack of adequate unit and integration testing, missing and out-of-date requirements, and huge gaps between customer expectations and delivered product—are often symptoms of more deeply seated problems in the enterprise. We're not saying XP is a solution for those root causes. We're saying that if you're a testing/QA professional and can get involved with a team practicing XP, these problems will be minimized. We've found that these are major factors in determining the quality of life for professional testers.

## Wolves in Sheep's Clothing

Having touted the problems XP practices can solve, remember they work only if practiced diligently and consistently. A team that pays only lip service to XP practices is not an XP team and would have to be treated like a dysfunctional traditional development team. Not all traditional development teams are dysfunctional, of course, but those that are almost always claim to follow some methodology while violating it at every juncture. This would be the worst type of situation in which to try out the role we advocate in this book.

For instance, if a team claims to be using XP but doesn't have an onsite customer, then a massive, out-of-date requirements document will be replaced by pure ignorance, which is probably worse. Likewise, if a team doesn't use pair programming or automate unit tests, the code will be just as rife with unit- and integration-level bugs as that coming out of a traditional software development project. The "acceptance" testing will be the first time the code is ever tested. Make sure a team is really practicing XP before you attempt to apply these XP testing techniques.

## Summary

- XP is a lightweight but disciplined approach to software development that has testing and quality at its core.
- XP is based on four values: communication, simplicity, feedback, and courage.
- Twelve practices comprise the rules of XP:
  - Onsite customer
  - Pair programming
  - Coding standards
  - Metaphor
  - Simple design
  - Refactoring
  - Testing
  - Continuous integration
  - Small releases
  - Planning game
  - Collective code ownership
  - Sustainable pace
- XP solves three major testing and quality assurance problems:
  - Unit and integration bugs during system and acceptance testing
  - Lack of requirements from which to develop tests
  - Large gaps between customer expectations and delivered product

# *Chapter 2*

# Why XP Teams Need Testers

Much of the published material on Extreme Programming is aimed at programmers, customers, and managers. Some purists may argue that a tester role is unnecessary in XP projects: customers can write the acceptance tests and programmers can automate them. This can work, and certainly some successful XP projects don't have testers.

We believe, however, that more XP teams can be successful by doing a better job of defining, automating, and running acceptance tests when someone is focused on that role and that this focus helps in other areas as well. If you don't like to think of someone in the tester "role" on an XP project (because the only true roles defined in XP are programmer and customer), think of having a programmer with a "tester focus."

We'll illustrate this point with a true story about a remodeling project Lisa recently experienced, but first let's define what we mean by the term "tester."

## *Definition of Tester*

By the term **tester,** we mean a person who not only develops and runs tests but has quality assurance and development skills as well. Testers spend a portion of their time actually testing, but they also help customers write stories, and they define acceptance tests and take the lead in automating them.

We're combining what would traditionally be described as both quality *assurance* and quality *control* activities. The classical distinction between these two is that quality assurance (QA) aims to avoid the introduction of defects in the first place, and quality control (QC) aims to detect defects that have already been introduced. QA is process oriented; QC is product oriented.

While this distinction is useful for manufacturing, it's less so for software, and our experience has been that either activity alone is generally useless. In any case, XP tries not to overly classify people, because to do so implies that they alone are responsible for coding, testing, analysis, and so on, when XP is all about integrating these activities.

If you're used to thinking of a "test developer," "quality analyst," or "software quality engineer," please mentally substitute your own term for ours. We're using "tester" mostly because it's short, but also because it's an instantly recognized term among software teams. Usually followed by "Oh—*them*."

## The Tester's Contribution, Illustrated

Almost all software teams include testers in some form. We want to talk a little about why this is so and then move on to how this plays out in XP. Consider the following story about Lisa's experience with a construction contractor:

> When I decided to put an addition on my house, I wanted the basement extended as well. I signed a contract with my contractor that specified many details. I'm a pretty detail-oriented person, a quality assurance professional, and I thought I read this contract carefully.
>
> When the contractor built the new basement and cut a hole for the door into the old basement, he didn't install a door to close it off. When I asked why, he pointed out that I hadn't said I wanted one. I could access the new basement—it was functional—but had no way to close it off. Since the door was not included, I'd either have to do without or pay extra.
>
> Naturally, I had assumed the new basement would have a door I could open and shut. But since I hadn't specified it, the contractor hadn't included the cost of the door or the labor to install it in the contract. My contractor is terrific (call me if you live in Denver and need remodeling), but I couldn't expect him to just give me a free door.
>
> How nice it would have been if someone had looked at the contract and then said, "No door is specified here—don't you want one?" Then I could have decided whether to spend the money, and it wouldn't have been a less than pleasant surprise later.

This remodeling project unfolded right before Lisa's eyes, so the omission of the door became apparent long before the project was complete. But with a software project, this wouldn't necessarily happen. In fact, for traditional software development, the "missing door" would probably not surface until the house was finished and the contractor had ridden off into the sunset.

The use of Extreme Programming would improve on this outcome, because the lack of a door would become obvious at the end of the iteration (short development cycle, usually two weeks), and the customer could choose to have it included in the next iteration. In fact, with XP, you could do even better: ask questions the first day of the iteration that would uncover the hidden assumption of the missing door.

As Lisa points out, what we really want as customers is for a builder to understand that when we specify a doorway in the requirements, we also expect a door to go in the doorway. This seems so blindly obvious to us that when a builder omits it, we might assume he's either stupid or dishonest.

The problem is that, as customers, our view of the proposed doorway is, first, something you can go through, and second, something you can close off. We get to the idea of a door in the doorway pretty quickly. But the contractor is thinking of the many other attributes of the proposed doorway, such as the size (30, 32, 34, 36 inches?), the shape (square or arched?), the moldings (profile, material, finish), the threshold and transition between floor materials, the framing required (especially in a bearing wall), the electrical and plumbing runs, location of light switches, and so on. The aspects the contractor is naturally going to pay the most attention to are the ones that affect construction, not the ones that affect the livability of the result. That's because the contractor "lives in" the remodeling process itself: this month our remodeling project, next month another, and so on.

This type of thing happens a lot in software development projects. As developers, we tend to focus on items that are important or interesting to the development process. How often have you been involved in projects that got the really hard part right but missed the easy stuff—which, unfortunately, turned out to be the very thing that mattered most to the customer?

This is where a tester can make the biggest contribution to a software project: by thinking about the system from the viewpoint of those who have to live with the solution but with the grasp of details, possibilities, and constraints of those building it.

In XP, for example, it would be someone in the role of tester who, during the Planning Game or while writing acceptance tests, would think of the obvious things one would do with a doorway and how to test if they're working.

This person would ask the customer, "How about a test for whether the room can be closed off?"

If the customer wants the door, the tester makes sure this was included in programmers' estimates. If not, the estimates are changed, and the customer may have to pick stories again for the iteration. The tester helps the customer write a test to make sure the door works as desired; then the team executes the test and reports its result. Before the end of the iteration, the customer knows not only that she needs to ask for the door but also that it's there and working properly.

In addition to providing this double-vision view, incorporating both programmer and customer sensibilities, the tester also has an outlook that differs from the programmer's in terms of the assumptions they make about correctness.

Programmers naturally assume that, in general, "things work." After all, even the simplest method or function involves the execution of millions of low-level microcode instructions or hardware circuits, and each one has to work flawlessly every single time or that piece of code could never work. As each method of an object is implemented and the objects are assembled into packages and applications and the applications into systems, which are then maintained, extended, and evolved, each piece in each level has to perform correctly every time for the whole system to work. Since programmers achieve this almost impossible-seeming level of reliability most of the time, that shapes their experience and world view.

Testers, on the other hand, are all descendants of Murphy and assume, in general, that things "don't work right." This is because testers live in a world where, no matter how many things are working right, some things always aren't. This is the same world, by the way, we all inhabit as customers. Our new electronically controlled, fuel-injected road machine may be a marvel of modern engineering, but if the cup holders are too small for a can of pop, that's what we notice. And even though 50 billion microcode instructions in our system may work flawlessly every second, if highlighted text is invisible because it's the same color as the background, that's what the customer will notice.

## Shun the Dark Side

Just as we had a caveat for testers on the potential of XP to solve quality assurance and testing problems, we also have one for XP teams on the potential of testers to help XP projects. The tester role we advocate in this book is not the traditional quality assurance/testing role. It follows a much more integrated, team-oriented approach and requires adapting one's skills and experience to function in an XP environment.

Just as you wouldn't want to be in the tester role on a team that claims to be XP but doesn't follow the practices (see "Wolves in Sheep's Clothing" in Chapter 1), you also wouldn't want to have a tester on your XP team who doesn't understand and buy into the methodology. A tester who views programmers as adversaries or doesn't believe in test automation or expects to spend more time planning than doing is likely to cling to techniques honed on traditional software projects. This will, in the best case, fail to help and, in the worst case, undermine the rest of the team's adherence to XP practices. Find a tester who understands and is committed to XP.

## Summary

- We define a "tester" as someone who not only tests but who has QA and development skills.
- Our use of the term "tester" involves both QA and QC activities, and we drop the distinction between the two and encompass both in the integrated testing activities of XP
- A tale of remodeling in which the contractor did not appreciate how the presence of a doorway in the plans should imply a door illustrates how customers' assumptions get missed in the development process.
- A tester makes a contribution by viewing the system from the stand point of the customer but with the grasp of details, possibilities, and constraints of the developer, avoiding the "missing door" syndrome.
- A tester provides a skeptical outlook on the correctness of the system that helps keep the team from overlooking things that will make the customer unhappy.

# Chapter 3

# How XP Teams Benefit from Having Testers

Anyone who has participated in a major software project knows that it takes a village to get a software release out the door. Lots of people with many different job titles contribute. Although much of the published material on Extreme Programming focuses on the roles of customers and programmers, most XP projects still depend on multiple players to succeed: testers, quality assurance engineers, requirements analysts, project managers, product managers, technical writers, marketing professionals, and (yes) salespeople. In XP projects, the lines between most of these roles blur: every programmer is also a requirements analyst and a tester, for example.

We all need someone to keep the books and write the checks, and the practices of Extreme Programming should not be limited to just customers and programmers. Many aspects of business can benefit from ideas such as "the simplest thing that could possibly work," even those peripheral to the main activity of software development.

Testing, however, is not a peripheral activity in XP. Four of the twelve practices, fully one-third, involve testing as a major component. With a savvy professional in the tester role, an XP team will produce a better product, more efficiently, and with a better quality of life for all concerned.

## Checks and Balances

The business world turns on checks and balances. Accountants don't audit their own books. Builders and architects have their plans reviewed by structural engineers. Contracting work is always inspected and approved by building inspectors. There is a reason for this: call it selective focus, separation of concerns, or just plain human nature. We all focus on some things and block out others, depending upon the task at hand.

For example, consider why building inspectors find code violations when they inspect a remodeling job. Sometimes it may be because the carpenter was lazy or incompetent, but usually it's because he was focusing on the construction: is the frame plumb and square, is the miter clean with no gaps, are the nails set properly under a shaving, so they can't be seen? All accomplished, but when the inspector arrives: whoops—code requires a minimum width of 34 inches for a doorway providing egress from a room below grade, and this doorway is only 32 inches wide.

It's true that by simply focusing on finding the defects rather than building the system, the tester can be much more effective at finding defects. It would be a mistake, though, to conclude that this is the main way a tester benefits the team. In fact, putting too much emphasis on this aspect can lead to a dysfunctional team, where responsibility for testing and quality are placed solely on the tester.

Sure, the tester is focused on the testing and finding defects and quality. But so is everyone else on the team. For instance, one hallmark of XP is the "test-first" pattern, in which programmer pairs write the unit tests first, before they write one line of code. This focuses the programmers on testing and finding defects before they become so involved writing the code that testing becomes an afterthought. These automated unit tests must pass 100% before the code goes into the repository and then for each subsequent integration.

So it's not just the focus on finding defects that provides the benefit. After all, the carpenter who built the wrong-size doorway in our remodeling example was no less focused on finding defects than the inspector; he was just looking for a *different type* of defect.

The tester will be looking for a different type of defect too. Instead of defects in the function of individual programming objects and methods, which are the focus of the programmers' unit tests, the tester will be looking for disconnects between what the system is and what the customer wants it to be. This is acceptance testing, as opposed to unit testing.

Is this really a benefit? If the unit tests are comprehensive, automated, and pass 100%, doesn't this guarantee that the system is what the customer wants?

No. No. And No. Traditional software development, where unit testing is so haphazard that the systems are literally teeming with low-level bugs that show up in user-apparent problems, might leave room to think so. When you eradicate these, as you can by using XP practices, you're still left with the user-apparent problems. In fact, you may have more, because all those low-level bugs can mask the real gaps between what the customer wants and what the system does.

## Acceptance Tests versus Unit Tests

Okay, you may say, but what's the benefit of having a team member dedicated to this? Why not just adopt the test-first pattern and have programmers write acceptance tests at the very beginning, even before they write unit tests? And automate those acceptance tests, just as with the unit tests, and require all code to pass 100% of them before going into the repository and after each integration, just like unit tests? Then XP could eradicate those user-apparent defects just as it does the unit-level defects.

Well, that, in a nutshell, is exactly why we advocate the dedicated testing role. If acceptance tests were just like unit tests, programmers could write and automate them and then build the system too. However, unit tests and acceptance tests are different in important ways that affect how a test-first approach can be carried out.

Unit tests are written in the same language as the code they test. They interact with the programming objects directly, often in the same address space. A programmer pair can switch seamlessly between writing tests, writing code, refactoring, and running tests without even getting out of the editor. And the unit tests correspond almost exactly to the programming objects. It's perfectly natural for a pair of programmers to write the tests for the object they're about to code and then make sure the tests all run 100% when they're done. From then on, those tests are invaluable in validating that the code still working after refactoring.

Acceptance tests, on the other hand, correspond to the programming objects in a much looser way. A single acceptance test will almost always rely on many different programming objects, and a single programming object will often affect the outcome of multiple unrelated acceptance tests. Also, acceptance tests are frequently run through an external interface to the system, perhaps the user interface, requiring specialized tools to validate behavior visible to a human being, as opposed to another programming object.

It isn't possible to switch easily between acceptance tests and coding the way it is with unit tests, because the acceptance tests won't run until all the required code is ready, even when the piece the pair is working on is completed. Because of this, acceptance tests can't be relied upon after refactoring the same way as unit tests can.

Due to these differences, acceptance tests don't fit as naturally into the programmers' workflow and don't provide as much immediate benefit in finding defects in new or refactored code. It isn't surprising, then, to meet with resistance when asking programmers to spend the time writing automated acceptance tests before writing the code. It might be an easier sell if acceptance test automation were quick and easy, but it requires a high level of concentration and attention, sustained throughout the course of the project, to develop and maintain a set of tests that can both validate the system and be carried out in the available time.

A tester brings this level of focus to the team, along with a crucially different viewpoint that combines the prejudices of the customer with the technical skills of the programmers. As programmers, we're aware of the customer issues and do what is (minimally) necessary to satisfy them. But as a tester, we *care* about what it will be like to use and own the system over the long haul, while still being aware of the programming and technical details. This allows us to find the missing door as soon as the doorway is conceived rather than after it's constructed.

## *Navigating for XP Projects*

In *Extreme Programming Explained* and *Planning Extreme Programming*, Kent Beck compares XP to driving a car: you have to watch the road and make continual corrections to get to your destination.

Who is driving this car? What keeps the team from getting lost or making a wrong turn? Who makes them stop and ask directions? Any member of the team can perform this role, but the tester is a natural. The tester is suitably equipped to act as the navigator, reading the acceptance test "maps," interpreting the customer's requests, watching for signposts in the form of acceptance test results, and letting everyone know how the journey is progressing. Like the XP coach, the tester has a level of independent objectivity; the tester is a coach for the team with respect to testing and quality.

Mastering XP practices, like learning to drive, isn't always a smooth process. Lisa's friend Melody was "taught" to drive by her dad. His teaching technique consisted of burying his nose in a newspaper. He didn't notice that whenever she made a left turn, she turned into the left lane of the new street, directly into oncoming traffic. Since he didn't mention her left turns, Melody believed this was the correct way to drive. She found out differently the first time she drove with her mom, who reacted dramatically to her first left turn. Testers needn't be dramatic, but they can help make sure the team obeys the rules of the road and arrives safely at its destination.

An old truism says that when everyone is responsible, nobody is responsible. Everyone is responsible for quality in an Extreme Programming project, but it sure helps to have one or two team members whose primary focus is quality.

## Summary

- Testers bring both specialized skills and a unique viewpoint that combine to enable the team to produce a better product more efficiently.
- Testers provide checks and balances and are more efficient at finding defects, because they focus on it.
- Testers find a different type of defect than programmers' unit tests do.
- A dedicated tester role adopting test-first acceptance testing can help an XP team eradicate user-apparent defects just as it does unit-level defects.
- If XP is like driving a car, the tester helps keep the team on the right road and makes them stop and ask for directions when necessary.
- However, the tester role and testing functions must be integrated an isolated testing function in which testers are involved only at the end doesn't work.

# *Chapter 4*

# XP Testing Values

When you get right down to it, most software projects succeed or fail based on the people involved, not the methodology or technology they use. For instance, after reviewing dozens of projects over a span of 20 years, Alistair Cockburn, in "Characterizing People as Non-Linear, First-Order Components in Software Development," states, "Peoples' characteristics are a first order success driver, not a second order one" and are "better predictors of project behavior and methodology success than other methodological factors."

It's easy to see how the characteristics of individual people bear on the success of the project. All things being equal, one would expect a team with more talented individuals to outperform another with less talented members. But a funny thing happens when people get together into teams: the whole is sometimes more and sometimes less than the sum of the parts. New factors begin to operate that involve how each individual feels about the team, what he thinks other individuals feel about the team, and how she thinks the team as a whole feels about her as an individual: team morale, in other words. The effects of morale can be stronger than that of the team members' individual characteristics.

A team that "clicks" can sometimes accomplish things far beyond what seems possible, given the capabilities of the individuals. At the other extreme, a dysfunctional team usually fails, regardless of how "good" individual members may be. As Kent Beck writes in *Extreme Programming Explained*, "If members of a team don't care about each other and what they are doing, XP is doomed."

Because of the important effect these human factors have on project outcomes, XP actively promotes a focus on the people involved in the project and how they interact and communicate. It articulates a set of shared values that bind the team in a way the 500-page methodology manual cannot: courage, communication, simplicity, and feedback.

Let's look at the way these four values apply to the tester role (the four definitions below are from Merriam-Webster OnLine, www.m-w.com):

## Communication

*A process by which information is exchanged between individuals through a common system of symbols, signs, or behavior*

Information is the resource all project activities ultimately depend on. If the development team has incorrect or insufficient information about the customer's requirements, this will be reflected in the final product. This makes human interaction and communication critical for the team's success. While everyone on the team will be asking lots of questions and needs good interaction skills, these skills are especially important for testers, who so often bridge gaps in understanding or assumption between customers and programmers. Have you ever taken your car to a mechanic and tried to describe the funky noise coming from the right rear wheel? Think of a tester as the person who knows just how to mimic that noise, so the mechanic can figure out what the problem is. Testers are interpreters in a land often strange to both programmers and customers, clarifying each group's requirements to the other.

Testers contribute to a project's success by asking the right questions. The movie and television show *M\*A\*S\*H* had a character, Radar O'Reilly, who knew before anyone else when helicopters were about to land with wounded soldiers. As a tester, you need some of Radar's prescient qualities. You need to know when customers are not saying what they mean. You need to be an analyst (sometimes you might need to be a psychoanalyst!) You need to detect when the programmers have missed something the customer wanted. You need to be alert to the incoming wounded, raising a flag when your gut tells you the programmers have underestimated or run into a roadblock that will prevent them from meeting a deadline.

Testers actively collaborate with customers. If you're using agile practices but aren't able to have an onsite customer who works with the programmers on a daily basis, the tester can shuttle between the customer and the development team, acting as a customer proxy. This book is intended to help you define your own tester role. You can boil down the information and present it in a nutshell to the customer at the start of your project, so she understands your relationship to the team.

In addition to facilitating communication between other members of the team, testers have something of their own to communicate: a vision for testing within the project. This vision has to be driven by the major risks affecting the correctness of the delivered system. It provides a foundation and guiding light for the team's decisions on everything from what test tools to use, to which tests to automate, to when and whether to release. This foundation includes gradually realizing and adjusting the vision to the circumstances.

## *Simplicity*

*The state of being simple, uncomplicated, or uncompounded; directness of expression*

In *Extreme Programming Explained,* Kent Beck advises Extreme Programmers to always do the simplest thing that could possibly work. Please note that this *not* the "simplest thing that works" but the "simplest thing that *could possibly* work." In other words, nothing requires that the first thing you try must work. The admonishment is to make sure that the first thing you try is *simple*.

This can be hard for those who have worked as testers in traditional software development environments—who may feel an obligation to test every line of software as thoroughly as possible, to make sure it meets the highest standard for quality. The truth is, though, it's not about your standards. It's about the customer's standards. Do the simplest test you can to verify that a piece of functionality is there or that the software meets the customer's standard for robustness. If a unit test covers an acceptance test, don't repeat the test. If the customer raises the quality bar in the next iteration, you can add more tests or more complexity to existing tests to handle it. Why not test as much as you want (or more than the minimum necessary)? Because you don't own your resources, the customer does.

Simplicity with respect to testing also means choosing test tools lightweight enough for XP. Your tools should let you quickly automate testing for critical business functions and then add tests as your resources permit.

Embracing simplicity also requires a lot of courage. Testing "just enough," gaining the best value in a competitive situation without exceeding available resources, is tough. It feels safer to try to test everything. Deciding what needs to be verified can be daunting.

# Feedback

*The return to the input of a part of the output of a machine, system, or process*

It's interesting to note that, of the four core values of XP, feedback is the only one defined in terms of a machine. One interpretation of this is that success on a software project is three parts people and one part technology—which is not too far off, in our experience. Even the feedback on an XP project involves people. Kent Beck states in *Extreme Programming Explained*, "Concrete feedback about the current state of the system is absolutely priceless." Feedback is what testing is all about.

In another departure from traditional software development, XP teams want to know the results of testing. They get feedback every day from the unit tests, and as acceptance tests are completed, they'll grow to depend on the feedback from those tests as well. Customers tend to understand acceptance tests much better than they do unit tests, since they participate in writing them. You may even display the functional and acceptance test results along with unit testing results on a daily basis. You'll get a lot of satisfaction posting these for everyone to see, especially if the graphs continue in positive trends each day.

Who gives *you* feedback? How do you know the acceptance tests are adequate? Both the customer and the programmers can give you valuable input on test definitions. The short iterations help too. If the acceptance tests pass but the customer is dissatisfied with how the software works at the end of the first iteration, you know your team's communication with the customer about the tests was faulty.

Make sure you, the programmers, and the customer work together to write tests that truly show the customer that the stories are completed in the way required. If many acceptance tests are still failing at the end of the iteration, this, too, is a sign that your development team doesn't really understand what the customer wants and what the tests are checking. See what you can do to facilitate better communication between programmers and the customer.

One of the most valuable skills you can learn is how to *ask* for feedback. Ask the programmers and customer if they're satisfied with way the team is automating and running acceptance tests. Do they feel the acceptance test results are giving value? Are the acceptance test definitions easy enough to use? Are there enough tests for areas of high technical risk? In the day-to-day race to finish an iteration, we don't always stop to think what could and should be changed. The retrospective meeting and iteration planning are both good times to get the team to think about these issues and suggest alternatives.

## Courage

*Mental or moral strength to venture, persevere, and withstand danger, fear, or difficulty*

We left courage for last, but for a tester it may be the most important of the four values. XP can be scary from a tester's point of view. As a tester, the prospect of writing, automating, and performing tests at top speed in one- to three-week iterations, without the benefit of traditional requirements documents, feels at first like driving down a steep, winding, one-lane mountain road with no guardrails. Programmers who lack experience automating acceptance tests may find this prospect equally daunting.

A tester may fear looking stupid to the customer because she overlooked a giant defect. The fact that the customer's story and acceptance test did not cover the area of the giant defect will not mitigate this feeling. You need courage to help the customer define acceptance criteria and test to those criteria.

You need courage to let the customer make mistakes. Maybe he doesn't want to invest in some of the tests you recommend. You'll all find out quickly whether this was a good decision, and everyone's testing skills will improve with time.

A tester may fear looking stupid to the others on the team by asking for help. If you're pair testing with someone who's not familiar with your work and your test script stops working, you may feel defensive and embarrassed. You need courage to work in pairs.

As the tester—and everyone on an XP team is a tester to some extent—you need the courage to determine the minimum testing requirement proving an iteration's success. Does this mean you do an incomplete job of testing? Nope. As they say in the Air Force, if it weren't good enough, it wouldn't be the minimum. Testers can always find another test to do, another angle to check out. Knowing when to stop testing takes a lot of courage.

Testers have to help the customer decide how much testing is enough. A customer who has a lot riding on a software package is going to worry that no amount of testing can ever be enough.

Being the only tester on an XP project of four, six, eight, or more programmers can feel lonely at times. You may need courage to ask a busy programmer to pair with you to develop an executable test. You may need courage to convince your team to include test support tasks along with the other stories and assume responsibility for the acceptance tests. You may sometimes feel you're constantly asking for help and support from people who don't necessarily have the same immediate priorities you have. It may take more courage to ask for help than to try to soldier on alone. Ask!

Acceptance tests provide feedback, which is often good news. Your team might not take particular notice of that. What they notice is all the bad news you bring by discovering defects and bringing up issues. Bearing bad tidings as tactfully as possible is a courageous act. You need not just bravery but persistence and a thick skin, because programmers in the midst of an iteration don't always want to stop and look at bugs. You have the right to ask for help anytime, but this doesn't mean it will always feel good to have to ask.

If you're working on a project where something—the technology, the domain—is new to you, you may need courage to ask questions and learn something. Remember you're never alone on an XP team. If you have problems, your team is there to help you (although they may need gentle prodding). Embrace new challenges that come up, and enjoy the adventure!

## Summary

- Projects succeed or fail because of the people involved, regardless of the processes or methodology used.
- The way a team works together and feels about itself can have an effect on the outcome as big as or bigger than individual members' characteristics.
- Testers help facilitate communication among members of the development and customer teams.
- Do the simplest tests you can to verify that customer requirements are met.
- Don't work alone—partner with other team members for tasks such as test automation, and ask for help as needed.
- Be persistent, and keep your perspective.

# Chapter 5

# Overview of the
# XP Tester Role

Now that we've provided some reasons why we think XP projects need a tester, we'll describe what that job involves. When we talk about the tester role on an XP team, we don't mean one person is responsible for all testing, or even all acceptance testing. Keep in mind that XP strives to avoid specialization, so everyone on an XP team contributes to test development and execution. More than one person may often play the tester role, and the tester may also play multiple roles, using a wide variety of skills.

To quote Ron Jeffries, "XP is not about 'roles' at all. It is about a much tighter integration of skills and behaviors than is implied by the notion of roles" (e-mail). Acceptance testing in particular does not get done properly in XP unless the whole team embraces it as an essential collective responsibility.

Paraphrasing Ron again, the idea behind the XP testing practice is that testing is an integrated activity, not a separate one. Feedback should be continuous, with the customer expressing needs in terms of tests and programmers expressing design and code in terms of tests. In XP as it was envisioned, testing activities and skills are needed across the whole team, with no tester role into which we can plug a person and say we've accounted for testing.

While we acknowledge that the two official XP "roles" are customer and programmer and that testing is a team activity, our experience has shown us that on most XP teams, one or more persons need to wear the tester hat, focus on acceptance testing, and provide leadership in the areas of testing and quality assurance to the rest of the team. This is what we mean in this book when we talk about the tester role. We're not equating or comparing it with the customer and programmer roles. In fact, the tester will play both of these roles within the team. If you have a problem using the term *role* in this context, then think *focus*. We'll refer to a person in the tester role or with the tester focus as simply a tester from this point on.

The tester may pair to write production code or write test code alone. She'll certainly provide a quality assurance role in preventing defects from occurring in the future by learning from current failures. Testers raise the team's consciousness about quality and promote best practices in every stage of software development, from requirements gathering to launch.

Like everyone on the XP team, the tester has rights and responsibilities and many hats to wear. The tester's duties include two often conflicting roles: customer advocate—making sure the customer gets what he asked and is paying for—and programmer advocate—making sure the customer doesn't take unfair advantage of the programmers to the detriment of the project. (This could also be the job of the programmers themselves or the coach, but it's an area where testers can contribute.)

As a tester, you think about the system as if you were the customer. Not about how you're going to build it but how you're going to "live" in the end result. Use this viewpoint to figure the most important things to verify, then use your systems knowledge to come up with all the details the customer may not have thought of.

Yes, in XP the customer is responsible for specifying the level of quality needed via the stories and acceptance tests. But a customer may think he knows what he wants, just as Lisa thought she knew everything she wanted in her house addition. She *did* read scores of British home design magazines, but that doesn't mean she knew anything about construction.

Besides overlooking details they should care about but are unaware of, customers as a group are not terribly experienced in quality assurance and testing. If stories aren't well defined and acceptance tests are not thorough, you may get through plenty of iterations with everyone happy, and then BAM! A customer might not notice a missing door until an end user complains about it.

We've already talked about the value of courage as it applies to XP testing. Testers, too, have a lot of fear about XP. Much of this is due to misperceptions about XP.

Testers are afraid that

- There isn't enough process.
- They won't have enough detail to understand the stories.
- They won't be able to get the tests written fast enough to execute them in the same iteration.
- They won't be able to automate tests fast enough to keep up with the rapid iterations—or they won't know how to automate the tests, period.
- They'll have to sacrifice quality for deadlines.
- They'll get stuck between a demanding customer and frustrated programmers who argue over whether a function or performance criterion was really part of a particular story.
- The documentation won't be sufficient.
- Nobody will help them.
- They won't be able to pick up new technology fast enough.
- They won't have time to do thorough enough testing.
- The software won't meet their personal quality standards.

## XP Tester's Bill of Rights

Testers have rights that permit them to do their best work, as do all members of their XP team. Here's a Tester's Bill of Rights. Since testing involves programming, it overlaps with the Programmer's Bill of Rights defined in Kent Beck and Martin Fowler's *Planning XP*. Because testers see the application under development with a customer's point of view, their rights mirror some of the customer's rights

- You have the right to bring up issues related to quality and process at any time.
- You have the right to ask questions of customers and programmers and receive timely answers.
- You have the right to ask for and receive help from anyone on the project team, including programmers, managers, and customers.
- You have the right to make and update your own estimates for your own tasks and have these included in estimates for stories.

◇ You have the right to the tools you need to do your job in a timely manner.

Like the programmers, you have the right to do your best work. You can't do it without a commitment to quality from your whole organization. The fact that your organization is using XP (and that they hired a tester) is a good indication that they care deeply about quality. If you find this isn't the case and that they're just using XP halfheartedly because it's trendy, because management decreed short releases are now required, or to pay lip service to quality, consider searching for other job opportunities. You can't succeed if the team isn't dedicated to producing good stuff.

## XP Tester Activities

Here are some of a tester's activities on an XP project (we'll provide more details in Part II: Test Drive through an XP Project):

◇ Help negotiate quality with the customer.
◇ Help clarify stories.
◇ Help with estimates during planning.
◇ Advocate the customer's rights.
◇ Guard the programmers' rights.
◇ Work with the customer to write effective and thorough acceptance tests.
◇ Make sure acceptance tests (functional, load, stress, performance, compatibility, installation, security, anything not covered by unit and integration tests) verify the quality specified by the customer.
◇ Help the team automate maintainable acceptance tests, using lightweight tools and test designs.
◇ Make sure test results are reported in a timely manner, forming a continuous feedback loop for the team.
◇ Make sure acceptance testing keeps pace with development.
◇ Help the programmers design more testable code.
◇ Keep the team honest; if they sacrifice quality to speed ahead, they must reveal this to the customer.

## Summary

- Having an XP tester role does not mean one person is responsible for all testing or even all acceptance testing.
- Most fears about being a tester on an XP test team are unfounded.
- Testers have rights too.

# Chapter 6

## Quality and XP

It's impossible to talk about testing without mentioning quality, and vice versa. Testing is almost always performed with some implied level of quality in mind. While a 100% pass rate is required of unit tests, this is not necessarily the case for acceptance tests. It's up to the customer to decide whether all tests she defines are critical and must pass. Acceptance testing in XP requires some definition of quality levels and criteria. This is often an ongoing negotiation as the project proceeds.

## Defining Quality

To define quality, you have to ask the customer team lots of questions during the planning game. What *is* quality for this story? How will we know it when we see it? What one story in the iteration, or one part of a given story, absolutely must work? It's often easier to think about it the other way: "What's the worst thing that could happen here?"

For example, if you're developing a retail Web site, the ability to make a purchase may be the critical function. To go further, perhaps correctly validating the credit card is the most business-critical item on the purchase screen. These exercises help the customer prioritize stories and help you design tests and focus resources. This information will go into the acceptance tests to help the programmers estimate and plan each iteration and to ultimately meet customer expectations for completed stories.

What happens when you ask the customer questions for which he has no answers? "We don't really know which operating systems or browser versions should be supported." "Gee, we aren't sure how many concurrent users will log on to the system." The customer may not be familiar with the technical aspects of her application. Or perhaps you're developing a new product and the customer has no historical data to fall back on.

Make sure you're asking questions for which the answers really do matter. Although this may seem obvious, it's sometimes easy to get carried away with all kinds of scenarios that are just never going to happen. Assuming they do matter, help the customer find answers! However hard it is to come up with some kind of answer now, it can be much harder later to undo the result of a bad assumption. Even if you can't determine the answer at this point, at least everyone will know it's an open question and not make assumptions about it.

In XP, the customer's role is to make business decisions, not to be a quality expert. Face it, some people are always on the "happy path" (not looking for problems)...just as Lisa was when she signed a contract with a builder for a home addition. And although the customer may be conscious of budgetary limitations, he may not articulate them in a way programmers understand. Also, if he's not technically savvy, it might not occur to him that he can't have features A through Z plus 99.995% uptime in three iterations.

While the customer is responsible for coming up with quality criteria, the development team can help. Programmers can research and present several alternatives to the customer. For example, say you're developing a system where users are updating records in a database. If two users try to update the same record concurrently, a deadlock may occur. Your team can give the user three different ways to deal with the problem. The least expensive creates the risk of a race, while the most expensive provides record locking, to prevent such a condition. Now the customer can weigh the cost against the risk and decide what to do this iteration. Later, when other high-priority features have been taken care of, she can come back and implement a more expensive alternative if she wishes.

We've sometimes had customers who were passive and unsure of exactly what they wanted in terms of quality. Sometimes they don't have ready answers to questions like "How many concurrent transactions does this application need to support?" Your team needs full information from the customer to make progress. With your focus on quality, you can check to make sure the customer proactively defines the quality criteria. After all, he's usually paying the bills.

It's hard to build up trust between the customer and the development team, and easy to lose it. It's better for everyone to be clear on the standards for quality up front and make accurate estimates than to disappoint the customer with an unpleasant surprise when the end of an iteration or release rolls around.

## Setting Quality Criteria

The customer may define quality standards as a set of features. For example:

- ✧ Whenever the user makes a mistake, a user-friendly error screen appears.
- ✧ It's impossible to crash the server via the user interface.
- ✧ The system can handle a hundred concurrent logins.
- ✧ The system will stay up 99.995% of the time.

The customer asks for a certain level of quality, and the programmers account for that in estimating the risk and effort of the stories. Many quality criteria can become stories on their own. For example, the customer could write a story saying the system should handle all exceptions and print out a user-friendly error message.

## Who Is Responsible for Quality?

Quality should be a collaborative effort among the entire project team, which includes everyone involved in getting the software released. The tester is responsible for helping the customer make conscious decisions about quality during the planning process. If the customer is clear about her acceptance criteria and these are reflected accurately in the acceptance tests, you're much more likely to achieve the level of quality the customer wants without giving your time away.

How do various members of the team participate in producing a high-quality deliverable? Customers need to understand their responsibilities in defining quality and writing tests that prove it. If your XP team includes testers, they can help the customer with these tasks and act as customer surrogates if the customer can't sit with the team. Testers can pair with programmers to go over stories and review the finished tasks and stories to make sure the requirements are met.

Programmers can estimate technical risks of stories and provide alternatives to help the customer achieve a balance of quality and cost. By mastering XP practices such as test-first coding and refactoring, programmers build quality into the software. They shoulder their part of the quality burden by taking on tasks related to acceptance testing, such as writing automated test scripts and coming up with ideas on how to automate tests simply and effectively.

All teams need strong leaders. If the team is failing to master a necessary practice and takes no action on it, someone in a position of authority needs to get the team together and decide how to correct the problem. It's human nature to avoid doing things that are hard. We've often found, for example, that programmers who haven't done test-first coding before won't do it unless required to do so by a leader they respect. Once they try this practice, they see the value and keep going, but someone has to push them to start.

Lots of other people are probably involved in the delivery of your software project, even if you don't always think of them as someone "on the team." It's a common misconception that XP projects "don't produce documentation." Of course they do, and if your team is fortunate, you have a good technical writer to help with this task. Someone has to write the paychecks and approve the expense reports. Have you thanked your accountant lately? Someone recruited you into the company and told you how to file a medical insurance claim. Someone buys your office supplies. Someone set up your network, someone fixes your laptop when it dies a big blue death. All these people are on your extended team, and, though their services may be peripheral, they're important in enabling your core team to do its best.

## Summary

- ✧ Testers should help customers define quality by asking lots of questions during the planning game.
- ✧ Testers may need to push customers to define specifics about quality.
- ✧ Programmers can help customers define quality levels by offering estimates to achieve different levels.
- ✧ Quality may be defined as sets of features. Stories can be written to achieve particular quality criteria.
- ✧ Quality is a collaborative effort of the team.
- ✧ Teams need strong leaders to help the team recognize and address problems.

# Part II

# Test Drive through an XP Project

In Part I of this book, we discussed what XP can do for quality assurance and testing professionals and what a tester can do for an XP team. We described the tester's role at a high level, and now we're going to examine it in more detail, by taking a virtual test drive through a prototypical XP project in the role of an XP tester.

We'll examine what the tester should be doing at various points along the way and use examples to illustrate how the tester does it. In the course of our journey, we'll find out many of the testing, development, and quality assurance skills XP testers use. You'll get a chance to try these out yourself in the exercises provided.

Before starting out on a road trip, it's good to have a destination and route in mind (though we might change our minds anytime once we're on the road). Our test drive is modeled on a three-day trip from Chicago to Salt Lake City, via Denver. This is three solid eight-hour days of driving, through the heart of the Great Plains and over the Rocky Mountains. Here's our planned itinerary (see next page).

The first two days, we drive through gently rolling hills. The roads aren't hard to negotiate, but the long, open stretches can get tedious. We'll have to concentrate to keep our eyes on the road. We're likely to run into construction detours and the occasional traffic jam. Once we head up into the mountains, the drive can get downright dangerous, especially if the weather's bad. We need

Our itinerary

| Day | Road Trip | General XP Activities | XP Tester Activities |
| --- | --- | --- | --- |
| 1 | Leave Chicago on I-80 West<br><br>Lunch at Gringo's in Iowa City<br><br>Check in to the Quality Inn in Omaha; dinner at La Strada | User stories<br>Release planning | Help with user stories<br>Find hidden assumptions<br>Define high-level acceptance tests<br>Estimate acceptance testing<br>Enable accurate estimates |
| 2 | Leave Omaha on I-80 West<br><br>Lunch at the Brick Wall in North Platte<br><br>Check into the Castle Marne B&B in Denver; dinner at My Brother's Bar | Iteration planning<br>Coding and unit testing<br>Refactoring<br>Integration | Estimate testing and test infrastructure tasks<br>Nail down acceptance test details<br>Write executable acceptance tests<br>Organize acceptance tests |
| 3 | Leave Denver on I-70 West<br><br>Lunch at W. W. Pepper's in Grand Junction<br><br>Arrive in Salt Lake City | Acceptance testing<br>End of iteration<br>Next iteration<br>Release | Refactor acceptance tests<br>Get acceptance tests running<br>Execute acceptance tests<br>Make acceptance tests run through user interface<br>Perform retrospective<br>Perform regression testing<br>Release |

to make sure our car doesn't overheat on the long climb up toward the divide. A rockslide might hold us up. It's a mighty pretty drive, though. We'll enjoy our journey, especially the road food!

# Chapter 7

## User Stories and Release Planning

Most XP projects start with the creation of user stories and release planning. On an ideal project, the customer writes the user stories first, the development team estimates the time required for each story, and then the whole team develops a release plan that divides the stories up among several iterations.

The details for each iteration are then planned in a separate activity right at the start of the iteration. This "just-in-time-planning" technique, where details are left until the last possible moment, is used to avoid expending effort on something the customer later decides either to change or discard.

In practice, creating the user stories, planning the release, and planning the first iteration often overlap. The release plan changes as new stories are created and existing stories are revised throughout the project (one reason for leaving the details to iteration planning). In fact, writing stories, estimating them, and packaging them into iterations are activities that extend through the life of the project. In our in our test drive, however, we'll take them up in sequence.

In day 1 of our test drive, our goal is to answer the following questions about release planning and story writing:

&#10022; Does a tester have a role here? (We think so.)

&#10022; What goals should a tester focus on?

❖ What is the best way to accomplish these goals?

❖ How about some examples?

We'll also propose some exercises that will allow you to practice. You can find our answers in the back of the book.

## The Tester's Role in Up-Front Activities

The tester's contribution in planning for an XP project (or any software development project) is often overlooked. Consider the following experience of Lisa's:

> *My team once started a project without me. I was offsite on another contract when a project involving a new external customer began. They figured they could get through the initial Planning Game and first iteration without a tester. After all, they were senior Java developers, with years of experience on a wide variety of projects and several months doing XP. However, things didn't turn out quite the way they expected. Here's the story in the words of the team captains, Natraj Kini and Steve Collins:*
>
> *"One realization that we came to was the importance of a full-time tester to keep the developers honest. When we didn't have a full-time tester for the first iteration, we got 90% of every story done, which made the client very unhappy during acceptance tests—they perceived that everything was broken. When a developer attempted to take over the role of creating acceptance tests, we also found that there was a lot more to the art and science of acceptance testing than we had realized." (Natraj Kini and Steve Collins, "Steering the Car: Lessons Learned from an Outsourced XP Project")*

This project team learned that leaving the tester out until later in the project was a painful experience. The programmers were motivated to learn more about testing, so they could do a better job of delivering value to the customer. Lisa learned that as a tester, one of her most important functions is to transfer her testing skills and experience to the rest of the team.

It's true that even if they never put a tester on the project, a team would probably learn how to do a better job with the acceptance tests after a few painful iterations. Whether they learn to do it well enough to satisfy the customer depends on the team. In the case of Lisa's team, the customer was unhappy enough after that first iteration to consider canceling the project. Why risk that if you don't have to?

What kind of thinking could lead to leaving the tester out at the start of a project in the first place? We think it would go something like this:

*The tester runs tests, which requires the code, of which hardly any exists until the end of the first iteration, and possibly not a whole lot then. Therefore, the earliest we really need the tester is the end of iteration 1. That's only a day or two before the beginning of iteration 2, so how much trouble can we get into in 24 hours?*

Several assumptions here are questionable, and in Exercise 1 we'll ask you to identify them, but they start with the assumption that *the tester's main contribution is running tests.*

We're not denying that running tests and reporting the results are an important part of the tester role. As Kent Beck writes in *Extreme Programming Explained,* "An XP tester is not a separate person, dedicated to breaking the system and humiliating the programmers. However, someone has to run all the tests regularly, . . . broadcast test results, and to make sure that the testing tools run well."

As a tester, you may spend more time running tests and reporting results than performing any other single activity. But just because it absorbs such a chunk of your time and effort doesn't make it the most important thing you do. For instance, driving across the country takes a lot more time and effort than filling up the gas tank beforehand, but try leaving that step out and see how far you get!

Okay, we have half the answer to question 1: Does a tester have a role in release planning? We say, "Yes, and it isn't running tests." So what is it?

## Goals of Up-Front Tester Activities

Based on our experiences, we think the role of the tester during story writing and release planning is characterized by four goals:

1. **Identifying and making explicit hidden assumptions in the stories.**
   Remember Lisa's missing door from Chapter 2? That's what we're talking about here. As a tester, your goal should be to avoid the "missing door" syndrome by identifying the assumptions that the customer has hidden in the stories.

2. **Defining some acceptance tests for each story.** We recommend writing acceptance tests for the stories as soon as possible, before iteration planning. This turns out to be an excellent way—maybe the best way—to get the customer's hidden assumptions out into the open. These will just be high-level acceptance tests for now—you don't want to spend too much time fleshing out stories the customer may never choose. By including acceptance tests along with the narrative of the story, the team can make much more accurate estimates of each story's cost during release and iteration planning.

3. **Including time for acceptance tests in story estimates.** It's your responsibility to get the time required for acceptance testing into the planning game in some form. You can add your estimates to those of the programmers or create additional stories that represent acceptance testing activities and put the estimates there.

4. **Enabling accurate estimates of time and velocity.** You can help programmers with their estimates on the user stories. While remembering that you're part of the development team and not an adversary, you can still afford to be a bit more pessimistic than the programmers (e.g., more like Nostradamus than Pollyanna). You can make sure estimates include enough time for automating and debugging tests, running tests, fixing bugs, and retesting.

We've found that accomplishing these goals during story writing and release planning has a big payoff later in the project. Is the tester the only one working on these things? Absolutely not: XP calls for programmers and the customer to do these things. But in practice, these goals can be overlooked in the rush to produce. A tester who's focused on them helps the rest of the team meet them.

Flushing out the hidden assumptions in the stories helps programmers implement more accurately the first time around, which makes for happy customers. XP may be self-correcting in terms of bringing these things out in the open eventually, but clearing them up earlier allows for more velocity later on.

Specifying acceptance tests up front with the stories is really a type of test-first development. It helps avoid some types of defects altogether and gives the team a head start on test automation and test data acquisition. This allows functional testing to keep up with the programmers at crunch time, when the end of the iteration approaches.

Including acceptance test tasks in the stories and enabling accurate story estimates makes release and iteration planning more accurate and provides time to automate the tests, which pays off many times over in later iterations.

In the next chapters, we'll expand on each of these goals, discuss effective ways to accomplish them, and provide examples.

## Summary

- ❖ Testers do some of their most important work during story writing and release planning.
- ❖ During story writing and release planning, a tester should
  - Identify and make explicit hidden assumptions
  - Define some acceptance tests for each story
  - Estimate acceptance-test time and include it in story estimates
  - Enable accurate estimates of time and velocity
- ❖ Accomplishing these lay the groundwork for
  - More accurate implementations
  - Time for automation
  - Testing that "keeps up"
  - Happier customers

Here's a warmup exercise.

## Exercise 1

Identify as many questionable or incorrect assumptions as you can in the following statement:

*Testers run tests, and running tests requires that the code be written, and no code is available until the end of the first iteration. Therefore, the earliest the tester is needed is the end of iteration 1.*

# Chapter 8

## Identifying Hidden Assumptions

Finding any old hidden assumption is actually pretty easy, because customers (usually) don't hide them purposefully. It's just a natural consequence of knowing their businesses too well. Mentioning one thing always implies a whole set of other things; indeed, this is fundamental to communication. If you had to explicitly list and define *everything*, you couldn't even talk to the customer, let alone build a system for him.

The goal here, though, is to find only assumptions where *A* implies *B* to the customer but implies *C* (or nothing) to the programmer. These are the ones that lead to problems later.

## A Process for Finding Hidden Assumptions

So if the stories are loaded with hidden assumptions anyway, how do you find the ones that are potential problems? We described the dual view of the tester back in Chapter 2, and that's the foundation for the basic approach: think about the story first from the customer's viewpoint, then from the programmer's viewpoint, and identify the mismatches.

You can go about this in a lot of ways. The process doesn't follow a strict linear progression; you tend to switch between viewpoints a lot and part of the time even gaze simultaneously from both. With a little experience you'll develop your own way of doing it, but for those who might have trouble getting started, we'll provide a step-by-step approach. It's helpful if the entire team is aware and supportive of this process, so get them involved and consider using this as a team exercise early in the project.

However, this is not a drawn-out analysis you perform alone for days (or even hours) and then write up in some tome "for review." This is real-time analysis, done on the fly while working with the team on stories or during the release planning meeting.

When we break this analysis down into steps, it looks as if it could be a lot of work. In fact, you'll do this in a minute or two for a given story and use it as the framework for targeting your questions in the discussion. While you go through this process, people will probably add notes to the story cards. You'll take your own notes as needed to remind you and the customer about these points when writing the acceptance tests. Here are the steps:

1. Imagine you're the customer and think about how this story relates to your business. Think how the customer would answer the following questions and what those answers imply: What business problem is it solving? How does it solve the problem? How could the system implement the story and not solve the problem? Are there alternate solutions? Are there related problems?

2. Now imagine yourself as a user of the system in this story. What would be the worst thing for you that could happen? How about the best thing? What would really irritate you? In what ways can you, as a user, "screw up"? How would you want the system to respond? How often will you be involved in this story? What are you likely to have just previously done, and what are you likely to do next?

3. Forget the customer and the user. Imagine you're the programmer. Based on what's written in the story, what's the simplest and easiest way to implement it that could possibly work?

4. Now it's time to be the tester. How likely is it that the simplest implementation will really solve the customer's business problem? Solve the related problems? Be the best solution? Avoid the user's worst-case scenario and achieve the best case? Integrate with the user's workflow? And so on.

5. Whenever the answer to a question in step 4 is "Not very likely," imagine what additional information is needed to change the answer to "Likely." This is the type of hidden assumption you're seeking.

During this process, you'll inevitably be asking lots of questions of both the customers and the programmers. You'll usually need to ask more than either group wants to answer, and you have limited time. Be disciplined and think things through first, so you get the maximum bang for the buck from each question.

Take a look at the following example.

## Example 1

Our customer team (a regional telephone company) has defined the following story for a business-directory application:

> **Story:** Create a screen that will allow the user to search on the Web for businesses by category of business and location.

**Step 1:** Think about the system from the customer's view. Remember, you're going through these points quickly, writing notes on story cards as appropriate.

- ◆ **I'm the customer. How does this relate to my business?** The phone directory is crucial to the phone system for both residential customers and business customers. Business listings and advertisements in the directory generate revenue.

- ◆ **What business problem is it solving? How does it solve it?** It's expensive to print and distribute a hard-copy directory, so I don't do it very often. This means new businesses can't get in for a long time, and I can't charge them. Plus users of the directory can't find them, so they call a directory operator, which is an expensive service to maintain.

  The Web directory can be updated cheaply, so I can afford to do it daily. This allows me to add new listings and realize the revenue right away as well as reducing directory-operator staffing and costs.

- ◆ **How could the system implement this and not solve the problem?** If people don't use the system, the problem isn't solved. Businesses won't pay if they still have to wait for the hard copy, and I won't be able to reduce the number of operators.

- ◆ **Are there alternate solutions? Are there related problems?** Can't think of any alternate solutions. Finding residential listings is a similar problem, but I can't get any revenue from that. If it works out as expected with the business listings, may try residential next.

**Step 2:** Think about the system from the user view. Keep up your momentum and skip over questions where you don't come up with ready answers.

⬧ **I'm a user, searching for a business. What are the worst and best things that can happen? What would really irritate me?**
**Worst thing:** I find a business and drive to its location, but it's been out of business for a month (should have called ahead!)
**Best thing:** I find the business, click a few times, and accomplish my goal (purchase/order/complaint) online.
**Irritating:** I'm looking for a particular business and know the name (approximately), but I can't just search on the name. I have to figure out how some idiot categorized it and search on that, then pick it out of a hundred others. (I get irritated just thinking about it!)

⬧ **How can I screw up? How should the system respond?** Misspell something, like the category. The system should correct it for me or at least offer some correction alternatives.

⬧ **How often will I do this? What will I do before and after?** Not very often. A couple of times a week at most—that's how often I use the hard-copy phone directory. What I've done before will usually be completely unrelated. Next thing is probably to call the business (if I found one) or get out the hard copy (if I didn't).

**Step 3:** Think about the system from the programmer's view for a moment.

⬧ **I'm the programmer. What's the simplest implementation that could possibly work?** A form with text input fields for category and location; a Search button in the browser. A server program gets all the businesses that match the category and location from the database and sends a list in response. Each item in the list has the business name, address, and phone number.

**Step 4:** Identify any mismatches between these views.

⬧ **How likely is the implementation to solve the business problem?** Not very likely, because solving the problem requires a significant percentage of customers to use the system. Say 20% of 20 million twice a week. That's over a million uses a day, or about 13 per second. The system needs to handle a peak load of ten times that, about 130 uses per second. Since each use will probably involve more than one search (say 1.5) and each search will involve multiple server interactions (say 5: presenting the form, loading images, and so on), 130 uses per second means about 200 searches and 1,000 hits per second. This is a fairly high performance requirement that the simplest implementation is not likely to deliver.

- ✧ **How likely is the implementation to solve the related problems (residential listings)?** Not very likely, for the same reason, and even more so (more users, higher performance requirement).
- ✧ **How likely is the implementation to avoid irritating the user? Respond appropriately to user mistakes?** Not very likely, because the simplest implementation has no search by name and no way to narrow the search or otherwise deal with a large number of returned results. The software has no provision for a pulldown list; users have to type in the category. It doesn't offer potential spelling corrections if a category is misspelled.

**Step 5:** Identify the assumptions. All your discussion up till now has led to this goal.

- ✧ What information is the customer assuming we know?
  - That the system will be able to handle a significant load, about 200 searches and 1,000 hits per second at peak.
  - That users should be able to search for a business by a number of things besides category, like name and address, and can search within the results when a large number is returned.
  - That users should be able to browse and select the category from a list. If they do type in a category that isn't on the list, the system should say so and offer the closest match.

Already we can see that so many requirements are coming to the fore, we'd need several stories to implement all this search functionality. That's just the kind of issue you want to come out of these release planning discussions.

As you begin asking your questions about the assumptions, try to avoid phrasing them as direct questions right off the bat. You don't want to put words into someone's mouth. For instance, thinking back once more to the "missing door" story, the question "Will you want to close the old basement off from the new addition?" is better than "Do you want a door in that door-way?" The reason the former is better is that it allows the customer to make the connection himself: "Yes, the old area won't be finished, so I want to be able to close the door. It should match the doors upstairs, which are six-panel oak, and have the same kind of doorknob (antique brass)."

When they make the connection themselves, customers often think of the details and share them with you. If you mention the door first, they may say yes, but they're likely to assume you know all about the door they have in mind, since you brought it up, and you have another set of hidden assumptions to worry about.

Later on, when we get into iteration planning, we'll want to make it easier on customers (and programmers) by providing choices between alternatives whenever we can. At that point, we'll be narrowing down and focusing in on the details, but here we're still in the gathering phase, using open-ended questions more frequently. This discussion will produced better-defined stories and may bring up the need for new stories.

Here are some of the questions you might want to ask in Example 1:

## Assumption 1

- ✧ How many concurrent users do you expect for this in production?
- ✧ What kind of response time is required?
- ✧ What values for category searches and locations would produce tests representative of production use?

## Assumption 2

- ✧ Is this story just for the category searches, or can the user search for a business by name?
- ✧ What do the search results look like?
- ✧ What sort of error handling is desired?

## Assumption 3

- ✧ What fields should be on the screen? Which ones are required?
- ✧ What happens if a given search produces no results?
- ✧ What edits may be required for the fields?

Once you've identified hidden assumptions, what do you do next? One way to proceed is just to write those assumptions right into the story, but this can have some disadvantages. We'll offer an alternative in the next chapter, which deals with defining high-level acceptance tests for the user stories.

## Summary

✧ Stories have loads of hidden assumptions. The ones to worry about are those that will cause problems.

✧ To identify the potential problems:
  ▪ Think about the system from the customer's viewpoint.
  ▪ Think about the system from the programmer's viewpoint.
  ▪ Identify the mismatches.

✧ Expect to ask lots of questions, but be disciplined. There's a limit.

✧ Ask tangential but targeted questions that allow the respondent to make connections and think of the details.

OK, now it's your turn to try these ideas out with an exercise.

## Exercise 2

### Introducing the XTrack Application

This and subsequent exercises will be based on a simple but useful XP tracking application named XTrack. XTrack is a Web application that allows our XP team to maintain information about projects, such as their iterations, stories, tasks, and tests, in a central online repository available to all project stakeholders. This application serves several objectives:

✧ The project's tracker has a simple way to maintain information about a project, such as estimated and actual time to complete stories, who owns which tasks, and which stories are assigned to each iteration.

✧ These data and metrics are available to all interested stakeholders online. For example, if an upper-level manager of the business wants to know how the current iteration is progressing, he can log into XTrack and see.

✧ Teams split across various locations can track tasks, stories, and iterations for a project. Using index cards or some other offline means of documenting these artifacts won't work if team members aren't all located in the same place.

✧ It maintains historical information about each project. For example, the team can look back during a retrospective and see whether they're getting better at accurately estimating stories.

Figure 8.1 is a screen shot from the XTrack system, showing some early versions of the stories written when the system was being developed.

You can access an instance of the XTrack system at http://xptester.org/xtrack.

**Story:** User can create, read, and update a story via a Web interface. The data fields in a story are number, name, author, description, estimate, iteration, timestamps, and state.

1. Given the above XTrack story, use the process we describe in this chapter to find hidden assumptions.

2. Identify the questions related to these assumptions that you'd ask in discussion.

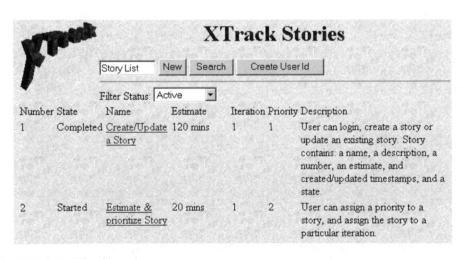

**FIGURE 8.1** XTrack stories

# Chapter 9

## Defining High-Level Acceptance Tests

Our trip is well underway, we just made our first pit stop for a tank of gas and a veggie sub (aren't Subways great!), and we're back on the road. Other than a minor disagreement about whether to put on a CD of Tony Rice on guitar or Sergei Nakariakov on trumpet, it's all been smooth sailing (first Tony, then Sergei).

Now we're ready to think about acceptance tests. Acceptance tests put meat on the bones provided by user stories. We start defining these tests during the initial release or project planning sessions but don't expect to get into too much detail at this point. What you're primarily after right now is to identify a few basic things that illustrate that a story has been acceptably implemented: the "happy path." After the stories have been selected in iteration planning and during the iteration is the time to lead customers off the "happy path" and dig into handling errors, unexpected paths through the system, unusual or unexpected data, and so on.

You want to avoid doing more than you absolutely need to now, because the customer could change his mind and not choose these stories. But you need enough details to get accurate story estimates. As always, asking questions will help ensure that the acceptance tests are a true reflection of the customer's requirements.

Keep in mind that the unit tests and test-first design practices of an XP project cover many of the testing needs. Acceptance tests show the customer that the story is complete, but they don't have to exercise every line of code or every possible test case you can think of. Different projects need different levels of testing. Your customer will decide the minimum she feels comfortable with. If you don't need to use all our suggested techniques in your project, skip them. We're presenting you with a toolbox for your own road trip. If the box is too heavy to carry around on your project, leave out the tools you don't need.

## Basic Acceptance Test Definitions

Defining tests at this level is usually pretty straightforward. Tests often come to mind just by reading the story and posing the question "How could you tell if this was in the system?" Go ahead and write down what immediately comes to mind. It's probably going to be, at a high level, exactly what needs to be tested. If not, noting it is still productive, because you're going to learn something as soon as someone else sees it.

With some experience you'll find this intuitive, but getting started can be intimidating, especially working within a short time window. If you have trouble coming up with acceptance tests for a story, try the following algorithm:

- ✧ Identify all the actions in the story
- ✧ For each action, write two tests in the form shown in Table 9.1.
- ✧ For *somedata,* supply inputs that should make the action succeed, and fill in whatever a successful result is for *result.*
- ✧ For *otherdata,* supply inputs to make the action fail, and fill in what the *response* should be.

**TABLE 9.1** Acceptance test template

| Action | Data | Expected Result |
|---|---|---|
| 1. *action* | *somedata* | Success: *result* |
| 2. | *otherdata* | Failure: *response* |

For instance, the story from Example 1 has just one action: Search.

## Example 2

Of course, this was pretty obvious from the story (see Table 9.2). It's about searching. If you search for something that's there, you should find it. If you

**TABLE 9.2** Acceptance tests for directory application story 1

| Action | Data | Expected Result |
|---|---|---|
| 1. Search | A category/location combination for which some businesses exist | Success: a list of each business within the category and location |
| 2. | A category/location combo for which no businesses exist | Failure: empty list |

search for something that's not there, you'd better not find it. Yes, it's easy, but don't let that bother you. Remember, you'll be doing this right at the beginning, after having read the story for the first time, maybe on the fly during the release planning meeting.

Just because these are high-level tests doesn't mean they aren't useful. When these tests pass, you'll have demonstrated *one* case where you can search for something that exists and find it, and *one* case where it doesn't exist and you don't find it. On the other hand, if these tests fail, you know without a doubt that the story isn't finished.

For a traditional software development project, this would be a long way from saying the story is acceptably implemented, because of all the low-level defects in the code when tests like this are run. The fact that one search returns results when it should and another doesn't when it shouldn't doesn't provide much confidence in that case.

The code on an XP project will be much cleaner by the time you run acceptance tests on it. It'll be doing what the programmers intend it to—not just programmers individually but with a separate pair of eyes verifying each assumption, confirmed by a 100% pass rate on the unit tests. You'll be adding additional cases with more detail later but not nearly what would be required for a traditional software project, where the acceptance tests often do the job of unit and integration tests as well.

Even defining acceptance tests as simply as in Example 2 will generate beneficial discussion during release planning. Take, for instance, the "empty list" result when no businesses match the specified category and location. The customer is likely to pick up on this and ask what, exactly, an "empty list" is. Does it mean no response at all? How will the user know the request has been processed? How about some kind of message like "No business matched your search criteria. Please try again"? How about some suggestions of related categories for which the database contains businesses?

Don't feel that all these questions need to be answered at this point, or even documented. What's important is that they become part of the team's public discussion rather than being privately interpreted in different ways by different members. The discussion is the key element. We may decide that having the search respond with suggestions of related categories is too expensive at this point and we're not going to do it. We've still accomplished something by bringing the questions up early and discussing them.

Another thing we can accomplish with these high-level acceptance tests is making the hidden assumptions visible. As we discussed in the previous chapter, once these have been identified, one approach is to write them right into the stories. This works just fine in some cases. For others, hidden assumptions might affect more than one story, or including them may make the story too long, or you might find it hard to phrase the assumptions correctly within the story.

In these cases, it's often quicker and easier to define the assumptions as acceptance tests. For instance, we can take the assumptions we identified in Example 1 and add them to the base acceptance tests for the story.

## Example 3

This isn't difficult if you don't get hung up on the details (see Table 9.3). Notice that in both Examples 2 and 3, we're not trying to define *how* we're going to go about performing the test. We don't, for example, need to worry about whether we have to log in to the system first, or how long the fields on the search screen are, or exactly what a location is, or what information is included in the list for a matching business.

Likewise, we're not trying to specify any particular values of test data—we're just saying we want some with this type of characteristic (searches with hits) and some with that (no hits, more than 20 hits, and so on).

As soon as we get a chance, though, we're naturally going to start thinking about how we're going to simulate 6,000 concurrent users or make up searches with a misspelled category and determine if the returned list contains the right one. Similarly, the programmer will be thinking about how to write the code that makes these tests pass, and the customer will be thinking about what else has to work before it's acceptable.

We want these things firmly in mind when estimating during release planning and also later on in iteration planning. We'll think them over while we're enjoying our first lunch break on our test drive.

**TABLE 9.3** Additional acceptance tests for directory application story 1

| Action | Data | Expected Result |
|--------|------|-----------------|
| 3. | Enough concurrent users and category/location combinations to generate 200 searches and 1,000 hits/second | Success: each user gets appropriate results list within a reasonable response time |
| 4. | Business name/location combo for which some businesses exist | Success: list of businesses that match the name at the specified location. |
| 5. | Business address/location combo for which some businesses exist | Success: list of businesses that match the address at the specified location |
| 6. | Search that retrieves more than 20 matching businesses | Success: list has a "Search within these results" option |
| 7. | Misspelled category/location combo for which businesses exist | Failure: contains a "Did you mean?" type message and a list of categories that includes the correct category |

This is actually a lot of tests for one story. We're doing this for the sake of example. In a real project, we'd start with a much smaller story, probably just basic search functionality. Things like searching within results and suggesting other searches need to be separate stories. We could write stories about handling load and performance now, but they'll probably be implemented in a later iteration. If stories that came out of release planning discussions are still too big in scope, defining the high-level tests will help show your team where you need to break them into smaller chunks.

In the next chapter, we'll discuss estimating the time for the acceptance tests.

## Summary

- ◇ Define the acceptance tests at a high level as soon as you read/see a story.
- ◇ Write down the obvious things that come to mind.

- ❖ If you get stuck, try this:
  - ▪ Write two tests for each action in the story, including descriptions of the inputs and system outputs:
    - – One that makes the action succeed
    - – One that makes it fail
- ❖ When you've identified hidden assumptions, write them into the acceptance-test definitions.
- ❖ Concentrate on what, not how, and don't sweat the details.

The following exercise gives you a chance to try this out for yourself.

## Exercise 3

1. Define high-level acceptance tests for the following story from the XTrack application (same project as Exercise 2 in the previous chapter). Don't look for hidden assumptions; just do it based on the bare bones of the story:

> **Story:** The user can provide an estimate for how long it will take to implement a story, prioritize the story, and assign the story to an iteration.

2. Use the technique from the previous chapter (or your own) to identify problematic hidden assumptions in this story and define additional acceptance tests that make them explicit.

# Chapter 10

# High-Level Acceptance
# Test Estimates

During release planning, programmers estimate the relative effort and technical risk for each story, using some kind of point system. At the start of each iteration, customers choose stories whose points add up to no more than the total number the team has said they can complete for that iteration. The units used to estimate stories aren't important; what's important is the consistency of the estimates, so it's clear how much relative effort each story requires. If a story turns out to take ten times the projected effort, you're going to have one messed-up iteration. The estimates don't have to be exactly right, but it helps if they're in the ballpark. Estimating the effort to complete high-level acceptance testing for each story will help make the story estimates accurate enough for useful iteration planning.

Acceptance testing is going to take time, regardless of whether testers, programmers, the customer, or some automated tool is doing it. Programmers typically include unit test time when they estimate a story, but they don't always think too much about acceptance testing requirements, which may be allocated as a fixed block of "a day or two" at the end of an iteration. They also may forget to allocate time for fixing defects and retesting.

When we planned our road trip, we built in time for everything that marks a successful trip: coping with unexpected delays, visiting some interesting sights, and making regular rest stops, so we can remain alert. On our XP test drive, we want to build in enough time for a safe and sane journey.

Here's why we want to consider acceptance tests when we're estimating stories during release planning. The time to develop and unit test a story is highly dependent on the story. This is true for acceptance testing time as well. However, they don't necessarily track together. Some things are a lot harder to code than to test; some are the other way around. The only reliable way to make sure you avoid a big problem near the end of an iteration (or one that bleeds into the next iteration) is to have some estimate during release and iteration planning of the acceptance-test time required for each story. Then, as you pack the iteration bin full of stories, you can make sure the acceptance test time fits as well.

The high-level acceptance tests you've already defined pay off in more ways than one. They give more detail about the requirements for the story, which helps the programmers estimate development time more accurately. These high-level test definitions also help you estimate the time required for acceptance testing.

If you think too much about how to account for acceptance testing time, it can get confusing. It seems that development time is the main driver of the iteration, since you can't execute acceptance tests before the code is ready and the time spent preparing for acceptance testing overlaps development time.

Sequencing problems may also arise. You may not be able to do some of the preparation until another story in the iteration is completed. That part of the preparation becomes an obstacle if the needed story is not completed enough in advance. Certain tests may only run in a limited window. For instance, a 6,000-concurrent-user test may need access to a production database that's available only late at night or on weekends. And what about when a test fails and you have to rerun it? How do you account for that?

Well, we've found it best not to worry about any of this, especially at this point in the process. All the dependencies, overlaps, and contingencies would be really difficult to figure exactly. If you did, you'd be wrong anyway, because everything would change by the time you actually got there.

The overlap between acceptance-test tasks and development tasks is no different from the overlap between different development tasks. Just estimate the time the testing tasks will take in the same units of measurement as the development tasks. As long as acceptance-test estimates get into the planning process, the team's velocity will account for them, and the fact that some tasks overlap or appear to be dependent on others won't matter.

## Ways to Estimate Acceptance-Test Effort

All you need to do now is come up with a ballpark estimate for completing all tasks related to acceptance testing. The approaches to doing this are probably infinite. You need a quick way to estimate, because you may have to do it in a few minutes per story. Remember, this is release planning, and you're participating in a discussion. You probably won't have time to go off by yourself and study it.

In the best-case scenario, you've had experience testing the type of application being developed and have a gut feeling for about how long it's likely to take. Of course, a lot of us don't live in the ideal world. If you have a hard time coming up with estimates on the fly, here are a couple of suggestions. Both involve looking ahead at a more detailed view of the activity. Even though this is release planning and no tasks have been defined yet (that will happen in iteration planning), you need to imagine what some of those tasks are going to be.

### Quick-and-Dirty Approach

Lisa's experience, based on years of keeping track of testing time versus developing time, is that testing usually takes about a third of the time spent on development. For a brand-new application that uses new technology, bump this up to half. For a simple application that isn't likely to change much, cut it down to 20%.

### Example 4

We'll use this method for a story to add a user to the repository and assign the user to a particular user group. Let's say the programmers estimate the development tasks at 78 points.

This is a pretty basic user interface. We've tested lots of user interfaces that involve creating, updating, deleting, or displaying records. On the other hand, this story involves a security model where users are associated with particular groups, which is a little different. Our customer is not sure yet how the screen should look and is still fuzzy on some of the details about how the user groups will work. It's best to pad the estimate to be on the conservative side. We decide time for testing tasks will add up to about 40% of the development time, or about 31 points.

We could stop at this point and just use 31 points as the estimate, but if the programmers' estimate is way off, ours will be too. What if testing this story reveals something unusual? It doesn't take much time to do a quick check by thinking ahead to what the testing tasks are going to be and splitting the 31 points among them, as shown in Table 10.1.

**TABLE 10.1** Example 4 estimate

| Task | Estimate (points) |
|---|---|
| Finish defining tests, obtain test data, get signoff from customers | 8 |
| Load test data | 2 |
| Automate tests | 18 |
| Execute tests, report results | 3 |
| Total | 31 |

This gives you a "reasonableness" check for your estimate: can you fit the likely tasks into the 31 points and reasonably expect to complete them?

## A More Detailed Estimating Method

Sometimes you may not be comfortable using the development time as a starting point, or you may have to come up with the testing estimates at the same time, or you may have trouble deciding if the likely tasks will fit or even if you've thought of all the likely tasks. Perhaps you have a project where the customer feels considerable risk is involved and wants detailed and complex acceptance tests to prove that every possible scenario works correctly.

Here's another approach in which you start with acceptance tests and think about the tasks associated with each test to come up with the estimate. This is something you normally wouldn't do until iteration planning, but if you need accurate estimates during release planning, you can use this technique:

1. For each acceptance test, estimate the time needed for the following:
   a. **Preparation.** Defining, creating, and validating test data; designing coding; debugging automated tests
   b. **Running tests.** Setting up, running, evaluating the outcome, and reporting the results
   c. **Special considerations.** A limited test window, for example
2. Add these three estimates to get the complete estimate for this test.
3. Add the estimates for all the acceptance tests to get the total for the story.

You can combine these two approaches as well, using one to complement and validate the other. Use whichever one seems to work best in a given situation, and don't sweat the details. Either method, as well as any other that involves thinking about what needs to be done, even for one minute, is better than no estimate at all.

We're showing this example in units of "ideal time": how long you think it would take to accomplish a task if you had absolutely nothing else to do. If the programmers use some other unit of measurement for estimates, use the same unit or use ideal time and convert later to the same units the programmers use.

## Example 5

Here's an example of using this method for the directory-application search story from the previous chapter:

> **Story:** Create a screen that will allow the user to search on the Web for businesses by category of business and location.

Table 10.2 shows the first acceptance test.

For preparation time, we'll allow half an hour each for defining details of the test and creating test records to support the test in the database. We'll also plan for half an hour each to write this as an executable acceptance test (see Chapter 16) and make it run through direct calls to the system code (Chapter 22). Finally, we'll allow 2 hours for interfacing to a test tool to make it run through the HTTP interface (Chapter 23). That's a total of 4 hours for preparation.

The test doesn't need any real setup, and it should run pretty quickly. We'll use the smallest unit we have, 0.1 hour (6 minutes), to represent both setup and execute time. We'll use the same number for evaluation and again for reporting, because those don't seem to have any special considerations either. Same for the test window—we don't see any particular limitations.

**TABLE 10.2** Test 1

| Action | Data | Expected Result |
|---|---|---|
| 1. Search | Category/location combination for which some businesses exist | Success: a list of each business within the category and location |

The total estimate for this acceptance test is 4.4 hours. Table 10.3 shows it in summary form.

Once you think this through for test 1, all the others except test 3 are similar, and you can use the same estimates without going through all the steps. Table 10.4 shows a summary of the estimate for all acceptance tests for this story.

**TABLE 10.3** Estimate for test 1 (in hours)

| Test | Preparation | | Execution | | Special | | Estimate | |
|------|-------------|-----|-----------|-----|---------|-----|----------|-----|
| 3 | Define details | 0.5 | Setup | 0.1 | | | | |
| | Create test records | 0.5 | Run | 0.1 | | | | |
| | Write tests | 0.5 | Evaluate | 0.1 | | | | |
| | Make tests runnable | 2.5 | Report | 0.1 | | | | |
| | **Total** | 4.0 | Total | 0.4 | **Total** | 0.0 | **Total** | 4.4 |

**TABLE 10.4** Estimate for all acceptance tests (in hours)

| Test | Preparation | Execution | Special | Estimate |
|------|-------------|-----------|---------|----------|
| 1 | 4.0 | 0.4 | 0.0 | 4.4 |
| 2 | 4.0 | 0.4 | 0.0 | 4.4 |
| 3 | 12.0 | 4.5 | 8.5 | 25.0 |
| 4 | 4.0 | 0.4 | 0.0 | 4.4 |
| 5 | 4.0 | 0.4 | 0.0 | 4.4 |
| 6 | 4.0 | 0.4 | 0.0 | 4.4 |
| 7 | 4.0 | 0.4 | 0.0 | 4.4 |
| | | | | Total: 51.4 |

So the acceptance-testing estimate for this story is 51.4 ideal hours (6.43 ideal days). The estimate for test 3 is a lot more than the others, so let's look at how we came up with it. Table 10.5 shows the details.

Preparation will be fairly extensive. We have to figure how many concurrent users we need to get the expected throughput and define "reasonable" response time. We say 2 hours. It will also take longer to create the test records, because we need a lot more—say another 2 hours. We also expect a longer spike for the automation because of all the concurrent users, so we'll allow 4 hours for that and another 4 hours to write the tests and get them running through the HTTP interface (you can't do load simulation through direct calls). That's a total of 12 hours.

The test will take a relatively long time to execute—we think 2 hours. We'll spend some time on setup tasks: make sure nothing else is going on in our test system, clear out the log files, set up monitoring tools. That's another half hour. We expect to spend an hour evaluating what happened: noting response times and throughput data, counting failures, preserving log records. We'll spend another hour producing a graphical results report for the team.

Special considerations come into play. As we mentioned earlier, system limitations often dictate a limited window for running load tests. We'll assume we can run this test only between midnight and 8:00 A.M. That means the worst-case time we'd have to wait to run the test would be 16 hours, if we were ready to test at 8:00 A.M. and had to wait until midnight. We estimate the average case at half that, or 8 hours.

Based on experience, we expect to have some kind of problem running a large test like this. We'll probably have to restart it or rerun part of it, not because the system fails the test but because something goes wrong with the test. We account for this with a half hour restart time. Special considerations total 8.5 hours.

**TABLE 10.5** Test 3

| Action | Data | Expected Result |
| --- | --- | --- |
| 3. Search | Enough concurrent users and category/location combinations to generate 200 searches and 100 hits/second | Success: each user gets appropriate result list within a reasonable response time |

**TABLE 10.6** Estimate for test 3 (in hours)

| Test | Preparation | | Execution | | Special | | Estimate | |
|------|-------------|------|-----------|-----|----------|-----|----------|------|
| 3 | Define details | 2.0 | Setup | 0.5 | Window | 8.0 | | |
| | Create test records | 2.0 | Run | 2.0 | Rerun | 0.5 | | |
| | Write tests | 4.0 | Evaluate | 1.0 | | | | |
| | Make tests runnable | 4.0 | Report | 1.0 | | | | |
| | **Total** | 12.0 | Total | 4.5 | **Total** | 8.5 | **Total** | 25.0 |

Adding this all up, we get a whopping 25 hours! Wow. That's a good thing to know up front! This story's a whopper in terms of acceptance-test time and will consume a lot of velocity if it's included in an iteration, unless it can be broken into smaller stories. Table 10.6 shows it in summary form.

You can't do accurate release and iteration planning without good estimates of both development and acceptance test time. In the next chapter, we'll talk about how to make your estimates even more accurate for planning purposes.

## Summary

 ⬧ The time required for acceptance testing tasks varies with the story and needs to be accounted for in story estimates.

 ⬧ In our experience, acceptance test tasks generally take anywhere from 20% to 50% of development time, depending on how dynamic the application is, how new the technology is, the team's experience with testing that type of software, and other factors.

 ⬧ Either start with a percentage of the programmers' estimate and work backward to fit in your tasks or start with the high-level acceptance tests and add up the estimates for the related tasks.

 ⬧ Do your estimate in whatever units work best for you, such as ideal hours, then convert to the same units the programmers use.

 ⬧ Add the acceptance test task estimates to the programmers' estimates for the stories.

Try it out yourself in the following exercise.

## Exercise 4

1. Define high-level acceptance tests for the following story from the XTrack application, using the techniques from the previous chapters or your own favorite method:

> **Story:** The user can create, update, display, and delete a task. A task has a name, description, assignee, estimate, actual time spent, state, and created/updated timestamps.

2. Assume the programmers have estimated that it will take $D$ ideal days to develop this (we're not going to tell you what number $D$ is, so it doesn't influence your answer to question 3). Using the first method in this chapter, estimate the acceptance-test time (hint: your answer will be in terms of $D$).

3. Use the second method in this chapter to estimate the acceptance-test time in ideal days.

# Chapter 11

# Enabling Accurate Estimates during Release Planning

The farmland in eastern Iowa has given way to rolling hills and prairie as we approach the end of the first day of our test drive. We've covered a lot of miles fast! We've been identifying hidden assumptions in stories, defining high-level acceptance tests for the stories, and estimating acceptance test times. The results of this work will improve the accuracy of release planning and iteration planning and thus provide better steering for the team. But wait! You, as the tester, can do even more to help the team estimate accurately.

## Why We Care about Estimates

Why all this emphasis on accurate estimates?

Because they have a powerful influence on our team's journey. If they're too low, we'll have to drive like maniacs to get to the finish line, risking spinning out of control and crashing. If they're too high, it's not such a bad problem—we might end up finishing early but at the wrong place. This beats crashing, and we can always have the customer pick more stories for a short additional drive. But if we get the estimates right, we'll get to the right place at the right time and have a great trip along the way.

Do the estimates have to be perfect? No. The reason we're emphasizing estimates is that over and over we've seen teams underestimate the time needed for testing. In fact, they often leave testing time out of story estimates altogether.

Here's a common scenario we've witnessed: Team X uses up all the time they'd estimated for stories without completing any of the testing tasks. Maybe they even dropped a story, but they're still short of time. Only a day or two is left in the iteration, so they panic and run the acceptance tests manually. Now iteration 2 starts. Not only do they have all the testing tasks for iteration 2, they still have to automate the acceptance tests for iteration 1. The problem snowballs into an avalanche.

If our story estimates include enough time for all the testing tasks, our team won't take on more work than they can actually complete in an iteration. Remember, no story is finished until the acceptance tests have run. That means time for the automation too.

Experienced XP teams can take estimation in stride. They have so much experience, they have a good feel for the effort each story will need. They might be high on some estimates and low on others, but everything will average out, and they can adjust as they go along. If you're working on a team that doesn't have a track record with XP projects, we think you need to pay more attention to the estimates.

## How You Can Improve Estimate Accuracy

Before we pull off the road and head for dinner, we're going to look at some more things you can do to help improve the estimates. The start of a new release is lot like a going down a good buffet line: all the stories look good. The team wants to make the customer happy, and programmers tend to be (and we are, and have been, programmers too) incorrigible optimists. We can't resist taking some of every dish, and we tend to overestimate our velocity.

You can help offset this tendency, but you need to be diplomatic about it. Nobody likes dieting, and the last thing you want to do is become an adversary. We've chosen the term *enable* to suggest that what you're doing *allows* others to be more accurate instead of somehow forcing them to be. Once again, a tangential approach is best.

You can, for instance, challenge estimates (politely): "Are you sure you can do that story in one day?" This is much preferable to challenging the estimator, as in, "Carol, there's no way you can get that done in one day, and you know it."

You can also point out aspects the estimator may have overlooked and allow her to draw her own conclusions. You can do this without making her feel stupid. For instance, "Carol, when you made that estimate, did you realize category names and codes don't have a one-to-one relationship?" may make Carol defensive if, in fact, she did overlook it. A better approach might be, "You know, Carol, I didn't realize until now that category names and codes don't have a one-to-one correspondence. Does that have any impact on how long it will take?"

When all else fails, play dumb and have someone (preferably the customer) explain things to you in the presence of the estimator. This gets the information to the estimator and lets her absorb it and take it into account while everyone is focused on you instead. Don't do this too often, though, or it will undermine your credibility.

This process begins in release planning, as soon as a story is written, but continues as the project progresses. You can ask in every daily standup meeting, where team members discuss their progress (we discuss standups in Chapter 30), "Are we sure we can finish all these stories? Do we need to go to the customer and have him remove a story?" And you can make a pest of yourself in other helpful ways: "Don't forget, these stories have to be finished the day *before* the end of the iteration, so we can run all the tests on the completed packages."

Please note that we encourage the use of the pronoun *we* in these questions. You don't want to exclude yourself from the problem. Not only will this cause resentment, it just isn't true. You're just as likely to be overly optimistic when you estimate, and you have to be diligent in keeping your own estimates realistic.

Another technique you can use is to question estimates that differ significantly from each other when the stories seem similar. For example, "I don't understand why the estimate for story 3 is twice that of story 2 when it seems they ought to take about the same amount of time. Is the estimate for story 3 too high?" Do look for estimates that are too high. They're rare, but watch for "padded" estimates that have been inflated for no valid reason. Your goal is more accurate estimates, not just higher ones.

Accurate estimates are important, but unfortunately, we don't have an algorithm we can give you to get you started. You'll acquire these communication and "people" skills by working with team members individually and in groups. The best we can do is suggest a few guidelines:

⬥ Challenge the estimate, but don't get personal.

⬥ Point out things you think were missed but not who missed them.

⬥ Phrase comments in terms of "how long it will take," not "the estimate" or "your estimate."

- ✧ If someone has to look stupid, make sure it's you, but don't do it often.
- ✧ Question widely differing estimates for stories that seem similar.

## Summary

- ✧ The accuracy of estimates has a big impact on how the project plays out.
- ✧ The tester can offset the programmers' natural optimism but must do so tactfully.
- ✧ Question estimates that seem too low or too high.

Finally! We've arrived at the end of the first day of our test drive. Time to check into the motel, get some dinner, and check out the pool. Let's hope they have a hot tub! Here's an exercise where you can have a little fun while trying out some of the ideas from this chapter.

## Exercise 5

For each situation, pick the best question to ask or statement to make:

1. Joan, a programmer new to the team, has provided an estimate for a directory service that you think is way too low. You say:
   a. "You dolt! Where did you learn to program? Wal-Mart?"
   b. "Can I smoke some of what you're smokin'?"
   c. "Not!"
   d. "Wait, let's look at the acceptance tests for that story. I think the validation is pretty complex. What do you think, maybe we need to build in more time just in case?"
2. Jim, the project manager, says, "This is a new client, and we really want to impress him. Let's forget about automating the acceptance tests this iteration, so we have time to squeeze in an extra story." You say:
   a. "Have you lost your #$%@!*&^ mind???"
   b. "Oh, heck, why not just do away with testing? Then maybe we can squeeze in two more stories."

c. "Let's think about this. We might save a little time this iteration if we skip the test automation tasks, but next iteration it'll take us longer to perform the regression acceptance tests from this iteration. We won't be able to keep up the same velocity, and the customer will be disappointed. If we automate tests for this iteration now, that'll save us time later, and we can provide the customer with consistent, high-quality deliverables."

3. Bob and Tom, both programmers, have come up with widely different estimates for two stories that clearly seem to require about the same effort. Tom is one of the younger team members, recently married, and his estimate is less than half of Bob's, who has over 20 years in the business. You say:

   a. "I don't know which of you is the idiot, but there's no way one of these can take twice as long as the other. Maybe you both are."

   b. "Tom, aren't you worried you'll have a mighty short marriage if you're in here all night getting that story right?"

   c. "Doesn't it seem like these should take about the same amount of effort? Maybe one of these is too high or too low  what do you think?"

# Chapter 12

# Planning the First Iteration

As the second day of our XP test drive trip dawns (what a lovely sunrise!) we're ready to begin the first iteration of the project. During the release planning on our first day, we pored over the system functions with the customer in the form of high-level user stories, asked a lot of questions, flushed out as many hidden assumptions as possible, and sketched the basic set of acceptance tests. We calculated the risks and technical difficulties and made estimates of the time required for each, including the time for acceptance testing.

Most of what we did in release planning was **widening** activity: we cast our net as widely as possible to make sure we caught all the requirements. We weren't concerned with which stories would be completed during the course of the project. Now, in iteration planning, we'll start **narrowing** things down. We'll tell the customer how much work our team can complete in the first iteration: our velocity. The customer will choose the stories, whose total estimates can't exceed our velocity, for us to complete in the first iteration. On the first day we enjoyed a smooth, speedy, open four-lane interstate. Today, our guidebook says the road is level and straight. But truck traffic is heavy, and we've heard the highway is under construction. Things could get a bit bumpy.

If you're used to traditional software development artifacts such as requirements, master test plans, and functional specifications, you'll naturally feel some trepidation here. You may be asking yourself how your team can possibly deliver a tested and production-ready software package in about two weeks, the end of the iteration.

The lack of heavyweight artifacts and the speed at which we'll be moving are related. The user stories and high-level acceptance-test definitions we do have are simple, so we won't have to spend time formatting, updating, reviewing, distributing, and/or approving them. We'll just get on with it. We have the best possible, always up-to-date reference: our customer.

## Overview of Iteration Planning

Iteration planning is selecting the set of stories to be implemented in an iteration, breaking down the implementation of each story into a set of tasks, and estimating the effort required to accomplish each task.

Prior to planning the first iteration, the development team will establish their velocity, the number of estimated units of ideal time they can accomplish per unit of actual elapsed time. For the first iteration, this will have to be something of a guess, based on past experience. For subsequent iterations, velocity is always equal to the number of units 100% completed in the immediately preceding iteration. This velocity, in combination with the length of the first iteration, will set an upper limit for the combined estimates of the stories selected for the iteration.

The customer or customer team chooses stories for this first iteration, based on what's most important to them. They're constrained, however, by what will fit into the iteration. No matter what, the stories' combined estimates can't exceed the development team's established velocity.

Once the customer has selected stories for the iteration, the development team takes each story, breaks it down into a set of tasks required to implement the story, and estimates the time required for each task. The customer is involved in this activity as well, available to answer the many questions that arise as the team examines the stories in more depth.

The end result of the iteration planning is a detailed activity plan that includes all the tasks to be accomplished to implement the selected stories by the end of our first iteration.

## The Tester's Role in Iteration Planning

In a lot of ways, iteration planning is like release planning on a more detailed scale. You'll be looking at some of the same stories but will see more of the specifics involved in each, because you're taking a closer look. Since the story estimates include time for acceptance testing (thanks to you), the velocity will, in theory, include the resources for acceptance testing. Keep the Tester's Bill of

Rights in mind during this process. You may realize, as you see more of the details, that the initial estimate was too low.

## Thinking of All the Tasks

Your priority during iteration planning is to help the team think of all the tasks they'll have to do to finish a story. Finishing a story means not only coding and integrating it into the system but also developing and executing the acceptance tests that demonstrate that the story is present, correct, and complete. You'll tend to think of tasks along those lines, whereas the programmers will likely focus on the coding, integration, and unit testing.

You can help get several categories of often overlooked tasks into the iteration plan. Some of these are one-time tasks that can be taken care of in the first iteration or so; others might extend over multiple iterations.

- **Development infrastructure**. These tasks usually come up when you have a brand-new team and project. Your team needs to decide what source-code control tool to use, what to use for building packages, what integrated development environment (IDE) to use, how to track defects, whether to use a particular development framework—anything related to coding and building the system. The programmers will probably be making the decisions and so are likely to think of some of these tasks, like evaluating and purchasing, but often overlook those involved with training, learning, and tweaking, especially with new technology.

- **Release packaging**. At the other end of the process, these tasks relate to how the system is delivered to the customer at the end of each iteration and release. This may be trivial, like zipping the code up into an archive and handing it to the customer on a CD, or it could involve any amount of specialized formats and delivery mechanisms. Since one of the strengths of XP is that the customer can decide at the end of any iteration to walk away with the functional system he has at that point, consider release packaging even during the first iteration.

- **Production environment**. These are tasks that may be required by the customer to integrate the delivered system into an existing production environment. For a brand-new, stand-alone system, these would be trivial. For an extension to a currently functioning system or a new system that integrates with an existing production environment, extensive regression and performance testing could be required, to validate that the newly delivered iteration will not cause problems.

- ✧ **Test infrastructure**. These tasks are associated with creating and maintaining a functional test system and obtaining and using test tools.
- ✧ **Acceptance testing**. These tasks are associated with defining tests, creating test data, developing test automation, and with executing, evaluating, and reporting tests.

These last two, test infrastructure and acceptance testing, are the areas where the tester has primary responsibility for defining and estimating tasks. We'll talk about these in detail a bit further on.

## Enhancing Communication

In addition to actively identifying tasks, you have a role in facilitating communication and understanding between the customer and development teams. You also strive for the best possible estimation of all tasks, as you did in release planning.

During iteration planning, you often need additional explanation of some or all of the stories the customer team selected. Sometimes they'll find they didn't completely understand a story, and now that they have all the facts, they need to reestimate it. It's much better to do this now than to come up short at the end of the iteration. Remember that getting even 90% of each story done still equals zero percent completed stories—and a velocity of zero for the next iteration!

Be alert for assumptions by development and customer teams. If you remember that the customer wanted a confirmation screen for sending a message and the programmers don't have a task to create it, bring up the issue. If the programmers misunderstood something that has a major impact on a story estimate, the story has to be reestimated. If the estimate is large enough to exceed the velocity for the iteration, the customer has to choose a story to leave out. Remember that although it's hard to have to ask the customer to ditch a story for now, it's much better than coming to the end of the iteration with stories not 100% complete! The deadline in XP is never negotiable. You have to collaborate with the customer on scope and make adjustments whenever needed.

The development team, including testers, may find estimating tasks to be hard at first. Estimating is tricky in the first iteration; you have no history for this particular project on which to base your estimates. Your team may estimate in time-independent points, pair hours, ideal programming hours, or some other system. Take your best shot—experience will improve your estimating ability. Your priority during iteration planning is to help the team think of all the tasks they'll have to do to finish a story.

The person estimating the task may be the one ultimately responsible for completing the task. However, some teams simply put all the tasks back into a bucket, and the person picking up the task later may not be the same one who estimated it. The person responsible for the task can reestimate it later if necessary.

## Summary

- ✧ Where release planning is a widening activity, iteration planning is more of a narrowing-down activity.
- ✧ Scary as it is to race ahead without artifacts like requirements documents, the simplicity of stories and availability of the customer makes speeding safe.
- ✧ Iteration planning is
  - Selecting the set of stories to be implemented in iteration
  - Breaking down the implementation of each story into a set of tasks
  - Estimating the effort required to accomplish each task
- ✧ The tester's primary responsibility during iteration planning is helping the team think of all the tasks necessary to finish the story, especially those related to
  - Development infrastructure
  - Release packaging
  - Production environment
  - Test infrastructure
  - Acceptance testing
- ✧ The tester also has the responsibility to help foster understanding between the development team and the customer and to strive for accuracy in task estimates.

Here's an easy exercise to get us going.

## Exercise 6

For each of the following questions, indicate whether it's more of the "widening" or "narrowing" type:

- ✧ "Does the user need to log in to use the system?"
- ✧ "When a user clicks that link, should the document display in the current browser window or pop up in another?"
- ✧ "How many search terms should the user be able to enter on this page?"
- ✧ "Would a user ever have to change any of this information?"
- ✧ "What's the maximum length for the customer name?"

# Chapter 13

# Defining and Estimating Testing and Test Infrastructure Tasks

As the first iteration gets underway, you're helping the programmers clarify details in the stories with the customer, looking for assumptions that may blow up the story estimate and require reshuffling of the iteration, raising questions about usually overlooked tasks, and generally holding everyone's feet to the fire for accurate estimates. But (to quote the late-night gadget commercials) that's not all! You also need to identify and estimate (as accurately as possible) the tasks associated with testing and test infrastructure that are your primary responsibility.

Don't be scared off by our geeky-sounding term *test infrastructure*. We aren't after a heavyweight infrastructure here. We simply mean that to help your team move at maximum speed, you need a stable test environment and some means of automating tests, capturing test results, and leveraging automated tests. The test infrastructure can be built incrementally: build what you need when you need it. We've had the unfortunate experience of working on projects that, at least in the first few iterations, had no environment apart from the development environment in which to do acceptance testing. Your project team probably won't succeed in delivering acceptable software without an independent test environment and some means of automating the tests.

## Identifying and Estimating Test Infrastructure Tasks

The test infrastructure provides a controlled environment in which to run your acceptance tests and tools to aid test execution, evaluation, and reporting.

Here are some of the things your test infrastructure should allow you to do:

1. Automate the acceptance tests.
2. Have a separate system you can load any time with the latest successful integration or an earlier one, without regard to what the programmers are doing.
3. Save test data and other state information from test sessions, to be restored and used as the starting point for subsequent sessions.
4. Keep track of which tests have passed and failed for each story in a given software build.
5. Incorporate automated acceptance tests into the build script, to validate that previously delivered stories aren't broken by refactoring.

You probably won't have the luxury of putting one infrastructure in place that has all these features, so use this as a starting point and negotiate. Hopefully, you won't have to start from scratch. Some or all of these features may already exist and be familiar to the team, or they may be inherent in the development environment or the nature of the system being developed.

For instance, when the team has just finished a similar project and is satisfied with the tools and techniques used for testing, it's natural to use them again. This probably doesn't require any specific planning.

Suppose the system is completely self-contained, with an interface consisting of only an application program interface (API)—for example, a statistical methods library. In this case, the test system would consist only of the code itself, and the functional tests could be automated in the source language of the system. Again, no need for defining and estimating specific tasks.

In many cases, your project will require test infrastructure tasks that must be identified and estimated in the iteration plan. If the tasks are overlooked, the iteration will fall behind schedule. Either unplanned tasks steal time allocated to other tasks or an inadequate test infrastructure results in longer-than-expected test development, execution, and evaluation times.

For a new project and/or a new project team, you may have to spend a significant amount of time setting up your environment and the tools you need. You could find that you have to tweak not only your test tools but your build and release process and related tasks as well. All these infrastructure-related concerns can make estimating pretty tricky for the first iteration of a new project.

For a way to handle this difficulty, consider the experience of one of the teams on which Lisa was the tester. For the first iteration, they decided to create an infrastructure story for this bootstrap time that would collect the "overhead" for the entire project. They thought at the time this would be a one-time occurrence, because of the number of tasks that happen only once during the project. As Lisa remembers:

> *This worked fairly well for the first iteration, but later we realized we should also have had an infrastructure story for similar tasks that appear in subsequent iterations. We found that we always spent some time on infrastructure and that it remained fairly constant in each iteration, because we were constantly adding to and adjusting the infrastructure. Based on this, we modified our approach to fold the average of these costs into our team's velocity. We worried about separate estimates only for stories that required a large infrastructure cost, such as creating a relational database.*

We recommend using this approach for the identifying and estimating test infrastructure tasks: for the first iteration, identify and estimate all the individual tasks necessary to get the appropriate tools and techniques in place. We recommend tracking the actuals on these, so they become part of the velocity calculation for subsequent iterations. Then, for subsequent iterations, break out separate tasks only when it's clear the infrastructure cost will be exceptionally large. Tracking actuals seems like a big demand, and it might not be necessary on your project. Our personal experience is that time needed for setting up a test environment and acquiring or writing test tools is often overlooked.

## Identifying and Estimating Functional and Acceptance Testing Tasks

While listing, estimating, and assigning programming tasks, make sure to include testing tasks. When you estimate tasks and stories, include time for both testing and test support. For example, you might need a script to load test data. No matter who is ultimately responsible for the task, it should be included with other tasks for the story. Thinking about testing tasks will help lead the team to a test-friendly design and serve as a reminder that testing is the responsibility of the entire team, not just the tester. In Chapter 10, we discussed a couple of ways to estimate high-level acceptance tests. The same principles apply when estimating detailed test-related tasks for an iteration's stories.

The testing tasks associated with a story usually involve some or all of the following:

- **Clarifying acceptance criteria.** You'll need a task for this when a story includes subjective criteria—for example, a phrase like "good response time" or "easy to use." It's vital to spend the time with the customer to quantify these aspects of the system before attempting to build or run a test for it.

- **Defining, acquiring, and validating test data.** You almost always need some form of test data. The customer should provide this, because she's likely to have representative data on hand or be able to easily define it. You may still need to spend time acquiring test data and may need to build some specialized tools for generating and loading it.

- **Automation design spike.** When using test tools to run automated tests through a user interface, you might have to try a variety of approaches to find the approach for a given application or test. If you're using a new tool or automating for the first time, you'll definitely want to include these tasks. Even when the tool and application are old hat, certain types of tests may still require experimentation. Examples include load and performance tests, tests that require synchronization of simultaneous access, tests that require a specific behavior or response from an interfacing system, and tests of failure and recovery behavior.

- **Automation.** These tasks include building and verifying the automated tests. Since creating automated test scripts is a form of programming, these often look like programming tasks. Just as you do with any code your team develops, you'll need to test and debug the automated tests before they're ready to run against the system.

- **Execution.** Automated tests usually run so quickly that it may not be necessary to break out a separate task for each test, but you'll still need to spend some time setting up the test and making sure it runs. The test may be run many times over the course of the iteration. In some cases, a single test (such as a large-scale load test) may warrant its own separate execution task.

✧ **Evaluation and reporting.** Most tests don't have specific tasks for evaluation and reporting, but there are a few exceptions. Load and performance tests are notorious for requiring lots of analysis during and after the fact, to determine what went wrong and how to remedy it. Another situation often arises in later iterations, as the system moves toward release: careful record-keeping of which version of the software build passed which tests becomes important, because so much already-present functionality can be broken at each integration.

If these look a bit familiar, they should. They're the same general areas we looked at in Chapter 10 when we made high-level estimates of acceptance-test time during release planning. Iteration planning provides the place to take a closer look and break out and estimate each task individually.

When we were estimating stories during release planning, we looked ahead to what we thought the tasks were likely to be, even though we waited to actually define the tasks until now. We probably missed some and maybe included a few we really didn't need. We may not have thought long enough about the ones we did foresee to estimate them accurately. That's what estimating is all about: prediction based on incomplete knowledge.

This technique of anticipating a future step to provide partial information in the present not only allows you to plan for that step more accurately, it also makes the step go more quickly when you get there. It gives you a sort of dry run. We'll use this same technique again in iteration planning, this time by looking ahead to what our test modules are going to be, even though we won't actually define them until we get to test design.

## A Note on Separate Test Teams

Some XP teams choose to have a separate test team and keep the acceptance testing tasks separate from development. We disagree with this approach, for several reasons:

✧ Testers on a separate team have no input into the team's velocity and thus no control over their own workload.

✧ Time for acceptance testing tasks becomes invisible when they aren't included with story tasks. As the end of the iteration comes up, everyone but the testers tends to forget about testing tasks.

- Writing, automating, and running acceptance tests is the responsibility of the entire XP team, including the customer.
- No story is complete until the acceptance tests have passed.

We're not saying this can never work, but it requires strong leadership and communication. It's simpler to include testers as part of the development team and testing tasks as part of the story tasks.

Iteration planning is best learned by doing. You'll find lots of pointers in XP publications, but they may not specifically address testing tasks. Here's an example of breaking out and estimating test infrastructure and testing tasks for the phone-directory application used in the preceding examples. For the purpose of a clear example, we're using a story containing functionality that, in a real project, might be broken out into multiple stories.

## Example 6

> **Story:** Create a screen that will allow the user to search on the Web for businesses by category of business and location.

In Chapter 9, we defined the acceptance tests shown in Table 13.1 for this story.

**TABLE 13.1** All acceptance tests for directory application Story 1

| Action | Data | Expected Result |
| --- | --- | --- |
| 1. Search | A category/location combination for which some businesses exist | Success: a list of each business within the category and location |
| 2. | A category/location combo for which no businesses exist | Failure: empty list |
| 3. | Enough concurrent users and category/location combinations to generate 200 searches and 1,000 hits/second | Success: each user gets appropriate results list within a reasonable response time |

**TABLE 13.1** All acceptance tests for directory application Story 1 (Continued)

| Action | Data | Expected Result |
|---|---|---|
| 4. | Business name/location combo for which some businesses exist | Success: list of businesses that match the name at the specified location |
| 5. | Business address/location combo for which some businesses exist | Success: list of businesses that match the address at the specified location |
| 6. | Search that retrieves more than 20 matching businesses | Success: list has a "Search within these results" option |
| 7. | Misspelled category/location combo for which businesses exist | Failure: contains a "Did you mean?" type message and a list of categories that includes the correct category |

Let's say this is the first story in our first iteration. Below is the way we broke out and estimated the tasks in ideal hours. Remember, this is just an example. If your stories aren't this complex, you won't necessarily need all these tasks. We just want to illustrate all the possibilities.

## Test Infrastructure Tasks

We need to select and implement a test tool that will allow us to run tests through the user interface. Assume we have a short list of tools we've used before, so we'll be able to decide on one fairly quickly. We estimate 3 hours.

Now, say we have a machine allocated for a test system. We need to install the base software on it and create some shell scripts to pull over our software from the integration system whenever we have a new build. We estimate 3 hours.

We also need some shell or database scripts to load, save, and restore the data in the test environment. We estimate 2 hours.

We want to find or create a tool to save and report results for each run of our functional tests. The whole team needs to look at this and decide the best approach. We estimate 8 hours.

## Acceptance Testing Tasks

We know we'll need to work with the customer to define categories and business names. The customer should also come up with the searches to retrieve the various types of results. While we're compiling that, we'll also define error messages, the look and feel of the search form and results list, and probably come up with additional typical and potentially tricky user scenarios. In addition to all this, we'll need to figure out how many concurrent users we need for the load test and determine what "reasonable" response time is. We estimate 4 hours.

Once we've defined the details, we'll need to load test data into the test system and also into whatever format is necessary for the test automation to access it—especially the load test, which will require a lot of different searches. We expect to obtain test data from the user and load it into the system using standard database utilities. Once again, we estimate 4 hours.

We're going to break out the test automation tasks for this story by anticipating writing an executable version of the test. We'll do that for real later on in the iteration (Chapter 16). For now, based on the acceptance tests we've defined, it appears we can handle all of them, except test 3, with a single `search` module.

This module will be parameterized with the search specification as a category and location, a business name and location, or a business address and location. It will perform the search according to the parameters and return the results list. We expect to first build a version of `search` that calls the system code directly (half hour) and later one in the test tool that goes through the user interface (2.5 hours), for a total of 3 hours to code and test this module.

Four variations on the expected results are possible:

1. A list of businesses that match the criteria
2. An empty list when no matches exist
3. A list with a "Search within" option
4. An empty list when a term has been misspelled, with a "Did you mean?" suggestion

We expect to need a `verifyList` module to recognize each of these variations. We estimate 1 hour to code and test this module.

Because test 3 involves multiple users and has performance criteria besides the functionality validated by our `search` module, we'll need a different module for that test, which we'll call `multiSearch`. This module will use `search` and `verifyList` to perform the searches and validate the results. It will coordinate the concurrent users doing the searches and will collect and validate the response times. Because we aren't as comfortable with multiuser automation, we expect to have to experiment to find the best way to do this, so we'll estimate a 4-hour design spike and another 4 hours to code and test this module.

Finally, setup and reporting for all tests except test 3 are trivial; we won't even estimate those. For test 3 to be valid, we need a good 2 hours at peak load and additional time to analyze the results, especially if the response times aren't good enough. There's a good chance we may have to do this test twice, so we'll plan for two execution tasks of 2 hours each and two analysis tasks of 2 hours each.

Table 13.2 shows our tasks and estimates.

**TABLE 13.2** Example 6 tasks and estimates

| Task | Estimate (hours) |
|------|:----------------:|
| Select test tool | 3 |
| Set up test system | 3 |
| Create scripts to load/save/restore test data | 2 |
| Find or build test results reporting tools | 8 |
| | |
| Define search test details | 4 |
| Load search test data | 4 |
| Code and test search module | 3 |
| Code and test verifyList module | 1 |
| multiSearch design spike | 4 |
| Code and test multiSearch module | 4 |
| | |
| First load test execution | 4 |
| First load test analysis | 4 |
| Second load test execution | 4 |
| Second load test analysis | 4 |
| | |
| Total | 52 |

## Summary

✧ The test infrastructure allows you to
  ▪ Automate execution of functional tests
  ▪ Automatically determine if the automated tests passed or failed
  ▪ Load the system at any time with the latest successful integration or an earlier one, without regard to what the programmers are doing
  ▪ Save test data from one test session for use in another
  ▪ Keep track of tests that passed or failed for a story and software version
  ▪ Incorporate automated tests into the build script
  ▪ Break out test infrastructure tasks in the first iteration, then fold them into the team velocity
✧ Testing tasks fall into the following areas:
  ▪ Clarifying acceptance criteria
  ▪ Defining, acquiring, and validating test data
  ▪ Automation design spike
  ▪ Automation
  ▪ Evaluation and reporting
✧ Anticipate the test design to break out testing tasks, especially automation tasks.
✧ Segregating acceptance testing tasks from development using a separate test team is usually a bad idea.

Try these ideas out yourself in the following exercise.

## Exercise 7

Break out and estimate testing tasks for the following story from the Xtrack application. This is the same story for which you defined acceptance tests in Exercise 4, so use those or our answer to that exercise as a starting point:

**Story:** User can create, update, display, and delete a task. A task has a name, a description, assignee, estimate, actual time spent, state, and created/ updated timestamps.

# *Chapter 14*

# Acceptance Tests and Quality

We thought we had the Great Plains figured out in yesterday afternoon's drive through western Iowa, but today we find out that was just the beginning. The rolling tallgrass prairies of Nebraska beckon us westward under an endless sky, and we begin to notice other things besides grass. As we look more closely, flowers, trees, birds, mammals, and insects (yuck! turn on the windshield wipers) become apparent.

The acceptance tests we defined on the first day of our test drive were at a high level. They were just enough to document an assumption and hang a ballpark estimate on for release planning. During iteration planning, we took a closer look at our tests and all the tasks required to accomplish them, giving us a better understanding and more detailed estimates in iteration planning. Now that we're done estimating for this iteration, we're ready to get down to doing the work.

This iterative approach is important to being able to move with sufficient speed through an XP iteration. At each step, you must defer as much detail as possible to the next, dealing only with items you absolutely can't put off. Without a risk of being left by the roadside in a cloud of dust, you can't expect to nail down every detail to the last gnat's eyelash before moving on. Our lunch stop today is at a place called the Brick Wall. Let's not run into any of those on our test drive.

## Acceptance Test Details

It's time to hammer out the details for each high-level test we've already defined or will discover as we go along. Just enough details, that is. We'll still defer lots of details to writing the tests and getting them to run.

The details we want to nail down now are those visible to the customer. For instance, a story may have some mention of "reasonable response time." You definitely want to work with the customer to quantify this. Once you've done so, you may still have details to work out about how you go about setting up the test (how to simulate a load, how to capture the response times, doing what, which response times are measured, and so on), but leave those to the next step, writing the tests.

We'll discuss how to go about getting these details down, but first we want to talk some more about the relationship between the customer, the acceptance tests, the quality of the delivered system, and the development team's quality of life.

Defining the details of the acceptance tests is really defining the quality the customer expects of the system. This should be a collaborative effort of the customer team and the development team, with the tester serving as the interpreter and the acceptance tests acting as the contract. General quality standards should be set during planning, but the acceptance tests contain the details that certify that the system meets the standards.

Quality is both a buzzword and an emotionally charged term for many. A lot of pitfalls beset an overly glib use of the term, and those of us in the "quality" profession are by no means immune. For example, experienced testers suffer the occupational hazard of always wanting to push for "higher" quality. Leaving aside the ambiguity of the term "higher" (assume it means "more"), the truth is, it's not up to the tester or QA engineer to set the quality level. That choice is reserved for the *customer*.

Which leads to the question: wouldn't customers always want the highest-quality system they can get?

No. Customers with time and money constraints consider a lot of other things. Is a Mercedes higher quality than a Ford or Toyota? Which do you own? Here's Lisa's experience from a team she worked with:

*Our customer was a startup with a Web-based product. They were in a crunch: they needed to show their application to potential investors in a few weeks but had nothing running. They just needed a system to be available an hour or two a day for demos. They weren't looking for a bulletproof 24 x 7 production server. In fact, they couldn't afford to pay for a bulletproof system right then. Their priority was to have enough features to show off, not to have a completely stable system. Of course, if they could get it for the same price, they'd love to have it bulletproof. It generally takes significantly more time and/or resources to produce a system with guaranteed stability.*

Here's another example. Our sample application, XTrack, is intended for use internally by our own team. We don't expect more than one or two users to be logged into the system at one time. Our users are trained and will not do too much weird, unexpected stuff. If they do, they're savvy enough to work around problems that arise. We don't need to produce the most robust user interface in the world. We're more interested in being able to track the project than in having a pretty, user-friendly interface.

Customers can't make intelligent choices about quality without understanding the cost of producing software that contains the desired features at the desired level of quality. The development team provides this information in the form of story estimates as well as in the details of the acceptance tests.

When the customer is looking for a bargain (and who isn't?) it may become demoralizing for the development team if they begin to feel they're producing a bad product. Understanding how to produce the customer's desired level of quality when the team has a "higher" standard is key to successful XP projects and requires making the distinction between *internal* and *external* quality.

## Internal and External Quality

In *Extreme Programming Explained,* Kent Beck writes, "There is a strange relationship between internal and external quality. External quality is quality as measured by the customer. Internal quality is quality as measured by the programmers."

He goes on to explain the human effect on quality: "If you deliberately downgrade quality, your team might go faster at first, but soon the demoralization of producing crap will overwhelm any gains you temporarily made from not testing, or not reviewing, or not sticking to standards."

In this light, it looks as if we should always strive for the highest standard of quality. However, this often comes at a cost. Is the customer—whether an external customer, if you're an outsourcing shop, or an internal customer, representing the business—willing to pay?

An important XP concept is the difference between internal and external quality. One of the reasons that members of XP teams love coming to work each morning is that they know they'll be allowed to do their best work. If you took that away, XP just wouldn't work. Internal quality tends to speed up development time; if your unit tests must always run at 100%, your programmers will be able to go faster, because they'll catch mistakes immediately. Internal quality is a given in any XP project. It doesn't cost customers more; in fact, it's saving them time and money.

External quality can be defined as a set of system features. For example:

⬦ Whenever the user makes a mistake, a user-friendly error screen appears.
⬦ It's impossible to crash the server via the user interface.
⬦ The system can handle a hundred concurrent logins.
⬦ The system will stay up 99.995% of the time.

Internal quality can be defined as a set of process attributes:

⬦ 85% of unit level defects are found by automated unit tests.
⬦ 80% of estimates are within 20% of actual.
⬦ 90% of the stories picked for an iteration are completed, on average.
⬦ 100% of projects deliver a product to the customer.

Negotiating with the customer on external quality doesn't mean skimping on acceptance tests or deliberately producing unstable code. It means the customer asks for a certain standard of quality and pays for it. If he wants a system to handle all exceptions, that should be in the story—or multiple stories. For instance, story 1 says to implement this functionality; story 2 says to make the functionality work with $N$ concurrent users hammering it.

## Summary

⬦ An iterative approach to acceptance-test definition is essential to keeping up on XP iterations.

- After iteration planning is the time to work on details visible to the customer, but leave those that aren't (how-to items) to test design and execution.
- Defining details of the acceptance tests is really defining the quality the customer expects of the system.
- The customer does not always want the highest-quality system.
- Producing the customer's desired level of quality when the team has a "higher" standard requires the distinction between internal and external quality.
- External quality is quality as measured by the customer. Internal quality is quality as measured by the programmers.

Try these ideas out yourself in the following exercise.

## Exercise 8

Indicate for each of the following whether it pertains more to internal quality or external quality:

- Number of defects in the code
- Number of overtime hours spent
- Customer satisfaction
- Development team morale
- System reliability
- Code readability

# Chapter 15

# Nailing Down the Details

Drilling down for acceptance-test details really requires getting out all the hats in your wardrobe. You need to be able to look at the system through the eyes of the customer to come up with a lot of the detail yourself, so you don't overwhelm the customer with questions. Likewise, you'll need to reason about the system from a programmer's viewpoint, to predict some of what the system is likely to do without overwhelming the programmers with questions. Finally, you need to put on the tester's hat and determine the set of tests that can be realized in the time available and that will best distinguish an acceptable system from an unacceptable system.

When you're defining all the details of the acceptance tests with the customer, you might find he needs a more robust system than was discussed during the Planning Game. This is an indication that he needs to write new stories for the remaining iterations to get what he wants. As we discussed in the previous chapter, higher external quality often means more time and/or more cost.

Remember, XP is a team effort. Programmers also provide input into the acceptance tests. They know what areas of the system have the most technical risk. They can propose alternative solutions to a problem, so the customer can decide on the best approach. When you ask questions of them or confirm what system behavior will be, a disconnect may become obvious between what the customer said and what the programmer heard.

The more quickly you can write the acceptance tests, the better. Not only does this help the programmers know exactly what they're programming, it also gives everyone time to build the necessary bridges into the system code. We'll talk about this more in the next chapter.

As we've pointed out before, XP calls for the customer to define the acceptance tests. If your customer is capable of writing tests and is willing to do this on her own on the first day of the iteration, great. If she's available the first day of the iteration to sit down with you to write the tests together, that's ideal. If you need to get the tests written and the customer can't start right away, start writing the tests yourself and arrange to meet with her by day 2 of the iteration at the latest. The guidelines in this chapter will help everyone who has to write acceptance tests. Since our experience is that we always end up writing the first cut of the tests, we've written the chapter this way.

## Picking the Customer's Brain (and the Programmers'!)

Some things will be obvious, and you should be able to come up with them yourself and not bother anyone, even for confirmation. Some things you'll have to run by the customer or programmer, but you can still do a lot of the work beforehand to make it easy for them. And some things will require them to really think about things that haven't yet occurred to them. This may not always be a pleasant experience, because in the process they may realize that other things they thought were done need more work.

The idea of coming up with even the most obvious acceptance detail on your own authority, without running it by the customer to approve, may be scary at first. Likewise with the predictions of how the system will work in a hypothetical situation. What if you're wrong? Who are you to say even one iota of how the system should work? Or how it will work?

Well, if you're wrong, you're wrong. No big deal. As programmers, we don't ask for every itty-bitty detail of how the system should work. We use our skills and experience to fill in all kinds of gaps; otherwise we'd never get anything done. As programmers, we get it wrong part of the time, and we will also as testers. As a tester, it's your job to fill in your set of gaps and bear some of the risk of being wrong too.

If the customer and programmers have limited time to answer your questions (which we've found is often the case), you want them to spend it answering the ones that make them think—that break new ground. The risks associated with never getting to these (because all the time got spent on the easy ones) are greater than those of getting a few easy ones wrong.

Deciding which items you can feel confident about, which require confirmation from the customer or programmers, and which require you to ask open-ended questions is something of an art, but the basic approach is easy to understand.

When you have absolutely no clue about what the answer should be or how to determine what it should be, you really have no choice but to ask the open-ended question (to the customer: "What should the system do if . . . ?" To the programmer: "What will happen if . . . ?").

If you have a pretty good idea that the answer is one of a few different possibilities and you have reason to pick one over the other (it's the simplest, quickest, easiest . . .), ask for confirmation of that possibility among the alternatives ("If . . . happens, the system should/will . . . , right? Or should it . . . ?").

And for the ones where you're pretty sure what the system should or will do, just go ahead and write those up without asking. The customer will be able to go over every detail of the tests if he wants, so you'll find out if you made incorrect assumptions.

## The Good, the Bad, and the Ugly

A lot of details fall out by going through a story on what we call the **happy path**. This is the path where all inputs are correct, nothing goes wrong, the moon is in the seventh house, and Jupiter aligns with Mars. Do this first and fill in all the details you can. A lot of this will be obvious stuff you don't need to ask anyone about.

Next, you need to get off this happy path and dig into the requirements for handling errors, unexpected paths through the system, and unusual or unexpected data. We call this the **sad path**. If a report has an input of a date range, ask yourself what should happen if the "end" date is earlier than the "from" date. Ask what the customer wants to see if the user types special characters into text fields in a GUI form and clicks the Submit button. Ask what should happen if it's a Web application and the user clicks the browser Back and Forward buttons. This is likely to raise cases where you can identify several alternatives, one of which is superior, and you can ask for confirmation.

Then think about serious failures and worst-case scenarios, the **bad path**. What should or will happen when the log fills up? When you run out of database sessions? What happens if someone reboots the system during a critical transaction? Sets the system date incorrectly? How about malicious use by a disgruntled employee? An attack by hackers? How about alien hackers?

Okay, the alien hackers scenario is probably a bit much. But it doesn't hurt to think outside the box here some, as long as you're not thinking out loud. Go ahead and imagine some wacky scenarios, and pay attention if the outcome could be catastrophic. Consider even a highly improbable event if the negative outcome is severe enough.

This is an area in which you really need to exercise professional judgment. On occasion, you may come across something that, though unlikely, would be so bad that you need to encourage the customer to consider it. Be careful, because if the system ends up with an alien hacker denial subsystem just because you spooked the customer, neither she nor the programmers may ever forgive you.

As you go through the stories along these three paths, examine your mental model of the customer's view of the system and the likely behavior of the system from more than one viewpoint. By all means, think about what sequence of things a user could do. Then think about the content and relationships among data items, both inputs and outputs. When you're stuck on one and can't think of anything new, switch to the other view. When you feel you've exhausted the possibilities of these two, consider external events, such as interacting systems, key dates (month-end, year-end, and so on), changes in underlying and supporting systems and technologies (e.g., new versions of browsers, Java runtime).

By driving down these happy, sad, and bad (or the good, the bad and the ugly) paths and looking through the various windows on the requirements, you can flush out the details you need pretty quickly.

Here's an example of how we would employ these techniques on the directory-search application we've used in previous examples:

## Example 7

**Story:** Create a screen that will allow the user to search on the Web for businesses by category of business and location.

First, we'll stroll down the happy path. Here are some simple user scenarios:

1. Enter a search, get results, see the desired business info, done
2. Enter a search, get no results, search again
3. Enter search, get page or less of results, don't see desired info, search again
4. Enter search, get more than one page of results, don't see desired info, go to next page of results, see info, done
5. Enter search get more than one page of results, don't see desired info, go to next page and some or all remaining, never find desired info, search again

Still on the happy path, here are various conditions in data we thought of:

1. Category/location combinations that retrieve a page or less of results
2. Category/location combinations that retrieve more than one page of results
3. Category/location combinations that retrieve no results

We couldn't think of any external events to deal with on the happy path. It's common for this view to become more useful on the sad and bad paths.

Now for the sad path. Here are some unexpected and unusual user activities:

1. Search with a misspelled category, get notice suggesting correct spelling, search again with correct spelling
2. Search with misspelled location, get notice suggesting correct spelling, search again with correct spelling
3. Search with misspelled category and location, get notice suggesting correct spellings, search again with correct spellings

Here are some error conditions in the data:

1. Category names misspelled by one and two letters
2. Location names misspelled by one and two letters
3. Pairs of misspelled category and location names for which the correct spellings retrieve one or more businesses
4. Pairs of misspelled category and location names for which the correct spellings retrieve no businesses

And an external event that could arise:

1. Changes to database records included in the search while search is in progress

Finally, the bad path. Here's what a user could do that might really mess things up:

1. Enter a search consisting only of special characters
2. Enter the maximum number of characters in each form field
3. Click for a search without selecting a category or city
4. Start a search, click the Stop button in the browser, start another search
5. Perform a search, click the Back button from the results screen, perform another search

Likewise, data conditions that would be disastrous:

1. Maximum number of database sessions reached
2. Database goes down during session

And external events:

1. Volume of concurrent searches exceeds server capacity
2. Server runs out of memory
3. Power to servers goes out

## Optional Tests

There are different schools of thought on whether optional tests should be included. One way to look at it is that if it isn't absolutely necessary that a particular test pass, you shouldn't bother with it. This is fair; after all, your goal is to test the minimum necessary. Still, there's no rule that acceptance tests must pass 100% before the end of the iteration.

If you have time to perform noncritical tests and they pass, they'll give the customer extra confidence. If they fail, the customer can decide later whether to make the defects into stories to address them. Including noncritical tests isn't necessary, but it gives the customer more flexibility. Customers always have their mental lists of "must-haves" and "nice-to-haves"; if the "must-haves" don't take as much as estimated in the way of resources, the "nice-to-haves" are already defined and can be completed too.

## Getting Creative

It can be difficult to write tests where the user takes strange and unexpected routes through the system, tries bizarre inputs, gets impatient and clicks a button ten times in quick succession, any kind of bad-path test you've identified.

In a way, these tests defy the whole idea of design, because if you can spec them out in advance, they aren't really unexpected, are they? This is definitely an area where you may need to wait for the system to be available and then play with it to get an idea of how to abuse it. These kinds of tests require a lot of creativity; have fun with them.

Sometimes it's tough to even think how to test a particular item. For example, what if a story implements a data model within the database schema but no story uses it in a user interface? It may be that this type of test is better handled by the unit tests—it may not even be appropriate to have a separate acceptance test. Consider whether it impinges on the customer in some indirect way, and design tests for that. After all, if the customer really can't tell whether the story has been implemented or not, *that* should be a pretty quick story to implement, eh? (wink, wink, nudge, nudge).

## Lights-Out Test Design

One of the pitfalls to avoid is paying equal attention to everything. This is the well-known "test everything" syndrome. The slowest moving, most bloated, most bureaucratic "waterfall" software project in the world didn't include time to test everything, so you can expect to have to skip something on a fast-moving XP iteration. The trick is in knowing what to concentrate on and what to ignore. We can't give you an algorithm for making this distinction, but we can sum up the key ingredient in a single word: risk.

Design your tests to minimize risk. Even if this seems obvious, it's still easy to fall into a trap where you devote an inordinate amount of attention to an area, not because it's especially risky but because it's an easy area for which to design tests. Maybe you just have a ton of detailed information about that area, like a list of fields with all the various types of allowable values and optional/required specifications. It's easy to design tests that go through lots and lots of combinations, but if this isn't a risky area, why bother? Here's one of Tip's favorite stories about this:

> *A man comes home after working late into the evening and notices his neighbor on his hands and knees under the light at the end of his driveway. When he asks what's up, the neighbor replies, "I dropped my key and I'm locked out till I find it."*
>
> *Being on good terms with the neighbor, the man immediately joins him on his hands and knees. After searching fruitlessly for a few minutes, he asks the neighbor how long he's been looking. "I just dropped it five minutes before you got here," the neighbor explains. "I can't believe we haven't found it yet."*
>
> *They search for another five minutes or so, and finally the man says, "Show me exactly where you were standing when you dropped it. Maybe we can reconstruct the trajectory it took." To his great surprise, the neighbor walks up the driveway and onto his porch. "I was just getting ready to unlock the door," he explains, "when I sneezed and dropped it."*
>
> *Exasperated, the man asks why in heaven's name they've spent the last twenty minutes looking under the light when the key was dropped on the bloody porch. The neighbor answers sheepishly, "Well, my porch light is burned out, and I was afraid I wouldn't find it in the dark."*

In the next chapter, we'll share our experience of useful ways to get all these details down into an executable form the whole team can understand.

## Summary

- ✧ Acceptance tests are a team responsibility that involve the customer, the programmers, and the tester.
- ✧ To get the details down, you need to wear all three hats.
- ✧ When questioning customers (and programmers):
  - Take the responsibility to define the obvious ones yourself; save the hard ones for them.
  - Ask them to select from alternatives where possible.
  - Ask open-ended to questions to break new ground and avoid going down the wrong path.

- Explore the happy, sad, and bad paths to enumerate the details:
  - Happy, where nothing unexpected happens and all is well
  - Sad, where users make mistakes and data is invalid
  - Bad, where all hell breaks loose
- Look at the system from multiple viewpoints on each path:
  - What the user could do
  - How the data could be compromised
  - External events
- Be creative when designing tests for unexpected paths and for features not directly evident to the customer.
- Don't try to test everything.
- Design your tests to minimize risk.

Try these ideas out yourself in the following exercise.

## Exercise 9

**Story 4:** The user can display and update information about an iteration. The iteration display shows the iteration start and end dates, the projected team velocity, all stories assigned to the iteration, and the total of the estimates for those stories. For completed iterations, it displays the sum of the actuals for each story and the actual team velocity for that iteration. The user can update the estimated velocity, start date, and end date.

1. For the above story from the XTrack application, identify which of the following details you would a) assume responsibility for defining yourself, b) ask for confirmation on, or c) ask open-ended questions about:
   - Constraints on the allowable inputs for start and end dates during update.
   - What should happen when invalid data is input during update.
   - The units in which to display the velocity, estimates, and actual totals.
   - What determines that an iteration is complete.
   - Which information will be included about each story.

- What happens when a story is moved from one iteration to another.
- Can completed stories in a completed iteration be moved to another iteration?
- The order in which the stories appear.

2. For the above story, identify some additional details based on
   - The happy path
   - The sad path
   - The bad path

3. Based on risk, where would you focus the most attention in designing tests for the following first four XTrack stories?

**Story 1:** Be able to create, read, and update a story via a Web interface. The data fields in a story are number, name, author, description, estimate, iteration, timestamps, and state.

**Story 2:** The user can provide an estimate for how long it will take to implement a story, prioritize the story, and assign the story to an iteration.

**Story 3:** The user can create, update, display, and delete a task. A task has a name, a description, assignee, estimate, actual time spent, state, and created/updated timestamps.

**Story 4:** The user can display and update information about an iteration. The iteration display shows the iteration start and end dates, the projected team velocity, all stories assigned to the iteration, and the total of the estimates for those stories. For completed iterations, it displays the sum of the actuals for each story and the actual team velocity for that iteration. The user can update the estimated velocity, start date, and end date.

# *Chapter 16*

# Writing Acceptance Tests

We have now accumulated quite a fair bit of information about the acceptance tests. If this were a traditional software project, we'd begin writing the information down in the form of an acceptance test plan or acceptance test design, and possibly both. But since this is an Extreme Programming project, we're going to skip all that and go directly to writing the tests. We aren't going to write documents *about* the tests; we're going to write the tests themselves, in an executable format, so we can start running them early and as often as possible.

This may seem a bit radical if you're accustomed to spending several weeks (or months!) writing, reviewing, and revising documents *about* testing prior to actually doing any. You don't have time for that on an XP project. The primary function of acceptance tests on an XP project is to pass or fail, and thereby provide feedback on the project's progress or lack of progress toward the customer's goals. The entire iteration will be completed next week, and the first running code is probably going to be available tomorrow. You must have a bias for getting tests running as quickly as possible.

You still have plenty of details to work out, and doing so with the customer and the rest of the team will increase their understanding of the stories. This will help them avoid some types of defects altogether and will take the place of the traditional review cycle on documents about testing. As you get the details about how the system should behave, you put them directly into the executable tests.

## Executable Tests

Writing executable tests requires the tests to be expressed in a form that can be interpreted by a machine. They don't necessarily have to be written in a programming language, but they do have to conform to a set of syntax rules and identify the information necessary to perform and evaluate the test. Usually a programming or scripting language works best, because it will provide ways to write tests at an understandable level while tucking the many details away in lower levels.

When picking a language in which to write the tests, look for the following:

✧ It's readily available on the platform(s) where your tests will run.
✧ You can hook it up to a user interface test driver, if applicable.
✧ An implementation of the xUnit framework exists in the language.
✧ You're reasonably fluent in it
✧ The system is being developed in the same language

We'll be using Java for our illustrations and examples, because it's available on all platforms, it's a common language used to develop the systems we test, it can be interfaced to just about any tool, and a Java implementation of the XUnit family of test frameworks is available at www.JUnit.org (JUnit for Java). If you aren't fluent in Java, don't panic. It's an easy language to use.

It's best to illustrate executable tests with an example. Take, for instance, a login story. We might have identified high-level acceptance tests for this as follows:

*Attempts to login with a valid id and password succeed; attempts with invalid ids and/or passwords fail.*

This captures the essence of the test but leaves out the details. The details can go into an executable test, as follows:

```
assertTrue( login("bob","bobspassword") )
assertTrue( login("BOB","bobspassword") )

assertFalse( login("bob","") )
assertFalse( login("","bobspassword") )
assertFalse( login("bob","wrong") )
assertFalse( login("bob","Bobspassword") )
```

Understanding this test is straightforward: `assertTrue()` verifies that the operand (whatever is between the parentheses) has a true value, and if not, fails the test. `assertFalse()` works in an analogous way, requiring its operand to be false. `login()` attempts to log into the system using the specified id and password, returning a value of `true` when the login succeeds and `false` when it fails.

The test includes two cases of logging in with a valid id and password and four cases of logging in with an invalid id or password. It should be clear from these cases that the id is not case sensitive, since both `bob` and `BOB` are expected to work, but the password is case sensitive, since `bobspassword` should work and `Bobspassword` should not.

This shows how the details of the login story can be put into the test itself. As we discover additional details, we can include them by adding more cases. The rest of the team, with the possible exception of the customer, will have no trouble understanding the test and using it as a reference when coding. You may need to spend some extra time with the customer to accustom him to this format. In the worst case, you can provide a less geeky version for the customer, which we'll illustrate in the next chapter.

If you know the cases you want to test when you sit down to write, which at this point you should, then writing this test takes about five minutes. For the sake of clarity, we've omitted several lines of Java directives and declarations that are essentially the same for every test, but even if you typed those in each time (instead of copying and pasting, which is how we do it), it would still take just a few minutes to write.

To run this test, you need `assertTrue()`, `assertFalse()`, and `login()`. You could develop your own `assertTrue()` and `assertFalse()`, but that isn't necessary, because they've already been developed (by Kent Beck and Erich Gamma) and are available free at www.jUnit.org. `login()`, on the other hand, will have to come from your project in one form or another.

The simplest thing, always a good place to start, is for `login()` to be a piece of the system. Then this test is runnable as soon as the `login()` piece (and everything it relies on) is programmed. You simply put it all together into one big program (your tests, `login()`, and anything `login()` requires) and run it. Of course, that works only if the system is being developed in the same language as the test, which is one reason why this is a consideration when choosing the test language.

When the tests and system development languages are incompatible, someone on the team will need to write a `login()` **bridge** in the test language that passes the operands from the test to the system's `login()` and ferries the return values back.

In fact, you'll often need to use something similar, even when the system development and test language are the same, because the actual pieces of the system are likely to have different interfaces from the ones one you want in the test. You'll need some kind of intermediate module to convert from one to the other.

In addition, when you want to run the tests through the user interface, as opposed to calling pieces of the system directly, you'll need a bridge to carry operands and results between your test and whatever tool you're using to drive the user interface.

Let's look at another example, the searching story for our directory application. One of the high-level acceptance tests we defined was this:

*A search with a category/location combination for which some businesses exist returns a list of those businesses; a search for a combination without businesses returns an empty list.*

Here's a first cut at the executable test:

```
assertTrue( search("woodworking","dublin ohio") )
assertTrue( search("horses","denver colorado") )

assertFalse( search("joy","mudville"))
assertFalse( search("U","team") )
```

Like `login()` in the preceding example, `search()` performs a search with the specified category and location. It returns `true` if the search returned a list of businesses and `false` if it returned an empty list. The test contains two cases of searches that should return lists and two cases that should return empty lists.

Now suppose one of the details we uncover is that when the location is a major U.S. city, the state can be omitted. We could add a case:

```
assertTrue( search("horses","denver") )
```

But this doesn't really express what we want. It just says that a search with `denver` for the location will return a list of some businesses. We want it to test that it returns the *same* list as the search with `denver colorado`.

To write the test we want to write, we need to refactor our `search()` so it returns, instead of simply `true` or `false`, the list of businesses that match the location and category combination. Then we can write the test as follows:

```
assertEquals( search("horses","denver colorado") ,
              search("horses","denver")            )
```

The `assertEquals()` verifies that its two operands are equal, and if not, fails the test. As with `assertTrue()` and `assertFalse()`, this is a module you get with the Beck/Gamma jUnit framework.

This example illustrates how the interfaces to `search()` and `login()` can be changed (refactored) as you learn more details about the desired system behavior. This is a further reason to use an intermediate module between your tests and pieces of the system, because even if the interfaces are the same at the outset, they probably won't stay that way as the tests and system are refactored.

Writing executable acceptance tests in this manner and at this point in the iteration will put you in an excellent position to begin running tests as soon as the requisite pieces of the system are programmed. Some additional work will probably be required to bridge between the tests and the system before the tests are actually runnable, but this can usually be completed quickly once the pieces of the system are in place.

Writing the tests in this manner greatly increases the probability they can be automated. It doesn't necessarily preclude your executing them manually, but we'll have more to say about that in Chapters 19 and 20.

This has been a high-level introduction to writing the acceptance tests. In the next several chapters, we'll take a closer look at some of the details and problems that commonly come up in when you actually try to do it.

## If You Have Trouble Getting Started

If you don't have a lot of experience with automating tests and the attempt to leap into coding acceptance tests leaves you with writer's block, here's an intermediate step to help you along. (This runs contrary to the XP philosophy of immediately writing test code, but there's no shame in the learning process.) Go back to the high-level tests we talked about in Chapter 9. Think about common *user scenarios*, sequences of interactions between a user and the system. Think about the actions, data and expected results of each test:

- **Action.** What the user does—for instance, "Login"
- **Data.** Specific inputs used in the action—for instance, "User id and password"
- **Expected results.** Minimum success criteria: screens, transitions, messages, data persists as a result of an action or step—for instance, "Invalid user ID or password"

If it helps you to think through the tests at first, lay these out in a format that's easy and clear for you (see Table 16.1). For example:

**Scenario:** Attempt to login leaving the user id and password blank—it should fail.

**TABLE 16.1** Simple scenario test

| Action | Data | Expected Result |
|---|---|---|
| Login | user id=blank password=blank | "The user ID or password is invalid." |

You can think of more complex scenarios whose steps you can translate into executable tests (see Table 16.2):

**Scenario**: Search with a misspelled category, get notice suggesting correct spelling; search again with correct spelling.

**TABLE 16.2** More complex scenario test

| Action | Data | Expected Result |
|---|---|---|
| 1. Login | Valid user id and password | "Enter your search criteria and click the search button." |
| 2. Search | Misspelled category | Suggestion of corrected spelling |
| 3. Search | Suggested correct spelling | List of businesses |

Whether you write the tests directly in executable format or use this method to help get you going, the tests will provide the signposts along the path of the team's XP journey. They need to be granular enough to show the project's true progress, so avoid unnecessary overlap. If you have a scenario with 300 steps and 10 of them fail, you probably have to fail the whole test case rather than come up with some complex formula for determining what percentage of it worked. Keep the tests simple.

You and the customer also have to come up with all the sets of data you want your tests to verify. Again it's best to code these directly into the tests, but if your customer has trouble conceptualizing that way or you just need a jump start, try any simple format to lay out the data you'll use to code the tests. Once you have more experience with automating, you can dispense with these extra steps. Table 16.3 shows a sample of test data you and the customer might have defined for a login scenario.

**TABLE 16.3** Sample test data

| Characteristics | User ID | Password | E-mail Address | Name | Expected Result |
|---|---|---|---|---|---|
| Invalid (missing) | (missing) | (missing) | | | "Please enter a valid user ID and password" |
| Invalid (missing) | jimbob | (missing) | | | "Please enter a valid user ID and password" |
| Invalid (bad id) | JIMBOB | Jumbo | | | "Please enter a valid user ID and password" |
| Invalid (bad psw) | jimbob | JUMBO | | | "Please enter a valid user ID and password" |
| Valid | jimbob | Jumbo | jim@azx.net | Jim Thornkj | "Welcome, Jim" |
| Valid | testuser1 | testpsw1 | test1@xptester.org | Test Userone | "Welcome, Test" |
| Valid | testuser2 | testpsw2 | test2@xptester.org | Test Usertwo | "Welcome, Test" |

We'll talk more about these formats for documenting tests in the next chapter, in case your customer isn't comfortable with having acceptance tests documented only in the automated tests themselves.

## Summary

- Don't spend time writing documents about tests; skip right to writing the tests themselves.
- Write executable tests in a language that, ideally:
  - Is available on the platform where you need to run the tests
  - Has an implementation of the xUnit framework
  - Will interface with the test tool you're using (if any)
  - You're fluent with
  - Is the same language the system is being developed in
- As you work out details with the customer and the rest of the team, put them directly into executable tests.
- Work with the customer so she's comfortable reading and understanding the tests.
- Use intermediate "bridge" modules to adapt the interfaces of system pieces to the interface desired for the test and to allow the test to execute through the user interface.
- Refactor the tests and the interfaces to the bridge modules as you learn more details about the desired system behavior.
- If you have trouble getting started, think about the actions, data, and expected results for various user scenarios.

Here's a chance for you to try out this format for yourself.

## Exercise 10

**Story:** User can create, update, display, and delete a task. A task has a name, a description, assignee, estimate, actual time spent, state, and created/updated timestamps.

For the above XTrack story, assume we've defined the following high-level acceptance tests in release planning. We know this isn't complete; it's just enough to illustrate the ideas (see Table 16.4).

**TABLE 16.4** Test data for Exercise 10

| Action | Data | Expected Result |
|---|---|---|
| 1. Add a new task | Valid values for the task fields | Success: the task is added |
| 2. Add a new task | Invalid values for task fields | Failure: invalid fields message |

Also assume we've come up with the following additional information while planning and beginning the first iteration:

◆ Users must be logged in to add, update, or delete tasks.
◆ The name and description fields are required.
◆ State has a fixed list of values: Not Started, Started, Completed.
◆ Estimate and actual time spent must be numeric.

Write these as an executable test in the style illustrated in the two examples in this chapter.

# Chapter 17

# Organizing Acceptance Tests

We've almost reached the end of the second day of our trip. The road's still pretty flat, but in the distance we can see the mountains we'll have to scale later in the iteration. The last stretch of today's road leaves us on the outskirts of test automation, where we'll start in the morning. Up to this point, we've been concerned primarily with *what* to test: which stories, what scenarios, which details, what inputs, what expected results, and so on. Now our attention is turning more to *how* to test these things.

We've already written some executable tests, and before we quit for the day, we'll take a look at how to keep them organized. There could be a fair number of them, and you and everyone on the team need to be able to call up the latest version of any test to run and/or refactor. The customer, meanwhile, may require a modified format if he can't work with the executable tests directly, and the two versions need to be kept in sync.

## Version Control of Acceptance Tests

Acceptance tests should be kept under version control, just like unit tests and the system code, and usually they can be placed into the same repository. For the most part, you can use the same methods for checking acceptance tests in and out as for unit tests and system code, but you may want different rules for integrating and refactoring them.

One of the cardinal rules for code and unit tests is that no integration of new or refactored code is complete until 100% of the unit tests pass. You can't require that 100% of all acceptance tests pass all the time, or you'd be back to the old "big-bang" integration, where the system isn't integrated until the very end when everything is done (and nothing works).

We recommend the following rule:

> *No integration is complete unless 100% of the previously passing acceptance tests continue to pass.*

In other words, once an acceptance test passes, it can never be allowed to fail. This is true when integrating both new and refactored code and when integrating refactored acceptance tests.

## Executable Test Files

You may have years of experience in organizing programming code; certainly someone on the team will. Organizing the tests will be pretty much the same sort of thing. It boils down to dividing up the tests into individual files. Some of how you do that will be driven by the language in which you write the tests. For instance, in Java, each class must be in a separate file whose name is the name of the class, so if you have a test named LoginStoryTest, it's just going to go into a file named LoginStoryTest.java—as simple as that.

We omitted some of the Java declarations and directives from our examples in the previous chapter, because we were focusing on the tests themselves. The stuff we omitted is the same every time (except for names), so it doesn't require any brainpower. This stuff actually organizes the tests, though, so we're going to look at it now.

Our example test of the login function is actually a Java class. Don't let this terminology scare you if you're not a Java programmer. A class (for our purposes) is just a blueprint for something—in this case, for our test. Here's some of the stuff we omitted:

```
public class LoginStoryTest {

    public void testLogin() {
   // This is where the tests were
     }
}
```

These declarations say this is the class (blueprint) for a `LoginStoryTest` and that a `LoginStoryTest` has a method (something it can do) named `testLogin`.

Our tests are in the `testLogin` method because (you guessed it!) they test the login. The login function is part of the login story, so it all goes into the `TestLoginStory` class, in a file named `TestLoginStory.java`. Pretty simple, eh? Well, logging in is pretty simple. Let's look at the exercise from the last chapter, which you should have studiously completed before reading ahead to this point. The story involved is, in part: *User can create, update, display . . . a task.*

We only asked you write an executable test for the create portion, but you can see that you'd also need to write tests for update and display. Here's how that would be organized:

```
public class TaskStoryTest {

    public void testCreate() {
// Create tests go here
    }

    public void testUpdate() {
// Update tests go here
    }

    public void testDisplay() {
// Display tests go here
    }
}
```

The tests for each major function within the story go into an appropriately named method. This keeps the number files associated with the tests manageable (one for each story) and puts closely related tests within easy reach of each other. One of the extremely useful features of the XUnit family of test frameworks is that no matter how many of these test methods we put into `TaskStoryTest`, the test runner will find and execute them all.

## Organizing Acceptance Tests in Spreadsheets

If the customer on your team is comfortable working with executable acceptance tests, this makes life a lot easier, because you'll be relying on her to provide you with realistic test cases or, at the very least, review the ones you make up. In the best case, you can even teach her to check out and update the tests directly. On the other hand, you may find she isn't disposed to work with the executable format and you need to provide some other format for her to review and update.

Spreadsheets are a good alternative format for presenting acceptance tests to a customer unwilling or unable to work with the executable tests. They're easy for just about anyone to maintain and manipulate, and they provide useful organizational features like hypertext linking and the ability to store more than one sheet in a workbook.

Since you need to keep the spreadsheet and the executable test in sync, the two formats require a more or less one-to-one correspondence. We've found it feasible use a single spreadsheet workbook to correspond to the class and separate sheets within the workbook to correspond to the methods.

In other words, corresponding to our `LoginStoryTest.java` file would be a spreadsheet file named `LoginStoryTest.xls`, and corresponding to our `testLogin` method would be a worksheet with the same name and the contents shown in Table 17.1.

**TABLE 17.1** The `testLogin` worksheet

| Outcome | Id | Password |
|---------|------|-------------|
| success | bob | bobspassword |
| success | BOB | bobspassword |
| | | |
| fail | bob | |
| fail | | bobspassword |
| fail | bob | wrong |
| fail | bob | bobspassword |

Likewise, for our slightly more complicated `TaskStoryTest`, we would have a spreadsheet file named `TaskStoryTest.xls` that would contain a worksheet named `testCreate`, one named `testUpdate`, and one named `testDisplay`. Table 17.2 shows what `testCreate` might contain.

**TABLE 17.2** The testCreate spreadsheet

| outcome | name | description | assignee | estimate | aotual | state |
|---------|------|-------------|----------|----------|--------|-------|
| success | User Gui | Create Gui | Bob | 2 | 3 | Not started |
| success | User Gui | Create Gui | Bob | 2 | 3 | Started |
| success | User Gui | Create Gui | Bob | 2 | 3 | Completed |
| fail | | | Bob | a long time | even longer | ohio |

You should be able to store the spreadsheets in the same source-control system as the executable tests. The customer can review and modify the spreadsheet files, and then you (or some other team member) can make the corresponding changes in the executable tests. If you don't want to keep the files in sync manually, reasonably simple programs can be written to extract the test cases from the executable tests into a format that can be loaded into the spreadsheets or to generate the executable tests from data exported out of them. This can severely limit your ability to refactor the tests, however, and should be undertaken with caution.

Well, that about wraps the second day of our road trip. We established the stories for the first iteration, planned and estimated all the tasks, and started writing executable acceptance tests, which we organized into files containing Java classes and methods and possibly corresponding spreadsheets for the customer. We've come a long way, and tomorrow we'll make the final push: finish writing the executable tests, make as many runnable as we can, execute them, report the results, and complete the iteration. Better get a good night's sleep!

## Summary

- The acceptance tests should be kept under version control, just as with unit tests and the system code.
- Use the same methods as for unit tests and system code, but a different rule: consider no integration complete until 100% of the previously passing acceptance tests pass.
- Organize the tests as you would any code.
- The executable acceptance tests for a story are contained in one or more methods of a Java class.

- If the customer can't work with executable tests, maintain corresponding spreadsheet files in which individual worksheets correspond to individual methods.
- Keep the spreadsheets and executable tests in sync. If absolutely necessary, use programs to move the test case/data back and forth, but this will limit your ability to refactor the tests.

Try these ideas out yourself in the following exercise.

## Exercise 11

> **Story 4:** The user can display and update information about an iteration. The iteration display shows the iteration start and end dates, the stories assigned to the iteration, and the estimated velocity for the iteration. The user can update the estimated velocity, start date, and end date.

For the above XTrack story:

1. Write an executable test for this story, and include the class and method declarations as illustrated in this chapter. Include at least one test case in each method, but don't worry about completeness. The point is the organization, not the details.
2. Pretend your customer can't stand the executable format. Create or mock up a spreadsheet for him that corresponds to the executable test in question 1.

# Chapter 18

# Test Design and Refactoring

On the last day of our XP road trip, we'll be leaving the Great Plains behind and heading up into the mountain passes. Hopefully, all the work we've done up to this point will keep us from getting buried in an avalanche or stranded like the infamous Donner party. (Customers may complain when the system isn't right, but they get awfully annoyed when you eat them ;-)

In this chapter, we're going to talk about some simple test design. "Whoa!" you may say. "We're already writing executable tests—isn't the time for design long past?"

No, actually, the time for *over*design is past. The right time for just-in-time-design is always "now," and that's the kind of design we want to talk about. We've been writing essentially the simplest tests that could possibly work for acceptance testing, and they *will work*, more often than you expect. But sometimes they won't. Sometimes they'll just have to get more complicated (don't you hate it when that happens?). Well, if you're lucky enough never to run into this situation, would you please buy our next set of lottery tickets?

## Establishing the Initial System State

The simplest tests tend to assume a great deal about the initial state of the system. For instance, take our sample login tests from Chapter 16. They assume a user defined in the system with the id bob and the password bobspassword. For another example, consider the searching tests from that same chapter. They assume certain contents of the database—for example, results for horses in denver but none for joy in mudville (mighty Casey has struck out).

Although we don't expect these particular tests to modify the state of the system, other tests will, and they can't be run again until the system is returned to that initial state.

Resetting the system to the initial state can be a simple set of instructions you execute before running the tests ("Now set the limburger attenuation parameter to 'Thursday' and hit Refresh"), but we've found it well worthwhile to build an automated reset—for instance, a shell script that shuts down the system, loads the initial state, and starts it back up.

## Tests That Leave the System State Unchanged

Unfortunately, in some situations, this simple approach doesn't work. One such situation is where the reset step becomes too costly. This could be because it takes a long time or because it has to be performed too frequently, or a combination of the two. If you find that running acceptance tests becomes a bottleneck and that most of your time is spent waiting on system resets, it's time to do something about it.

If you haven't already automated the reset, this would be a reasonable time to do it. If you've already done it, take a look at refactoring the tests that modify the state of the system, so they always leave it in the same state as when they started. For instance, a test of deleting records could create the records it deletes, and a test that creates records could delete what it created at the end of the test.

Suppose we've written the tests shown in Listing 18.1 for creating and deleting user ids (they have to come from somewhere, after all).

**Listing 18.1** Version 1.0

```
public class UserIdStoryTest {

    public void testCreate() {
        login("super","superpassword");
        assertTrue( createUserId( "new",
                                  "newpassword",
                                  "new@xptester.org") );
```

```
        assertFalse( createUserId( "fred",
                                   "",
                                   "") );
    }

    public void testDelete() {
        login("super","superpassword");
        assertTrue( deleteUserId( "bob" ) );
        assertFalse( deleteUserId( "doug" ));
    }
}
```

The create tests assume a user already exists with id of super and that
none exists with the id of new. The delete tests also assume the existence of the
id super as well as a user with id bob and no user with id doug. This is certainly
easy to arrange in the initial state of the system, but once these tests run, the
assumptions are no longer true, and the system must be reset.

The first attempt to createUserId has the expected result of true, because
we're including all the fields needed for successful user id creation. That's why
we use assertTrue. The second attempt, to add fred, fails, because we left off
two required fields. The expected result is false, so we use assertFalse. Chapter 22 will go into more detail about how we know what to code in these tests.

We can relax for the test so that, while it still has some assumptions about
the initial state, its execution doesn't affect the truth of those assumptions and
can be run over and over without resetting the system. Listing 18.2 shows how
we could do it (we've marked the changes with **bold** text).

**Listing 18.2** Version 1.1

```
public class UserIdStoryTest {

    public void testCreate() {
        login("super","superpassword");
        assertTrue( createUserId( "new",
                                  "newpassword",
                                  "new@xptester.org") );
        assertFalse( createUserId( "fred",
                                   "",
                                   "") );
        deleteUserId("new");
    }

    public void testDelete() {
        login("super","superpassword");
```

```
      createUserId( "john",
                    "johnspassword",
                    "john@xptester.org");
      assertTrue( deleteUserId( "john" ) );
      assertFalse( deleteUserId( "doug" ));
   }
}
```

As you can see, we've added actions to the test that undo the changes to the system state. In fact, we already had something like this at the beginning of the test: login. The login is necessary to set up the test, because only an already authorized user can create user ids. The createUserId we added to the testDelete method is just an additional setup step, creating the record we're about to delete. The deleteUserId we added to the createUserId method is a teardown step, done after the test to clean up and release resources. Some setup steps are mandatory, but the teardown steps aren't—they just provide the ability to redo the test without having to reset the system.

Don't worry that time spent automating the system reset is wasted if you then have to refactor the tests to include setup and teardown steps. You'll still need the reset because, even when every test is supposed to leave the system in the same state, not every test will. For instance, what if the delete function fails? The delete test will create the user id john but not delete it, and the assumptions will then be violated. In this case, you'll need to resort to the system reset.

## Coupling between Tests

Now that we've complicated things somewhat, we'll try to simplify them again. If you studied the above example long enough and closely enough, you'd eventually realize two things: a) you can simplify it as shown in Listing 18.3, and b) you really need to get a life already (just kidding).

**Listing 18.3** Version 1.2

```
public class UserIdStoryTest {

   public void testCreateDelete() {
      login("super","superpassword");
      assertTrue( createUserId( "new",
                                "newpassword",
                                "new@xptester.org") );
```

```
        assertFalse( createUserId( "fred",
                                    "",
                                    "") );
        assertTrue( deleteUserid( "new" ) );
        assertFalse( deleteUserId( "doug") );
    }
}
```

This version combines the `create` and `delete` methods into one, using the `create` tests as setup for the `delete` tests and the `delete` tests as teardown for the `create` tests. It's about half the size, will run in about half the time, and effectively executes the same test cases. It's even shorter than our initial version and can be rerun without a system reset.

Although this is all to the good, it has a dark side. The original test (version 1.0) would pass the `delete` tests if the `delete` function were working, without regard to whether the `create` function worked or not. Our latest version will fail the `delete` test if `create` isn't working, even if nothing is wrong with the `delete` function.

The loss of too much independence between tests can kill the effectiveness of acceptance testing. The acceptance test pass/fail can't be a useful measurement of the project's progress if the failure of one function causes every acceptance test to fail. So watch out for coupling between tests that can lead to this. You may introduce it on purpose in a case like this example after balancing the benefits and drawbacks, but interactions you didn't plan on may occur.

For instance, extra records that show up in the results of a `search` test could cause the `search` test to fail—not because anything was wrong with searching but because other tests that created records failed to delete them.

To deal with these types of interactions, imagine all the test methods are executing simultaneously and refactor your tests to provide consistent results in that environment. For example, use `search` queries in the `search` test that have no overlap with the values of the records created by the `create` test, so the records from one won't show up in the other, whether they're there or not. Not only does this avoid large numbers of failures resulting from just a few actual problems, it also allows you to execute the tests simultaneously.

## Summary

❖ Although you're already writing tests, you have an opportunity to use just-in-time design every time you refactor them.

- The simplest tests assume a lot about the initial state of the system, which must be established each time to have valid results.
- Use a shell script to reset the system to the correct initial state.
- If too much time goes into resetting the system, refactor your tests to leave the system in the same state at the end of the tests as at the beginning.
- Be aware of coupling you introduce between tests of different features.
- To avoid inadvertent coupling between tests, imagine they're all executing simultaneously and refactor them to provide consistent results in that environment.

## Exercise 12

1. Identify the assumptions about the initial system state in the following tests for XTrack story 4:

```
public class IterationStoryTest {

    public void testDisplay() {
        assertTrue( displayIteration("1") );
        assertFalse( displayIteration("2") );
    }

    public void testUpdate() {
        login("bob","bobspassword");
        assertTrue( UpdateIteration( "1",
                                     "10",
                                     "20041201",
                                     "20041215") );
        assertFalse( UpdateIteration( "2",
                                      "non-numeric",
                                      "bad date",
                                      "bad date" ) );
    }
}
```

2. Are these tests rerunnable without resetting the system?

# Chapter 19

# Manual Tests

No manual tests.

## Summary

  ✧ No manual tests

Here's a chance to try this idea out in the following exercise.

## Exercise 13

1. What about manual tests?

# Chapter 20

# What!?!!

Yes—we said, "No manual tests." All acceptance tests on an Extreme Programming project must be automated.

We could just say that and go on with the book. It's tempting. But if we did that, some of you wouldn't take it seriously, and you'd end up with a bunch of manual tests. Don't go there. On an Extreme Programming project, a manual test may be worse than no test at all. On our XP road trip, manual testing might lead us to a misadventure similar to that of the aforementioned Donner Party.

In this chapter, we're going to explain our stance on test automation. In the following few chapters, we're going to talk about various avenues we could take to automate our tests. Your team can consider the various options we present and adopt the ones that will help you on your own journey.

Do cases ever arise where you wouldn't automate a test? Our experience is that, indeed, we could have a valid reason not to automate a test. We might also find exploratory manual testing worthwhile. However, our experience is that acceptance-test automation isn't taken seriously, and XP teams can end up with way too many manual tests. Take it from us: this doesn't work.

When you start doing Extreme Programming, you must master all the practices defined in the Extreme Programming literature. Once you've mastered them, you may customize them if you have good reason. The practice of automating all your acceptance tests is no different. Start by automating 100%

of the tests. Once you've mastered test automation, and only then, you may find a good reason to do manual testing.

Does this sound really scary? Is your reaction, "Oh, great, I can't do XP then, because I don't know how to automate tests"?

Don't worry, we're not going to just say, "Automate all the tests" and leave it to you to figure out how to do it. The following chapters will walk you through it. Work through our examples and exercises and you'll be ready to try it in a real project, with the help of your team.

What if your reaction is, "I'm totally onboard with this idea, but my team doesn't understand why we should automate the acceptance tests. They think it'll take too long and won't be worth the effort"? We're going to give you the information to help you help them see the light and provide you with a means of automating that's palatable to the programmers on your team. Meanwhile, let's look at some reasons why we don't want manual tests.

## Manual Tests Are Unreliable

When manual testing is subjected to schedule pressure, the quality of the testing goes down. People begin to cut corners, omit tests, and miss problems. This is the kind of dysfunctional behavior for which traditional software development is famous. All those manual test cases look great on paper, but when crunch time hits, all the paper goes out the window. The warm, comfy feeling the manual tests gave us by promising to keep defects from getting through to the customer is replaced by the burning flames of perdition (which can be even worse than a bad hair day).

It's better to have no test at all than to rely on one that might happen or might not, depending on how the schedule goes and how attentive we are at four o'clock in the morning. Instead of counting on this dubious mechanism to eliminate defects from the system, we must omit the defects in the first place or find them immediately. Which is, of course, exactly what the XP unit testing practice is all about when it calls for the unit tests to be written before the code (omit defects in the first place) and for a 100% pass rate before code is integrated into the system (find defects immediately).

## Manual Tests Undermine the XP Testing Practice

If you know someone is going to be constantly scrutinizing the system looking for defects, the temptation to skimp on the unit tests can become irresistible:

*Bob*: "We'd better go back and add some unit tests for `formatRecord` *before we add this format.*"

*Ted*: "*Yeah, but John's checking each one of those displays in manually. He'll see it if anything isn't right, and if we don't finish this today, the story drops out of the iteration. I mean, you're right: ideally we should, but if we have to choose between delivering functionality to the customer and duplicating a test he's doing anyway, I say we serve the customer.*"

Hopefully, Bob will bring Ted to his senses and they'll write the unit tests first. The discussion could be avoided altogether if they weren't counting on John to eyeball the output of the module. It's amazing how good you imagine a manual tester is going to be when you're counting on his talents. Best case, it's approximately as good as you, the programmer, are when you look at the output from a module to find a particular defect. Maybe it would be this good if John were looking at just the one module, one time, for that particular defect. Now take that and spread it over all the modules, for every possible defect, over and over and over again, and you have a realistic idea of what you can actually count on from John.

## Manual Tests Are Divisive

Other than looking good on paper, manual tests do nothing on their own. When you find a defect with a manual test, *you* found the defect. When you miss one, *you* missed it. It's very personal, especially if *you* found it (or missed it) in *our* code.

Oh, we know—we're all egoless, have collective code ownership, and we're saintlike professionals. Nevertheless, we all know exactly what we were talking about here. It's possible a person might miss something because of some flaw in the test itself, but that will happen only when it doesn't matter. When the stakes are high and something is missed, it'll be because the person doing the test screwed up. Bank on it. The tester should have seen it—he just didn't, because he was distracted, under pressure, or having a bad hair day. If we had automated tests, the programmers could have caught the defect before any tester ever saw the code.

## The Wings-Fall-Off Button

One of our favorite Far Side cartoons shows a goofy-looking guy seated on an airplane, and on his armrest, next to the volume controls, is a toggle with two positions: one labeled "Wings Stay On," and the other labeled "Wings Fall Off." We just know this guy is going to switch it to the "Wings Fall Off" position because, first of all, he's goofy looking, and second, he isn't paying attention.

Who in his right mind would design a plane with a "Wings Fall Off" feature?

The sad thing is, this is airplane version 2.0. The first plane this engineer designed had only a "Wings Stay On" button, which had to be held in manually the whole time the plane was in the air (except when the wings were to fall off).

An Extreme Programming project with manual acceptance tests is like an airplane with a "Wings Fall Off" feature.

## What If You Have Manual Tests?

Are you really going to have no manual tests? What about testing for a consistent look and feel in the user interface? What if you've automated 80% of your testing by testing behind the front end and you just don't feel it's worth the effort to automate the remaining 20% of user-interface testing, because you don't expect those tests will find many defects anyway? What if your application is incredibly complex and can mean the difference between life and death, so you want subject-matter experts to intelligently explore the system and make sure it has no defects the automated tests weren't designed to catch? If you've mastered automating all your acceptance tests, you're qualified to decide if some excellent reason dictates performing a test manually. Maybe your hangar is small and you need the wings to come off your airplane for storage.

What do you do with tests you don't automate? Is a manual test intrinsically bad or useless? We don't think so, *if* your team has mastered test automation. There are right and wrong ways to automate tests, and there are right and wrong ways to execute manual tests. Tests that aren't repeatable or that don't produce timely, easy-to-read results are bad. If you have manual tests, use a test framework that lets you record the results as you go, and have a tool that translates these recorded results into visual, graphic reports, just as the automated tests do.

## Summary

⬥ All acceptance tests on an Extreme Programming project must be automated.

- On an Extreme Programming project, a manual test may be worse than no test at all.
- Manual tests are unreliable.
- Manual tests undermine the XP testing practice.
- Manual tests are divisive.
- An Extreme Programming project with manual acceptance tests is like an airplane with a "Wings Fall Off" button.
- If, having mastered acceptance test automation, you have an excellent reason for a manual test, it must be repeatable, with recorded results that can be viewed the same way as the automated test results.

## Exercise 14

Assume that the following four stories are in the first iteration of the XTrack project:

**Story 1:** User can create, update, and display a story.

**Story 2:** User can estimate a story and assign it to an iteration.

**Story 3:** User can create, update, and display a task

**Story 4:** User can update and display information about an iteration.

1. How many acceptance tests should be manual?
2. What about the tests you can't automate?

# Chapter 21

# Test Automation

You've probably surmised that we've finally reached the most intimidating mountain passes of our XP road trip. We've been climbing steadily for the last few chapters. We wrote executable tests, we talked about ways to organize them with spreadsheets if necessary, we discussed ways to refactor tests to maximize their effectiveness and how to set your system state before and after running tests to ensure valid results. We explored the reasons we're pushing for 100% acceptance test automation. We hope Chapter 19 didn't feel like a big bump in the road to you!

Now we're going to park the car and get out our climbing gear. There just isn't any way to demonstrate acceptance test automation without getting into a lot of technical detail and into the code itself. Hang with us through the rough parts. We'll get into the concrete examples before long, and you'll see that automating all your acceptance tests is not as daunting as you might have thought. In this chapter, we'll explain why and how we write tests that are modular, data-driven, and self-verifying. The next few chapters will get into more gory technical details of coding automated acceptance tests.

Since manual tests are out of the picture, you can get down to business with the automation. As we mentioned before, you'll have some additional work to do to before you can run the executable tests we described in Chapters 16 through 18. This should reassure you if you have any experience whatsoever in test automation, because if we said that's all there was to it, you'd know it was snake oil.

--------------------------------------------------------------------

In fact, if you've automated tests on a traditional software development project, you may find our approach pretty foreign. If you haven't done any test automation, you're going to find any approach mysterious. So before we go on, we want to point out the reasons for our automation approach.

Traditional test automation is a classic case of taking a manual process and automating it. Lots of time and effort goes into selecting a "test tool," which is then used to "capture" a manually executed sequence of interactions with the system. These captured scripts are then "replayed," and the results are either examined or compared to a baseline.

Tests created this way require manual execution the first time through. If the system changes much between the capture and the replay, the captured script will no longer run correctly (even if the system is working correctly) and must be recaptured or edited extensively. This can theoretically provide some automation on a traditional project, where weeks and months are spent in "system test," with the specifications frozen. On an XP project, where everything happens quickly and change is encouraged, constant recapturing becomes essentially the same thing as manual testing. Capture/playback may lead you off the high road and over a cliff.

It's possible to address the problems with traditional capture/replay–style test automation by using the captured scripts as a starting point, then breaking them into modules, replacing the hard-coded test data with parameters, and assembling the real tests using these modules as building blocks. This becomes a programming effort, working within whatever editing system and language the test tool supports.

While this works better than pure capture/replay, it still may take too long for an XP project. You still can't get started until the system is working, so you can do the capture. Creating modules from the captured scripts is time-consuming and tedious because of all the low-level details the tool records in the script for replay. The automation language, editors, and other development tools (if any) provided by the test tool are often insufficient, and the resulting automated tests end up completely specific to the test tool. If you're an expert user of your test tool, you can make it work, but if the programmers on your team aren't as familiar with it, you'll have problems (and grumbling in the ranks).

Many traditional software automation attempts start out with capture/replay and the intent to subsequently modularize the tests but never get there. The number of resulting automated tests is kept pitifully small because of the large amount of time required to maintain them.

To avoid this trap, we turn the process around. We start by writing modular, data-driven, self-verifying executable tests in an appropriate programming language instead of trying to reverse-engineer them from captured scripts in the language of the test tool. This allows us to immediately write the tests at the appropriate level without getting bogged down in replay details. Then we can take advantage of the full set of tools and features available in a commercial-duty programming language.

## Modular Tests

Modular tests don't have the massive duplication that results in captured scripts. The advantages of this should be obvious. In fact, these days, the idea of a creating a monolithic program with twenty chunks of identical code to do the same thing in twenty different places would probably never even cross your mind. Unless, of course, you can remember when people actually wrote programs that way. We can, unfortunately, still remember those programs (at least on good days we can. Some days, we can't remember where our teeth are). Uh . . . where were we? Oh yes—the sad thing is, people are still creating automated tests like that, even though we've known better for going on thirty years now.

Modular doesn't just mean breaking the test into any old pieces. It has to make sense and make you more productive. For instance, suppose you're working on a test for a forms-based Web application. After you do some capturing and start editing the scripts, you see lots and lots of code filling out forms, in whatever manner the test tool represents that. "Aha!" you think, "This cries out for some modularization" and create a module called FillOutForm. You parameterize it with the form to fill out, the fields to set, and the values to set them to, and replace all that code with calls to FillOutForm

Unfortunately, this modularization is not useful. For instance, it removes duplication in an area that isn't likely to change and leaves it in the areas that will (how you fill out a form won't change, but the fields you set and the values you set them to will). Also, how does FillOutForm relate to your test? It doesn't—it's just a means to an end. Try reviewing a test full of FillOutForms with your customer and you'll spend a lot of time trying to relate it to anything she cares about.

In fact we know *you* would never make *this* particular mistake, but it's a classic case of not seeing the forest for the trees. It's easy to fall into similar traps when trying to reverse-engineer. All that junk in the captured script can easily confuse you about what's important. So much has to do with the mechanisms of running the test that you focus on that instead of the test itself.

When you start with the test, the modules are obvious:

**Test that login with a valid password succeeds and a bad one fails**

```
assertTrue( login("bob","bobspassword") );
assertFalse(login("bob","wrong"));
```

What is the module? `login`, of course—it jumps right out at you. The `login` module can encapsulate everything possible about logging in, so this test never has to change, no matter how much the application changes (and it will change), and the test relates exactly to the feature of concern: logging in.

## Data-Independent Tests

Tests that are data-independent can run with different test data values; they're not restricted to hard-coded values. Data-independent tests allow you to cover as much of the input space as you feel is necessary. You can hard-code specific cases initially, add additional values and permutations in the future, and/or move the values out of the test and into a separate file, depending on how extensive you want the coverage to be.

We've said it before, and we'll probably say it again: it's essential that your customer provide realistic data for the tests and that you drive your tests with this data. Since the customer is likely (and encouraged) to change his mind, you need to be able to easily add to, enhance, and reorganize this data.

When you capture scripts, all the values you enter end up hard-coded into the script. So do lots of others you may not have entered but that were generated, returned by the system, or otherwise created as a side effect of your interactions. It's possible to go into the captured script, identify and separate these components, rewrite the hard-coded statements to use parameters, and develop an infrastructure for passing these parameters down and around to all the places where they need to be used. It just takes a lot of time, and it's easy to be distracted by low-level details and miss something, especially if you didn't capture a particular variation on the scenario.

When you start with the tests, the parameters to the modules jump out just like the modules do. What parameters does the `login` module in the above example need to have? It requires a login id and a password, obviously.

How about the `search` module for the following search tests:

1. Test that a search for a category/location combination with businesses succeeds and one with no businesses fails.
2. Test that a search for a business name/location for which a business exists succeeds and that one for which no business exists returns an empty list.

Obviously, it needs a category/location combination or a business name/ location combination and some means of knowing which it's getting:

```
assertTrue( search("Cat/Loc", "Horses","Denver"));
assertFalse( search("Cat/Loc","Joy","Mudville"));

assertTrue( search("Name/Loc","OCLC","Dublin, Ohio"));
assertFalse(search("Name/Loc","OCLC",""));
```

## Self-Verifying Tests

What do you want to know when a test runs? Whether it passed or failed. If it passed, you're happy—no need to look further. If it failed, you want to investigate and see if it's a real defect or an intended modification, which you'll need to accommodate with a change in the test. In other words, you want tests that tell you their outcome as part of running, as opposed to having to dig through the test output to determine what happened.

There's more than one automated way to verify a test, and some are better than others. For instance, test tools often include a feature where you can compare your latest result against a baseline file from a previous execution. The idea is that any differences represent potential problems. You could, in theory, include the comparison step in your automation, so that running the comparison doesn't require any extra interaction, and consider this a self-verifying test.

Trouble is, on an XP project, you just can't afford the time for this (that may be true for any sort of project). First of all, you'd have to make sure you masked out all the things that might be different but still not a failure: dates, times, session ids, dynamically generated record numbers, and so on. Then, a difference does show up, you have to study it and try to figure out exactly what it is and determine if it's okay or not. You're comparing everything, even items that have no importance. You're likely to get so many differences that the verification essentially becomes manual again.

The whole process may be faster than a purely manual test would be, but it has all the same weaknesses: it's slow, requires intense concentration on details, and is unreliable under heavy schedule pressure. Most systems and user interfaces developed on an XP project are way too dynamic to test in this manner—you end up spending all your time trying to deal with no-problem differences.

The problem with the baseline comparison method is that it starts out with the assumption that everything is equally important. Sure, you can modify that with "masks" or some other mechanism to ignore parts of a system response you don't care about or that you expect to be different each time. But if only a few things really matter (as is often the case), why spend all your effort trying to ignore what's unimportant? You should be focusing on identifying what *is* important, on recognizing those critical things in the response that determines whether the function you're testing actually worked. Remember, in XP we have time to verify only the minimum to show that the story is complete.

Self-verification is built right into the executable tests we described in Chapters 16 through 18:

```
assertTrue( login("bob","bobspassword") );
```

The `login` determines whether the attempt with the specified id and password succeeded or not, and the `assertTrue` verifies that in fact it succeeded (`login` returns `true`).

## Summary

- Automation on an XP project starts with writing executable tests immediately, not waiting for the system to be built and then capturing script, as with traditional test automation.
- Tests written this way fall into modules that naturally encapsulate system functions and relate directly to features being tested.
- The parameterization of the modules of tests written this way is obvious and allows the tests to be independent of particular test case values, making it easy to add to, change, and reorganize things when the customer changes her mind.
- The main thing you want to know when a test runs is whether it passed or failed, and you don't want to have to dig through test output to find out.

- ✧ The basic problem with the baseline comparison method is that it starts with the assumption that everything is equally important.
- ✧ Instead of spending effort on trying to ignore what's unimportant, focus on the critical things that determine if the function worked correctly.

It's hard to understand all these concepts when you're just reading about them. Working through the following exercise (or at least reading through our proposed answer) will help you see what we're talking about.

## Exercise 15

Given the following two Xtrack stories, identify as many modules and their parameters as you can:

**Story 1:** A user can create, read, and update a story via a Web interface. The data fields in a story are number, name, author, description, estimate, iteration, timestamps, and state,

**Story 2:** The user can provide an estimate for how long it will take to implement a story, prioritize the story, and assign the story to an iteration.

# Chapter 22

# Making Executable Tests Run

As we mentioned previously, the executable tests we've written can be run as soon as the corresponding code has been completed, if we can call those parts of the system (like the login code) directly from the tests. In this chapter, we're going to illustrate this with a simple example. We're going to use JUnit (www.junit.org) as our test framework. JUnit will provide a lot of the infrastructure we need, including a way to run the test and get graphical test results.

If you're using some other framework or test tool, no problem. You'll apply the same principles we show to your own executable tests, using the appropriate language and framework. Nearly every language has JUnit equivalents (collectively referred to as XUnit), which you can find at www.xprogram ming.com/software.htm.

If you're worried your programming skills aren't up to this or are concerned because you don't have an intimate knowledge of the application code you're testing, remember that you'll be able to pair with the programmers on your team to create these tests. At the very least, you can write up the tests as we showed in Chapter 16, and the programmers can take it from there. Check out Chapter 23 for more help if this is your situation. Once you walk (or climb) through our examples and exercises with us, you may feel more confident.

Suppose the XTrack system is written in Java and we've written the tests for the login function as follows:

```java
public class LoginStoryTest {

    public void testLogin() {
        assertTrue( login("bob","bobspassword") );
        assertTrue( login("BOB","bobspassword") );
        assertFalse(login("bob",""));
        assertFalse(login("bob","BOBSPASSWORD") );
    }
}
```

## Linking the Executable Test to an Application Test Class

To be able to run this test, we need to provide the `assertTrue`, `assertFalse`, and `login` functions. We could do this right inside each executable test, but then we'd be creating duplication. We want to do this in just one place for every test. The first step is to link this test to where those definitions are going to be. Here's how we do that (the **bold** text is what we need to add):

```java
public class LoginStoryTest extends XTrackTest {

    public LoginStoryTest(String name) { super(name); }

    public void testLogin() {
        assertTrue( login("bob","bobspassword") );
        assertTrue( login("BOB","bobspassword") );
        assertFalse(login("bob","");
        assertFalse(login("bob","BOBSPASSWORD") );
    }
}
```

On the first line, we added the phrase `extends XTrackTest`. This tells the Java compiler that our `LoginStoryTest` doesn't stand on its own but is actually a variant of another thing called an `XTrackTest`. This will cause the Java compiler to look in the definition of `XTrackTest` to find `assertTrue`, `assertFalse`, and `login`, since they aren't defined here in this class.

On the second line, we added a **constructor,** a special method the JUnit test runner will use to create and run our `LoginStoryTest`. Other than the name, which always has to be the same as the containing class (`LoginStoryTest`, in this case), this line will always be the same. It doesn't do anything itself—it just calls the constructor in the `XTrackTest` class (referred to as `super`).

## Defining the Application Test Class

Next, we need to define XTrackTest. We're using this name because these are tests for the XTrack application. If it were the Directory application, we'd name it DirectoryTest, and so on. Our definition of XTrackTest needs to provide, directly or indirectly, the assertTrue, assertFalse, and login functions (see Listing 22.1).

**Listing 22.1** XTrackTest.java

```
import junit.framework.*;
import xtrack.*;

public class XTrackTest extends TestCase {

    public XTrackTest(String name) { super(name); }

    public void assertFalse( boolean condition) {
        assertTrue(!condition);
    }

    public boolean login( String id, String psw) {
        XTrackSession session = new XTrackSession();
        return session.login(id,psw);
    }
}
```

The first line in this example, import junit.framework.*; , tells the Java compiler where to find the code for the JUnit framework. The JUnit framework contains assertTrue, assertEquals, and many other useful functions.

The second line, import xtrack.*; , tells the Java compiler where to find the code for the XTrack system. This is where the login code we want to test resides. More about this a bit later.

On the third nonblank line, we define XTrackTest and specify that it, in turn, does not stand alone but is a variant of something called a TestCase. This means that whatever methods a TestCase has, an XTrackTest has the same ones, plus whatever additional ones we define here. TestCase is defined in the JUnit framework, so we don't need to define it. Even better, it endows our XTrackTest with the assertTrue and assertEquals methods (among others).

The next line contains a constructor, just like the one in LoginStoryTest (except for its name). When LoginStoryTest calls super in its constructor, it actually calls this code. This constructor in turn calls `super`, which is the constructor of `TestCase`, where the work of creating an instance is finally carried out.

The next three nonblank lines are a definition of `assertFalse`. At the time of this writing, JUnit does not define an `assertFalse` method, so we have to define our own. Given `assertTrue`, however, it's pretty easy to build an `assertFalse`, as you can see.

## Calling the Code to be Tested

Finally, the next four nonblank lines are the definition of `login`. This `login` is a bridge to the `login` code we're going to test, part of the XTrack system. Our `login` method just calls that code and passes its id and password parameters on. Creating the `login` method required knowledge of how the XTrack code is written, because we're calling that code just the way the other parts of the XTrack system do. This is where pairing with the programmers on your team comes in handy.

Since we're the programmers on your team right now, we'll explain how this code works in the XTrack system. Your mileage may vary; the `login` code you'd be calling on your own application under test might not work this way at all, and you (or whoever creates your `XTrackTest` equivalent) will have to know how your `login` code works to write this method for your system.

The `login` code in XTrack is a method of a class named `XTrackSession`. The `XTrackSession` class is used throughout the XTrack system to keep track of user sessions. When a user attempts to log in, the system calls the `login` method of an `XtrackSession` object with the id and password the user typed in. Luckily, the `login` method of `XTrackSession` has exactly the parameters we want in our login—`id` and `password`—and returns `true` if the login attempt succeeds and `false` if it fails.

Consequently, our login creates an `XTrackSession`, then calls its `login` method, passing the same `id` and `password` parameters that were passed to it. Our login then returns whatever value the `session login` method returns.

## Running the Test

Whew! We're done making this test run. It may seems like a lot when you go through it line by line like this, but if you take a look back over what we've done, you'll see that we've just written (or modified) about twelve lines of Java code. This will take about fifteen minutes, perhaps less, once you get the hang of it.

We can now compile and run `LoginStoryTest`, assuming that the code for the JUnit framework and the parts of the XTrack system are in the place we specified.

The tests are compiled just like any other Java program, using the Java compiler (javac):

```
javac LoginStoryTest.java
```

Because `LoginStoryTest.java` references `XTrackStory` (in the extends clause), compiling `LoginStoryTest.java` will also compile `XTrackTest.java`.

The tests are run using the Java interpreter (java) and a utility from the JUnit framework named `TestRunner`. `TestRunner` has two flavors: a command-line version and a GUI version. The GUI version is run as follows:

```
java junit.swingui.TestRunner LoginStoryTest
```

When all the tests pass, the result looks like Figure 22.1.

**FIGURE 22.1** Result of all tests passing the GUI version

The command-line version runs the tests in the same manner, but it displays the results in a textual format and terminates when the tests are run (unlike the GUI version, which hangs around until you explicitly click the Exit button). You run it like this:

```
java junit.textui.TestRunner LoginStoryTest
```

When all the test pass in this version, it looks like this:

```
.Time: 0.01
OK (1 tests)
```

## Getting Additional Tests to Run

We make the remaining executable tests run just as we did this first one, except that we've already created the application test class, XTrackTest. We modify each test to add the extends clause and the constructor line, and we add definitions to XTrackTest for the other functions (like login) we use in the remaining tests.

For instance, consider the create and delete user id tests we used as examples in Chapter 18. If we've successfully made LoginStoryTest run as illustrated above, we need to do two things to get these tests running as well. First, we need to add the extends clause and constructor to the UserIdStoryTest, as we did to LoginStoryTest (see Listing 22.2).

**Listing 22.2** UserIdStoryTest.java

```
public class UserIdStoryTest extends XTrackTest {

    public UserIdStoryTest(String name) { super(name);}

    public void testCreateDelete() {
        login("super","superpassword");
        assertTrue( createUserId( "new",
                                  "newpassword",
                                  "new@xptester.org") );
        assertFalse( createUserId("fred",
                                  "",
                                  "") );
        assertTrue( deleteUserId( "new" ) );
        assertFalse( deleteUserId("doug") );
    }
}
```

Second, we need to add definitions of `createUserId` and `deleteUserId` to XTrackTest. As with `login`, this requires us (or whoever defines these in XTrackTest) to have knowledge of the code that creates and deletes user ids in XTrack.

To help you understand this example, we'll explain how this code works in XTrack.

XTrackUser is a class in the XTrack system that represents a user identity. It has a `create` method that defines the id, password, and email address of the user identity and adds it to the database. If the user identity is successfully added to the database, `create` returns `true`; otherwise, it returns `false`. XTrackUser also has a `delete` method that causes the user identity to be removed from the database (assuming it's in the database). If the `delete` succeeds, `delete` returns `true`; otherwise, it returns `false`. By default, when a new instance of an XTrackUser is created, it has zero-length values for the id, password, and email address. By supplying an id value to the constructor, you can obtain an XTrackUser representing the user identity in the database with that id.

Consequently, our `createUserId` needs to create an instance of an XTrackUser and then call its `create` method, passing the specified user id, password, and e-mail address. It can return whatever `create` returns. Our `deleteUserId` needs to obtain an XTrackUser for the id to be deleted and then call its `delete` method. Listing 22.3 shows the additions required to XTrackTest (marked in **bold**).

**Listing 22.3** XTrackTest.java

```
import junit.framework.*;
import xtrack.*;

public class XTrackTest extends TestCase {

    public XTrackTest(String name) { super(name); }

    public void assertFalse( boolean b) {
        assertTrue(!b);
    }

    public boolean login( String id,String psw) {
        XTrackSession session = new XTrackSession();
        return session.login(id,psw);
    }
```

```
    public boolean createUserId( String id, String psw,
                                 String email) {
        XTrackUser user = new XTrackUser();
        return user.create(id,psw,email);
    }

    public boolean deleteUserId( String id) {
            XTrackUser user = new XTrackUser(id);
          return user.delete();
    }
}
```

## Combining Multiple Tests into Test Suites

Now that we have these two executable tests running (logging in, maintaining user ids), we could manually run them one after another, but that would quickly become tiresome as we get more and more of the tests running.

A better way is to create a test suite that combines all the tests, so we can run them in a single operation. Listing 22.4 shows an example that illustrates this by defining a test suite with the `LoginStoryTest` and `UserIdStoryTest`, in a class named `AllTests`.

**Listing 22.4** AllTests.java

```
import junit.framework.*;

public class AllTests {

    public static Test suite ( ) {
        TestSuite suite= new TestSuite("XTrack");
        suite.addTest(
            new TestSuite(LoginStoryTest.class));
        suite.addTest(
            new TestSuite(UserIdStoryTest.class));
          return suite;
    }
}
```

The beginning and end sections of this file can always be the same; it's the text marked in bold that includes `LoginStoryTest` and `UserIdStoryTest` in the suite. As you get each executable test running, you add it to the suite by adding lines like this to `AllTests`.

For instance, to add the tests for the story about adding, updating, and displaying tasks (TaskStoryTest), you'd add the following line:

```
suite.addTest(new TestSuite(TaskStoryTest.class));
```

By continuing in this fashion, you can get the entire set of executable tests running and build a suite in AllTests.java that runs all the tests with a single operation.

In the next chapter, we'll show you how to take these same tests and run them through the user interface instead of calling the individual pieces of the system directly. That'll make for a more realistic end-to-end test.

## Summary

- To make the executable tests run:
  - Add to each executable test:
    - An extends clause that references your application test class
    - A pass-thru constructor
  - Define an application-test class that
    - Is named AppTest, where App is the name of your application Extends JUnit's TestCase
    - Adds a pass-thru constructor
    - Defines assertFalse
    - Defines a method that calls the system code you want to test (requires knowledge of how the code in the system works)
- Compile the executable tests with javac, just as with any other java program.
- Run your tests with java and JUnit's TestRunner utility.
  - The GUI version is junit.swingui.TestRunner.
  - The command-line version is junit.textui.TestRunner.
- Combine all the tests into a test suite in AllTests, so you can run them in a single operation.

We encourage you to try this out yourself in the following exercise and see that it isn't as hard as you might think.

# Exercise 16

1. Assume you've written the following test for creating tasks in the XTrack system:

```
public class TaskStoryTest {

    public void testCreate() {
        login("bob","bobspassword");
        assertTrue( addTask( "User Gui",
                             "Create GUI",
                             "Bob",
                             "2",
                             "3",
                             "Not Started" ) );
    }
}
```

Indicate the modifications required to TaskStoryTest to make it run.

2. Assume you've already gotten LoginStoryTest and UserIdStoryTest to run as illustrated in this chapter. Assume that the code in the XTrack system that creates tasks works as follows:

> An XTrackTask *class in the XTrack system represents a task. An* XTrackTask *has an* add *method that sets the task's name, description, assignee, estimate, actual, and status fields to values specified as parameters. If the specified values are all valid, it then attempts to add the task to the database. If the addition is successful, it returns* true; *otherwise, if the add fails or if any of the specified values is invalid, it returns* false.

Show what you'd have to add to XTrackTest to call this code and make the TaskStoryTest run.

# Chapter 23

# Running Executable Tests through Other Interfaces

Getting over these mountain passes isn't so hard if you've got good maps and the right equipment. In the last chapter, we showed you how to make the executable tests run by directly calling the code we want to test. This approach has several problems:

- ✧ The system must be written in the same language as the tests.
- ✧ You need to know how the code works to call it.
- ✧ The tests bypass potentially large and important sections of the system.

The first of these problems can be solved by choosing a suitable language in which to write the tests or by using special interfaces to call from the test language to the system language, such as the Java Native Interface (JNI).

If you have good programming skills, you can deal with the second point by reading the system code and/or spending some time on a programming pair developing it. If that isn't practical, have the programmers who *are* intimately familiar with the code write the methods in the application test class (XTrack-Test in our example from Chapter 22). This will be easy for them to do if you've already written the executable tests, because the executable tests completely specify how these methods (like login, createUserId, addTask, and so on) are to behave.

Once these methods are written, you can probably figure out how to make the necessary changes when you refactor the executable tests, as we described in Chapter 16. If you need help, ask a programmer to pair with you. In fact, once an acceptance test has passed, you may wish to treat the test like production code, making changes only as part of a pair.

## Code Missed by Direct Calls

That leaves the third point, which is the most serious and difficult of the three to deal with. To illustrate why this is such a serious problem, consider the `login` method of `XTrackTest` from Chapter 22 and recall our explanation of how the `login` code works that we're calling in XTrack:

> *When a user attempts to log in, the system calls the* `session` `login` *method with the id and password the user typed in.*

```
public boolean login( String id, String psw) {
        session = new XTrackSession;
        return session.login(id,psw);
    }
```

From our explanation, it's clear that some code in XTrack somehow takes what the user typed in for the id and password and calls the `login` method on that user's session object.

Does our test exercise that code? No—our method bypasses that code. It has its own version of that code. Possibly the code in our `login` method and the code in XTrack that does the same thing are similar. The point is, when we run this test, we're not executing that code. We can find defects in the `login` method of the session object, but we *can't find defects in the XTrack code that calls it*. It's easy for an XP team, especially one without an experienced tester, to fall into this trap.

What if the `session` `login` method works great but that code in XTrack that we're duplicating here has a defect that causes it to always convert the user's password to lowercase? Or what if that code calls the `login` on the wrong session object? Some users aren't going to be able to log in, and there's no way our test can find these defects.

## Expanding Coverage of the Executable Tests

This problem doesn't make the executable test implemented by direct calls bad, it just means these tests can't find a significant population of *potential* defects.

You absolutely want to get the executable tests running through direct calls first. These will both find defects and demonstrate the progress of the project toward the customer's objectives, which is what acceptance testing is all about.

Whether you then spend the effort to get the tests to run through other interfaces depends on the team's assessment of risk for not doing so. The system may be designed so very little code needs to be duplicated in the application test class (see the description of an XP team at BoldTech Systems at the end of this chapter), in which case the risk may be quite small.

The good news is that when you do need to run the tests through some other mechanism than direct calls, you don't need to make any changes whatsoever to the executable tests, since they're completely independent of the interface with the system being tested.

You may have a choice among several methods to interface the tests to your system, other than direct calls. Usually, the farther out toward the user interface you get, the more difficult it becomes.

Consider, for instance, a Web-based system like XTrack. Leaving the user's browser program aside, the system may still consist of discrete programs, such as the Web server itself, an application server, servlets, CGI scripts, database servers, backend hosts, and so on. The easiest way to interface your tests (after direct calls) may be to bypass, for instance, the Web server, and drive the servlet, CGI script, database server, and so on, directly. While this allows you to test all the code in, say, your servlets, you're still bypassing code in the Web server and application server, not to mention the communications layer (Internet) and the browser.

If you move back in the chain, so you're driving the tests through the Web server, you can cover more of the code with tests, but with greater effort—because interfacing to the Web server using HTTP protocol will probably be harder than just calling servlets. Going back another step and driving the test through the browser covers even more of the code but is even more difficult, because you have to deal with the GUI thing: mouse clicks, keystrokes, and screen layouts.

## Interfacing to a Test Tool

The farther you get from direct calls, the more useful some sort of test tool will be in interfacing your tests to your system. The test tool will "know" how to interact with your system at the level you want to interface, and you'll just need to interface the tests to the tool. What this boils down to is writing a different set of methods in the application test class (XTrackTest in our examples) that invoke the code in the system indirectly through the tool, rather than directly by calling them.

We're going to illustrate this by making the executable tests from the previous chapter run through the XTrack user interface (more or less) by interfacing to a Web testing tool called WebART (available at www.oclc.org/webart/downld.htm). This is an HTTP-based tool that interfaces Web-based systems at the same level as a user's browser, allowing us to test almost all the code in XTrack. The only code we'll be missing is what runs in the user's browser—JavaScript, for example. As it turns out, XTrack uses very little JavaScript, so this provides pretty good coverage.

WebART isn't the only test tool you could employ for this purpose. Once you understand our approach, you can use it with whatever tool is appropriate for your project.

As we promised, no changes are needed to the executable tests themselves (`LoginStoryTest`, `UserIdStoryTest`, `TaskStoryTest`, and so on). All the activity takes place at the application test class (`XTrackTest`) and below.

We could create an entirely new version of `XTrackTest` for interfacing the tests through WebART. This new `XTrackTest` would have different implementation of the methods `login`, `createUserId`, and `deleteUserId`, and we could swap the two versions of the file in and out, depending on which way we wanted to run the tests.

## Creating an Application Test-Interface Class

Although creating a separate version of XTrackTest for WebART could work, we'd have to recompile the tests each time we wanted to switch between direct calls and WebART, and we'd end up with duplication (more than one `assertFalse`, for instance). To avoid these problems, we'll create a new application test-interface class to hold just the methods (`login`, `createUserId`, and so on) that are going to be different between the two interfaces.

We'll call this class `XTrackTestInterface`. It looks like Listing 23.1.

**Listing 23.1** XTrackTestInterface.java

```
public class XTrackTestInterface {

    public boolean login( String id,String psw) {
        return false;
    }
```

```
        public boolean createUserId( String id, String psw,
                                      String email) {
            return false;
        }

        public boolean deleteUserId( String id) {
            return false;
        }
    }
```

You can think of this as a kind of null-test interface to the system. The methods don't do anything; they just unconditionally return false. Note that this class has no extends clause. It isn't based on any other thing, like the other classes we've used so far. Instead, it's going to provide the base for the two interfaces we need: the direct-call interface, which we already have working, and the WebART interface, which we're going to create.

## Refactoring the Direct-Call Interface

Next, we move the methods that directly call the system code into their own class, named XTrackDirectInterface, as shown in Listing 23.2.

**Listing 23.2** XTrackDirectInterface.java

```
    import xtrack.*;

    public class XTrackDirectInterface
                extends XTrackTestInterface {

        public boolean login( String id,String psw) {
            XTrackSession session = new XTrackSession();
            return session.login(id,psw);
        }

        public boolean createUserId( String id, String psw,
                                      String email) {
          XTrackUser user = new XTrackUser();
        return user.create(id,psw,email);
        }

        public boolean deleteUserId( String id) {
            XTrackUser user = new XTrackUser(id);
            return user.delete();
        }
    }
```

The **bold** text indicates what's new here, which isn't much. We're just wrapping a class around the methods we wrote to call the XTrack system code: you should recognize them as the code currently in XTrackTest. In fact, that's where we get it—we just copy the code from XTrackTest and paste it right into XrackDirectTestInterface. Note also the import xtrack.*; statement. We need this here because we're calling the XTrack system code in this class.

## Refactoring the Application Test Class

We know this is sounding complicated—just hang on and you'll see where we're going. The next step is to refactor XTrackTest by removing the code we moved to XTrackDirectInterface and replacing it with code that can use either the direct interface or the WebART interface (creating the WebART interface will be the last thing we do). Listing 23.3 shows what the new version of XTrackTest looks like after we've done this.

**Listing 23.3** XTrackTest.java

```java
import junit.framework.*;

public class XTrackTest extends TestCase {

    public XTrackTest(String name) {
        super(name);
        setTestInterface("direct");
    }

    public void assertFalse( boolean b) {
        assertTrue(!b);
    }

    private XTrackTestInterface testInf;

    public void setTestInterface(String interfaceType){
        if (interfaceType.equals("direct"))
        testInf = new XTrackDirectInterface();
        else if (interfaceType.equals("webart"))
            testInf = new XTrackWebARTInterface();
        else
            fail("Undefined interface " +
              interfaceType);
    }
```

```
public boolean login( String id,String psw) {
        return testInf.login(id,psw);
}

public boolean createUserId( String id,
                             String psw,
                             String email) {
        return testInf.createUserId(id,psw,email);
}

public boolean deleteUserId( String id) {
        return testInf.deleteUserId(id);
    }
}
```

We've removed the import xtrack.*; statement, because we no longer need it. That's because we no longer have a direct connection between XTrack-Test and the XTrack system. That direct connection is now encapsulated in XTrackDirectInterface (which now needs the import statement, as we pointed out above).

We've modified the XTrackTest constructor so it's no longer simply a pass-through to super (the constructor in TestCase). It still calls super, but after that it also calls the setTestInterface method to set its interface to direct. This means that by default, this version of XTrackTest will use the direct-call interface, the one we already have working.

We made no changes to assertFalse. The next new thing is the declaration of an XTrackTestInterface named testInf. Understanding how this is used is bound up in how the setTestInterface method works.

The setTestInterface method checks if direct was specified. If so, it creates a new XTrackDirectInterface and stores it in testInf. If webart was specified, it creates an XTrackWebARTInterface and stores that in testInf. In other words, this method creates an object for the appropriate type of interface (either for direct access or access via WebART) and stores that object in testInf.

Having created an object for the appropriate interface in testInf, our new version of XTrackTest simply needs to pass the parameters to corresponding methods of testInf in its login, createUserId, and deleteUserId methods and return the same values testInf's methods return.

## Creating a Tool-Specific Interface Class

The final step is to define XTrackWebARTInterface, which will hold the new methods we'll write to interface to XTrack using the WebART tool. Exactly what these new methods do depends on how you need to interface to a particular tool.

Unfortunately, there's no free lunch. While the direct-call method requires exact knowledge of the system code, the test-tool method requires expert knowledge of that test tool. You need to know not just how to use the tool but how to interact with the tool from the language of the executable tests—in this case, Java.

One of the reasons we picked WebART for this illustration is that a Java package is available (jWebART) that makes the interface to the tool fairly painless (although it's still necessary to know how to use WebART itself to drive the system). Using jWebART, XTrackWebARTInterface looks like Listing 23.4.

**Listing 23.4** XTrackWebARTInterface

```
import jWebART.*;

public class XTrackWebARTInterface
            extends XTrackTestInterface {

  public XTrackWebARTInterface() {
     super();
     project = new WebARTProject("XTRACK");
     script = new
         WebARTPersistentScript(project,"XTRACKIF");
  }

  public boolean login( String id,String psw) {
      return script.invoke("login","id=" + id,
                                   "psw=" + psw);
  }

  public boolean createUserId( String id, String psw,
                               String email) {
      return script.invoke("createUserId",
                           "id=" + id,
                           "psw=" + psw,
                           "email=" + email);
  }
```

```
    public boolean deleteUserId( String id) {
        return script.invoke("deleteUserId",
                             "id=" + id);
    }

    private WebARTProject project;
    private WebARTPersistentScript script;
}
```

Starting with the first line, the `import jWebART.*;` statement tells the Java compiler where to find the code for interfacing to WebART in Java. Next, the `XTrackWebARTInterface` class is defined as extending the `XTrackTestInterface` class. This is just like the `XTrackDirectInterface` class.

If you're wondering why we defined `XTrackTestInterface` and then based the two real interfaces on it, it's so we can store either one in `testInf` in `XTrackTest`. We can do this because they share a common base class. Otherwise, we'd have to have two different variables and duplicate code to call the methods of one or the other.

The next thing is the constructor for this class. The code following the call to `super` essentially does the following:

- Starts the WebART tool
- Tells WebART to put into effect a preexisting group of settings (preferences, file paths, options, and so on) named XTRACK
- Tells WebART to start a script running named XTRACKIF

In other words, if this interface is instantiated (`XTrackTest.setTestInterface` is called with a value of `webart`), it will start WebART, set the project to XTRACK, and start the XTRACKIF script. Of course, the XTRACK project and the XTRACKIF script will have to already exist, and we'll have to take care of that within the WebART tool itself.

Finally, we have the `login`, `createUserId`, and `deleteUserId` methods. These call the `invoke` method in the `WebARTPersistentScript` object to pass their arguments to a subscript in the XTRACKIF script. The first parameter of `invoke` is the name of the subscript, and subsequent parameters are the names and values of the parameters to be passed to the subscript.

At this point, we've completed interfacing our tests with the WebART tool. If we compile all our tests again, they'll still go through the direct interface because of the `setTestInterface("direct");` in `XTrackTest`. It would be good practice to do that and make sure the tests all still pass before going on.

Now we change XTrackTest to setTestInterface("webart"); , recompile it, and all the same tests now go to the WebART tool. Most of them fail, because we haven't done any work in WebART to set up the XTRACK project or create the XTRACKIF script. The next chapter will show you how to do that.

Don't worry, things will get easier. We'll start our downhill run pretty soon!

## One Team's Experience with Direct-Call Test Automation

Now that you have an idea of the problems with calling your code directly from the test and what's involved in doing it a different way, consider the following successful experience of one XP team using direct calls:

A small team at BoldTech Systems set about creating a generic Web-based content management system from scratch, using Java. The team started with five members, all experienced programmers and architects. They decided to automate most of the tests using Java and the JUnit test framework one layer beneath the user interface. These automated acceptance tests were developed right along with the code, with the acceptance tests written, automated, and run before the end of each iteration.

The user interface was made up of Java server pages (JSPs). The bulk of the application logic was put into a lower layer, Struts, a Web application navigation framework. Struts managed the form, the actions, the information that goes in and out of the session, and the errors. The automated acceptance tests used mock objects for forms, requests, responses, and sessions.

When a user pushes a button such as Submit, the Struts form calls a "button push" action, and the test methods emulate this with a mock object and the action. The action is where the business logic is located, and at that point the system code is called. The tests could verify that a Save button led to the correct validating and persisting data in the database and could emulate series of button pushes and verify that data persists between sessions.

This team designed their code specifically for ease of testing. By having well-formed code, so that all requests were processed in a central location, the amount of code missed by calling the system code directly was kept to a minimum. This was a great example of writing the system for testability.

For validation, the tests go into the session and validate the application state—what is actually in memory for that user session—rather than looking at an HTML table in the HTML user interface, for example. They validate how the data exists in the native structure before it's been rendered. Because the tests are written in Java, using the JUnit test framework, they're flexible and easy for the programmers to maintain. It's easy to drive the tests with data and create a variety of scenarios, including error testing. The tests can simulate multiple concurrent users as well. For example, they can write a test where two users try to delete the same record.

By testing below the user interface, the team finds the tests cost little to maintain. About 20% of the development effort is spent on creating and maintaining the automated acceptance tests, and most of that is on test creation. These tests cover about 80% of the application's functionality.

Team members report that the automated acceptance tests routinely find problems that the unit tests don't. They depend on these tests for confidence that their changes didn't break anything. They take about ten minutes to run, so they aren't run quite as often as the unit tests, but the programmers run them several times each day.

## Summary

- ✧ Problems with directly calling the system code from the tests include
  - ▪ The system must be in the same language.
  - ▪ It requires exact knowledge of the system code.
  - ▪ The tests bypass code and can miss defects.
- ✧ To address these problems:
  - ▪ Pick the right language for the tests, or use something like JNI.
  - ▪ Help programmers write the system code, have programmers write the application-test class, or both.
  - ▪ If the risk is high enough, make the tests run through an interface that covers more of the code.
- ✧ The tests can be run through a different interface without requiring any changes:
  - ▪ The changes take place in the application test class and below.
  - ▪ The farther out toward the interface you get, the more difficult these become, and the more useful a test tool is.
- ✧ To make the executable tests run through a higher-level interface using a test tool:
  - ▪ Create an application test-interface class.
  - ▪ Move the direct-call methods from the application test class into a direct-interface subclass of the application test-interface class.

- Refactor the application test class to instantiate an object of the appropriate interface type and call the methods on that object instead of implementing them directly.
- Create a tool-specific interface subclass of the application test-interface class and implement the methods that go through the tool.

✧ It's better to design the system up front to make direct-call testing less risky, if you can do so.

Try the following exercise, and these ideas will become clearer.

## Exercise 17

Assume you've made the changes to XTrackTest and created the additional classes, as illustrated in this chapter. Assume you're now going to add a third interface that will run the tests through a GUI tool called GUITAR.

1. Indicate the changes required to LoginStoryTest (warning: this is a trick question):

```
public class LoginStoryTest {

    public void testLogin() {
        assertTrue( login("bob","bobspassword") );
        assertTrue( login("BOB","bobspassword") );
        assertFalse(login("bob",""));
        assertFalse(login("bob","BOBSPASSWORD") );
    }
}
```

2. Indicate the changes required to the setInterface method of XTrack-Test:

```
public void setTestInterface(String interfaceType){
    if (interfaceType.equals("direct"))
        testInf = new TrackDirectInterface();
    else if (interfaceType.equals("webart"))
        testInf = new TrackWebARTInterface();
    else
        fail("Undefined interface " +
          interfaceType);
}
```

3. Are other changes required to XTrackTest or any other existing class?

# Chapter 24

# Driving the System
# with a Test Tool

In the previous chapter, we illustrated how to make the executable tests run through other interfaces besides direct calls to the code. Without making any changes to the XTrack tests themselves, we added a few lower-level classes to send the tests to the WebART tool, to be played through the XTrack browser interface. When we finished, we were able to send the tests to WebART, but the tests all failed, because we hadn't done anything in WebART to perform the tests. In this chapter, we're going to complete the process by doing exactly that.

The details of how this is done are, of course, highly tool-specific, so we're not going to get overly detailed. Our goal is not to make you expert (or even proficient) at using this particular tool but to prove by example that it's possible. We'll use the example to discuss validation issues that always come up when automating tests at or near the user interface, regardless of the tool used. You can apply this to whatever tool seems suitable to your project. See Chapter 29 for more about developing and selecting test tools.

We won't pretend this is easy to grasp upon first read. We recommend that you try working through the exercise for this chapter. Stick it out—it's not as bad as it looks. You might feel you're teetering on the edge of a cliff right now, but we have plenty of safety gear!

## WebART Overview

Here's a brief description of WebART, to help you understand the example. WebART interfaces to a Web-based application at the HTTP protocol level, just like a browser, and interacts with the system though pages, links, forms, and HTTP requests like GET, POST, and PUT. It has a procedural scripting language that provides basic programming constructs, including support for modules (called subscripts), and has a capture facility that allows scripts to be created by performing interactions manually with a browser.

WebART supports the traditional capture/reply baseline/compare test automation model, but it also provides a method for building modular, data-driven, self-verifying scripts. Creating scripts like this is pretty much a programming effort. You can capture some short segments of code and paste these into your test scripts. A set of utilities, called the MDS (Modular Data-driven Self-verifying) framework, provides functionality to get test and validation data from external files, route the test data to the appropriate modules, perform the validations, and log the outcomes. By using this framework, you have to code only the details of the interactions with the system.

The jWebART package provides an interface utility that integrates with the MDS framework, so that by using both packages, we just need to write the interactions for `login`, `createUserId`, and `deleteUserId`.

## Main WebART Script

The main script consists mostly of calls to the MDS framework and jWebART, with just a few statements to include the WebART versions of `login`, `createUserId`, and `deleteUserId`. Here's what it looks like:

```
xtrackif
!script xtrackif
!param cfile = ""
!param gTestCaseFile(Test Cases)="xtrackif.testcase"
!include zdutil
!include login
!include createuserid
!include deleteuserid
!include jwebart
! {
  init();
  getTestCase();
  getTestCaseName(gtTestCase1);
```

```
    jWebartInterface();
    log ( script, gOutCome);
    }
!end
```

The first line provides the name for the script (xtrackif). This has to match what we specified in the XTrackWebARTInterface in Chapter 23.

The next two lines declare two parameters for the script. Parameters are variables whose values can be specified to the script when it's run. The first, cfile, is the name of a file the jWebART package uses to pass parameters and results back and forth between the Java environment and WebART. It gets specified by jWebART when it starts the script. The second parameter, gTest-CaseFile, is the name of the file that contains test data and validation data. In this case, the test data is coded into the executable tests in Java, so this TestCase file is used only for the validation. We'll provide an example of this file later.

The next line, !include zdutil, includes the definitions for the MDS framework. The next three include our WebART versions of login, create-UserId, and deleteUserId. These are the files where we need to do the most work. We'll take a look at examples of these as well.

The next line includes jWebART utilities, peers to the Java versions we discussed in the previous chapter but written in the WebART scripting language. The executable tests pass parameters through the Java jWebART functions, which communicate with these versions in the WebART scripting language, which in turn passes them on to to the WebART versions of login, createUserId, and deleteUserId.

The remaining lines consist of calls to utilities in the MDS framework (init, getTestCase, getTestCaseName, and log) and to the jWebART package. These calls perform initialization, read the TestCase file, and parse out test and validation data. They then enter the jWebARTInterface to accept requests from the executable tests in the Java environment. When a request is received, one of the modules login, createUserId, or deleteUserId is called; it interacts with the XTrack system via HTTP, and the result is returned to the Java environment.

## Login Module

The modules login, createUserId, and deleteUserId share a similar basic structure. They have a fixed set of parameters defined by the MDS framework and make the same sort of calls to MDS utilities at the beginning and end. Here's what the login module looks like:

```
!subscript login *pOut pIn tData vLevel *outCome vCrit
!declare zzId zzPsw pPage
!declare myOutCome
! {
  trace (login, interface, pOut, pIn, tData, vLevel);
  myOutCome=UnKn;

  getField(zzId,id,tData);
  getField(zzPsw,psw,tData);

  >0>$get(pPage,
         "http://${zzorghostzz}/.../login.htm")[];

  form.pPage.0.superid.tb.0[0] = "zzId";
  form.pPage.0.password.pw.0[0] = "zzPsw";
  form.pPage.0.Submit.su.0[0] = "Logon";
  >7>$submit(pOut,pPage,0)[];

  doValidation(outCome, myOutCome, tData, vCrit,
               vLevel, pOut);
}
!end
```

The first few lines are declarations that define the parameters to the module and variables for use within the module.

- The `pOut` parameter will receive the XTrack system's response to the attempted login when login returns.
- The `pIn` parameter contains the current page (if any—the first time `login` is called, there will be no current page).
- `tData` contains the "real" parameters to `login`: the id and password.
- `vLevel` is an MDS variable that controls the level of validation.
- `outCome` will receive a value reflecting the outcome of the validations of the system's response to the login attempt.
- `vCrit` contains the validation criteria to check.

These last three are handled by MDS utilities and are just passed on to those utilities without requiring processing within `login`.

Next, a call to MDS utility called `trace` handles logging the test results. An assignment sets the variable `myOutCome` to `UnKn` (unknown—in the MDS framework, the outcome of a test can be pass, fail, or unknown).

The next steps are two calls to the MDS `getField` utility, which unpacks the values of the parameters from the `tData`. All parameters passed from an executable test in Java into a module like `login` are packed together into `tData`, and the `getField` utility unpacks them by name. This is why the parameter names were added to the parameter values in the calls to the `WebARTPersistentScript.invoke` method in the previous chapter. The names specified for the parameters there must match the names user here: `id` and `psw`.

The remaining lines, except for the call to `doValidation` at the end, are the scripting of the interaction with the XTrack system through the HTTP protocol. They are

- ❖ A `$get` that retrieves the page with the login form (we replaced a large chunk of text in the URL parameter to `$get` with ". . ." for clarity)
- ❖ Several assignment statements that set the fields in the `login` form to the specified id and password (the values that were passed in in `tData`, then extracted via `getField` into `zzPsw` and `zzId`)
- ❖ A `$submit` that submits the filled-out `login` form to the XTrack system

Finally, `doValidation` is an MDS utility that takes the response to the login (which was placed into `pOut` by `$submit`) and validates it according to the validation criteria in `vCrit`. If the validations pass, `doValidation` sets `outCome` to PASS. If not, it sets it to FAIL. The value of the `outCome` variable is then returned to the `jWebARTInterface` module, which in turn passes a value of either `true` (for pass) or `false` (for anything else) back to the executable tests in the Java environment. All this is to allow our tests to be self-verifying. If you see `pass` after this test runs, no worries. Otherwise, you need to investigate.

The other modules, `createUserId` and `deleteUserid`, are similar to this, as would be the others required to get all the executable tests running through WebART (`createTask`, `updateTask`, `createStory`, and so on).

## Validation Criteria

As promised, here's an example of the `xtrackif.testcase` file, with the simplest possible validations defined for `login`, `createUserId`, and `deleteUserId`:

**Listing 24.1** xtrackif.testcase

```
XTrackIf
  [
  Validation <validationTDI=Vlogin&
              text=XTrack Stories&>
  Validation <validationTDI=VcreateUserId&
              text=Record added.&>
  Validation <validationTDI=VdeleteUserId&
              text=Record deleted.&>
  ]
```

We've defined three validations here, one for each module. For the `login` module, the validation says, in essence, to look for the text `XTrack Stories`. When a login succeeds in XTrack, the user's browser is redirected to the list of stories, which contains this text. If it fails, the user remains on the login page.

In previous discussions, where we were making direct calls to the system code we were testing, the issue of validation didn't come up. The validation was there, but it happened inside the piece of code we were calling. The XTrack `session.login` method, for instance, returned `true` or `false` depending on whether the attempt passed or failed.

Now that we're interacting with the system through the user interface, we have to decide for ourselves whether an action was successful. In this case, it means examining the system's response to our login attempt to determine whether the attempt was successful. We'll have to do something similar for the attempts to create a user, delete a user id, and so on.

It's easy to get too detailed when specifying validations. The page resulting from a successful login has a lot more text than just `XTrack Stories`, as well as other kinds of things, like links, buttons, and other form elements. Wouldn't it be better to validate many, if not all, of these items? In fact, the MDS framework does provide primitives for validating the presence of links, forms, form variables, and tables, and a way to extend these to application-specific items. For an XP project, however, you probably don't want to take this route.

It's better to start with the simplest possible validation that distinguishes a success from a failure and enhance it only if it proves insufficient for some reason. Remember, we need only validate the minimum necessary to know if our story is correctly implemented. The more detailed and specific these validations get, the more difficult they are to maintain. This is why the MDS framework breaks them out of the code and into a separate file. The reason they tend to be so volatile is that they're completely dependent on the user interface, which is generally the most change-prone part of the system.

## Summary

- ✧ Our examples use the WebART test tool, but you can apply these same principles to any tool you choose if it supports this approach.
- ✧ Scripts written for the WebART test-tool interface use the executable tests written in Java and drive the XTrack system through the user interface.
- ✧ WebART is an HTTP-based tool, so the scripts interact with XTrack through pages, links, forms, and request primitives like get and submit.
- ✧ WebART scripts are interfaced to the executable tests by a set of utilities from the jWebART package implemented in the WebART scripting language.
- ✧ The jWebART utilities also integrate with the MDS framework, a set of utilities for writing Modular, Data-driven, Self-verifying scripts using WebART.
- ✧ The XTRACKIF script consists of a main script and a separate subscript for each module: login, createUserId, and deleteUserId.
- ✧ The subscript modules all share a similar basic structure, with a fixed set of parameters and the same sequence of calls to MDS utilities at the beginning and end.
- ✧ Unlike a direct-call interface, where the bulk of the validation takes place mostly within the system code, validation is much more of a task for the test when testing through the user interface.
- ✧ Validation criteria are specified in a separate file because of the high degree of volatility in the user interface.
- ✧ It's best to use the simplest possible validation that can distinguish success from failure. If it weren't the minimum, it wouldn't be enough!

Here's a chance to try these ideas out. If this chapter felt like it zoomed right over your head, work the exercise. It's not as bad as you think.

## Exercise 18

1. Assume you've done everything on the Java side to make the following executable test run through WebART:

```
public class TaskStoryTest {

    public void testCreate() {
        login("bob","bobspassword");
        assertTrue( addTask( "User Gui",
                             "Create GUI",
                             "Bob",
                             "2",
          "3",
                             "Not Started" ) );
    }
}
```

Indicate the changes that would be necessary to the WebART XTRACKIF.

2. Assume you obtained the following statements by capturing the process of adding a task to XTrack manually:

```
>0>$get(pPage,
       "http://${zzorghostzz}/.../createtask.htm")[];

form.pPage.0.name.tb.0[0] = "User Gui";
form.pPage.0.description.tb.1[0] = "Create GUI";
form.pPage.0.assignee.tb.2[0] = "Bob";
form.pPage.0.estimate.tb.3[0] = "2";
form.pPage.0.actual.tb.4[0] = "3";
form.pPage.0.status.tb.5[0] = "Not Started";
form.pPage.0.Submit.su.0[0] = "Create";
>7>$submit(pPage,pPage,0)[];
```

Using login in this chapter as a model, write the complete addTask subscript module.

# *Chapter 25*

# Bugs on the Windshield: Running Acceptance Tests

You've worked with the customer and the rest of your project team to define and automate acceptance tests. Now the team will run these tests as the stories are completed, providing concrete feedback about which stories are in fact completed and which require more work.

## How Often Do You Run Acceptance Tests?

Running acceptance tests is like voting: do it early and often. You defined acceptance tests before and during the iteration planning, then wrote executable acceptance tests during the first day or two of the iteration. As the stories are completed, the team makes the tests run through direct calls to the code, and you begin getting feedback immediately.

On our ideal team, the programmers responsible for the story are also responsible for making the executable acceptance tests for those stories run, which means implementing those methods in the direct-call interface required for the acceptance tests. The story isn't finished until the acceptance tests run successfully (except when the tests depend on other stories not yet completed).

If more work needs to be done to make the executable tests run, that should become the programmers' highest priority, not going on to the next story. Resist with all your might any temptation to give up on the executable tests and start testing manually. Once you step onto this slope, the only way out is down, and you'll never climb out of the hole. You'll end up spending more and more time on manual tests, until that's all you do.

In the worst case, if a test can't be automated, consider dropping it. As we discussed in Chapter 16, no test at all may be better than a manual test at this point. Keep in mind that with XP, unlike a traditional software development project, the acceptance test is not the primary method for assuring quality. We aren't looking for defects in how we carried out our intentions in the code. That's the job of our test-first, pair-programming teams and unit-test automation.

The job of acceptance testing is to uncover differences between our intentions and the customer's expectations. Consequently, the risk associated with not running an acceptance test is different from that of not running unit tests. This doesn't mean acceptance tests aren't critical to the project. Just remember that you have time to test only the minimum needed to prove that the story has been completed according to the customer's desires.

If you're beyond the first iteration, you also have acceptance tests (now regression tests) from previous iterations to run. Your team should have an integration environment already set up (if you don't, you're heading for big trouble), where the team can start doing builds containing new code for the iteration. Here's where you really get the payoff for test automation.

Run the automated acceptance tests for previous iterations each time a new build is done in the integration environment. Now your team knows right away if they broke something. The code may have passed the unit tests, but we know some defects can't be caught by unit tests. Running automated regression tests will keep development speedy.

"I read some other Extreme Programming publications that said customers should run the acceptance tests. What about that?" you ask. Good point. In XP Utopia land, our customers are right there with us executing the acceptance tests. In less ideal projects, the development team (including you, the tester) must take on this responsibility, at least initially. When you think the stories are complete, though, the customer always gets a turn.

On our projects, we've handled acceptance testing by the customer or user in different ways. Here are some alternative approaches:

- A tester and customer pair to execute acceptance tests; the tester may go around to a number of customers to repeat the process, each one running the acceptance tests that pertain to his part of the system.
- A group of customers meets in one room with several workstations and pairs with each other to run the tests.

✧ A group of customers meets in one room, but only one "drives" and runs tests, while the others watch via a projector (this scenario could be played out with remote participants, using a product such as NetMeeting).

When do you do this customer testing? Ideally, before the end of the iteration. If you're working with remote customers or in a situation where other teams provide parts of the final working system, you might be better off going through this process after the end of the iteration.

On one of Lisa's projects, the team had to compromise. They ran through the basic acceptance tests in a demo situation with the customer team a couple of days after the end of each iteration. Due to constraints in the availability of the user acceptance-test environment, the customers didn't get to do much hands-on testing until after each release. Each release consisted of two or three iterations, so this might mean several weeks went by before customers really got to test. As a result, some miscommunications between customers and programmers went unnoticed until it was too late to fix them before the release. You'll have to adapt your process to best fit your project and your customers.

Testing after the end of the iteration has one advantage for your development team: the iteration has already ended, and it's hard for the customer to say otherwise. Sure, you should have the customer sign off that the iteration is complete. In some organizations, that may even mean a formal signoff document. If a customer discovers that a story wasn't done according to her requirements (on which she also had signed off) or a significant defect is present, she can delay the signoff until her needs are met. However, that work will be part of the new iteration or a future one and may reduce the team's velocity that can be devoted to new stories.

Make sure your customer understands up front that he can't run a test on the last day of the iteration, decide the result doesn't look the way he wants, and delay the end of the iteration by a day or a week until it's fixed. The iteration is over when it's over. If a story isn't complete or has such severe defects that it can't be called complete, the team's velocity for the next iteration is lowered accordingly, and that story also has to be part of the team's workload for that iteration (unless the customer decides to postpone or drop it).

*Extreme Programming Installed* has an excellent chapter on handling defects. One suggestion is to report problems by writing them on story cards. The team can estimate how long fixing the defect will take. Fixes for low-priority defects can be scheduled in future iterations. Urgent problems need to be addressed right away, which could mean that one or more stories in that iteration may have to be deferred to make time for fixing problems. This is a thorny area that you, as an XP tester, may find difficult to deal with in spite of all these good guidelines for handling problems.

## Educating the Customer

This is an area where you want that ounce of prevention. Educating the customer so he has reasonable expectations is essential. Before you back the XP car out of the garage, talk with the customer about how you'll handle issues. Make him read the defect-handling chapter in *Extreme Programming Installed*. Better yet, produce your own XP owner's manual that describes your own team's development process and helps the customer get the most value out of the project. Your owner's manual could cover topics such as

- **Planning.** Describe story creation; explain that you defer in-depth discussion of each story until it's selected for an iteration or until it needs to be clarified for the purpose of making an estimate.
- **Iteration planning, story selection.** Outline the negotiation process involved in selecting the stories for an iteration that are both high priority for the customers and make sense for the programmers (in terms of dependencies between stories, creating an initial framework, and so on).
- **Acceptance tests.** List the input expected of the customer as she helps write the tests and the process for running and verifying results before the end of the iteration.
- **Defect fixes.** Define the policy on handling defects. You may choose to classify them into those that must be fixed to call the story complete and those that can be deferred to a future iteration. Fixes that will take up significant programmer resources must be written up as stories for the next (or a future) iteration. Whatever policy you decide on, make sure you and the customer agree on it.
- **Realistic expectations.** Set realistic expectations for the relatively low level of documentation and status artifacts generated as a byproduct of XP. If the customer feels lost without certain metrics or documents, you may be able to find a creative way to provide them without adding excessive overhead. XP is all about being flexible.

- ✧ **Communication tools.** Review what's available with the customer. For example, you might have a wiki (see Chapter 30) where he can learn about the status of the project and other general project information. Some teams capture information about iterations, tasks, and stories (as our XTrack system does) that can be used to generate reports of various metrics.

## Acceptance Criteria

Remind the customer that she defined acceptance criteria in the acceptance tests. Anything that causes an acceptance criterion not to be met is a defect. This is why you invest time in making sure the acceptance tests are thorough and that the development team has clearly understood the customer's requirements. The customer needs to understand that in spite of the best efforts and best XP practices of the team, some defects will probably be discovered by acceptance tests, and a few may even make it past both the unit and acceptance tests. Explain the options available for handling these defects.

Prepare the customer for issues that *look* like defects but are outside the scope of the iteration. It's one thing to imagine what a screen will look like and how it will work. When the customer sees the live software, he might wish it worked differently from his original description or might think of things he really wanted that he forgot to mention. Maybe this iteration's story didn't cover the ability for the system to handle a large number of users, and a large numbers of users causes a crash.

This is where your acceptance criteria come in handy. If it wasn't part of the acceptance criteria, it doesn't affect the successful delivery of the story. Fortunately, it can easily be included in the next iteration. The customer won't have to wait more than the length of the iteration, one to three weeks at most. It takes time for the customer to build trust in the XP team. She may be afraid to go on to the next iteration until all defects, even trivial ones, are fixed.

If the customer changes his mind about his standards for quality, those should be included in stories for subsequent iterations, along with new or changed ideas he's had during the iteration.

## Defect Management

Defects are the project's dirty laundry. Nobody wants to admit they'll happen, nobody wants to look at them when they do, and nobody wants to be the poor sucker who has to fix them.

Small teams may find that the simplest thing that could possibly work is to write all defects found during acceptance testing (note: not unit testing; those defects must be fixed immediately by the programmer who discovers them) on a whiteboard and check them off when they're done.

This works if your entire team is in one room and if you're doing an excellent job with collective ownership, test-first coding, and refactoring. In that case, if you find a bug during acceptance testing, your team writes an automated test for it (a unit test if possible), fixes it, and it never happens again—so you never need to remember what fixed it.

If your project is large, has teams in multiple geographical locations, or has not yet been successful in mastering some XP practices such as test-first coding, you need a central way to track who's working on a bug, a history of what was done to fix it, and what module was checked into the code base when it was fixed. You might need a way to help the customer track and prioritize problems, identifying issues that must be fixed before release.

Large, complex organizations may have their defect tracking and source-code control tightly integrated, making it difficult to get a fix into a code base without using a tracking tool.

Here's an experience Lisa might like to forget:

> *I worked on a team developing software for an external client—a large corporation. We had to use two separate bug-tracking systems. One was used during development, when most of the defects were found and fixed. During the corporation's post-development acceptance test and staging phases, which were tied to a separate source-code control system, we had to use a completely different defect management system. Having two source-code control tools and two separate bug-tracking systems required careful coordination and a lot of extra time.*

Avoid this situation if you can, but if you can't, plan carefully and brainstorm ways to mitigate the risks. For example, Lisa's team decided to transfer any defects left after development was complete to the post-development defect-tracking system and track all defects for that release in one place

## *Road Food for Thought*

Running tests and dealing with defects is as much art as science. Think about what you'll do for your next project. Brainstorm answers to these questions with your team.

- ✧ How will you educate the customer about what will happen during the project?
- ◊ Who will execute acceptance tests?
- ✧ Who will automate acceptance tests?
- ✧ How will you report and track defects?
- ✧ How will you handle fixing defects?
- ✧ How will you get customer signoff on the iteration?

## Summary

- ✧ Run acceptance tests as soon as code for a story or a testable component of a story is finished. Keep running the tests every build.
- ✧ Run acceptance tests from previous iterations as regression tests for each build in the development integration environment.
- ✧ Ideally, the customer runs the tests, but when he doesn't participate fully on a daily basis, programmers and testers run the tests until the customer has a chance to do so.
- ✧ Acceptance tests (except for those dependent on other uncompleted stories) must pass before the stories are complete. If the customer can't run them until after the end of an iteration, for whatever reason, the programmers must run them.
- ✧ Educate the customer before and during the project so she understands the testing, defect reporting, and defect-fixing processes.
- ✧ The customer defined quality criteria at the start of the iteration. Verify that these criteria were met.
- ✧ Outstanding defects should be written up as stories, estimated, and put in the bucket of stories from which the customer can choose for the next iteration.

## Exercise 19

Run the executable acceptance tests for the LoginStoryTest and UserIdStory-Tests for the XTrack system, which you can download from www.xptester.org/framework/examples/xtrack/downld.htm. What defects do the test results show?

# Chapter 26

# Looking Back for the Future

We made it through the first iteration! We safely navigated the curves and switchbacks, didn't lose too much time on the hills, and didn't need the runaway truck ramp on the downhill grades. We finished the stories, including the acceptance tests. We still have a few minor defects, but they're being tracked, and we'll be able to fix them in the next iteration. The customer is satisfied with the software. It's time to celebrate!

Some teams don't spend enough time celebrating successes. Even small wins such as completed tasks should be marked with some little reward. Successfully delivering an iteration ought to bring at least a box of doughnuts! We all work better with a pat on the back.

Yes, we're pleased with ourselves and deserve positive reinforcement. Still, there's always room for improvement. Now, while the iteration is fresh in our minds, is a good time to look back and see what we could change to help the next iteration go even more smoothly.

The definition of quality assurance is learning from our mistakes, so we can improve the quality of our product. Hold a retrospective at the end of each iteration to review what you did well, what new ideas worked out great, and what areas still need work. Martin Fowler included this as an XP practice in a presentation at XP Universe 2001. Yes, the retrospective is not a function of the team's tester but an activity involving the entire team. The reason we include it here is to give you another tool to help the team improve with each iteration.

There are a couple of simple ways to accomplish a retrospective (let's not call it a post-mortem—that sounds so negative). One is the iteration grade card, shown in Table 26.1.

By storing the grade cards online (simply keeping them on a wiki will do), you can track your progress over time. This feedback helps you, the team's quality watchdog, identify areas where improvements will lead to a higher-quality product.

Another similar and just as useful exercise is to have everyone on the team think about three areas:

✧ What we should *continue* doing

✧ What we should *start* doing

✧ What we should *stop* doing

**TABLE 26.1** The iteration grade card

| Category | Grade (0–10 or N/A) | Comments |
|---|---|---|
| Clarity of stories (planning game) | | |
| Customer/developer communication | | |
| Tester/developer communication | | |
| Standup meetings (developer communication) | | |
| Unit tests written (test-first programming) | | |
| Pairing | | |
| Design simplicity | | |
| Refactoring | | |
| Tracking | | |
| Build handoff to test | | |
| Documentation | | |
| Accuracy of estimates (risk assessment) | | |
| Overtime | | |
| Met customer expectations | | |

A common way to do this is to distribute reams of sticky notes to the team and have them write items for each category. Put these all on a whiteboard and start sorting them to see if they fall into any particular patterns. It's a good idea to have people think ahead on this subject, so they're ready when you hold the retrospective meeting.

Here's a sample result from a retrospective meeting held by Lisa's team early in a project. Note that this doesn't have to be a pretty document. We don't even really care about grammar and spelling. This is reproduced pretty much as it was recorded, except that the names of people who took responsibility for working on various areas have been changed.

## Retrospective for Release 1, Iteration 1

### Continue (What did we do well?)

- Wrote more tests
- It works—3 stories
- Pairing
- Adapt to change
- Better understanding of app, better documentation on stories and acceptance tests
- Development environment getting better
- Reduced travel—recognized where it wasn't working
- Build process has improved

### What did we learn?

- Looking at acceptance tests helps to make functionality clear and drive out "hidden" obstacles . . .
- Some acceptance tests written up front to help with iteration planning
- Communication better—getting team together to hear out vision of overall solutions
- Initial iterations are bumpy
- Architecture of overall system
- Build/integration environment

**Start (What can we do better?)**

**Most important issues**

- How we are distributing work between sites. Not a clear delineation between "front-end" work and "back-end" work. (Joe, Tom, Sue)
  - Remote facility not good for team development, not enough connections, get stuck in cubes
  - Problem with productivity (or feeling of productivity) when in remote facility
- Keep standups short (Joe, Betty)
  - Online—status only
  - Offline—pairing and tasks for the day
- Do travel on an iteration basis:
  - Travel for one iteration (2 weeks) for consistency across iteration
  - Try to get pockets of knowledge spread across the whole team so any work can be done anywhere (Ginger)
- Need more help automating and writing acceptance tests—(responsible parties)

**Medium importance**

- Difficult to learn what's going on as new person. Maybe have a team buddy?
- New people in main office for longer
- Split up the work better to help get outside team members involved

**Others**

- Testing strategy (Lisa, Sue)
  - Test first
  - For GUI work we can use WebART, but you can't "test first" with WebART
  - Need to look into setting up WebART for everyone to use easily
- Pair switching and using a consistant IDE, or at least a default—JBuilder
- Checklist that points to the right things on wiki (Tom)
- Teambuilding (Joe)

Standups and the wiki are discussed in Chapter 30.

Here are notes from a much later retrospective in the same project. The format of the report has evolved a bit over time. No people were assigned by name to any areas, because the team had decided to focus as a team on just a few areas, chosen by a vote. Your retrospective format might also evolve over time. The critical point is to work to keep your practices sharp and improve the team's effectiveness.

*Retrospective, Release 3, Iteration 2*
During our last retrospective, we defined these issues to work on:

- Knowledge sharing—brown bags (informal lunch meetings) about the application and general topics of interest (e.g., new approaches to acceptance testing used by Project XYZ)
- Testing—more on the integration box and using HTTPUnit for acceptance tests
- Demo machine
- How did we do?

**Stop (What slowed our progress?)**

- Code and coding—using multiple source-code control systems, checking in code without testing it on the integration environment, checking in non-compiled code
- Delivery—waiting for a pair or task to start working and take initiative if you have nothing to do
- Documentation—using old versions of requirements
- Iteration planning—starting the iteration with requirements that are not complete
- Pairing—switching pairs arbitrarily (only when pair has brought something to completion); using dialup for remote collaboration
- Shared resources—allowing outside parties to control the database
- Tasks—having uneven distribution of task ownership (each person should own at least one task, preferably a couple)

**Start (What can we do better?)**

- Code and coding—write code that communicates; organize code consistently; edgetting (checking out) files before modifying them; refactoring big units of functionality; creating/updating/sharing class diagrams; commenting all code; add history comments in source code
- Documentation—develop strategy for having current docs available to everyone; update functional specs regularly and distribute to all developers (developers should read and follow)
- Environments—have a demo machine so work is not slowed; do something about the environment as it takes too long to download latest code (tar file does not always contain latest code)
- General—reading e-mail and meeting announcements; having project manager more available and involved in local effort
- Knowledge sharing—haven't done brown bags yet; need brown bags or formal training around testing; when you sense somebody doesn't understand take time to teach them
- Requirements—talk with requirements analysts about stories not only at beginning but during development to check direction; updating reqs documents continually and distributing to each developer
- Standups—stagger the standups for the two teams so people on both teams can attend both (don't overlap with new SWAT standup)
- Tasks—have more diverse tasks to avoid a development bottleneck (and frustration)
- Teams—have both teams communicate occasionally so there is common direction
- Testing—ensure acceptance tests are robust and test records are valid; reviewing acceptance tests internally before reviewing with customers; consistently reviewing acceptance tests with users; running the past acceptance tests consistently (including 14.3 and 14.5 WebART tests) as regression testing at least once per iteration; refactoring tests; using naming conventions for acceptance tests and cases; solve the testing problem with Sue's machine; running tests on integration machine every time a build is pushed out

**Continue (What did we do well?)**

- Code and coding—refactoring test and production code
- General—the great work . . . this team rocks; snacks
- Pairing—effective pairing; remote pairing
- Requirements—challenge the requirements analysts with questions about unclear and missing requirements
- Standups—having them on time; keeping them short
- Tasks—having story leads
- Testing—automating as many acceptance tests as possible; getting tests working on integration machine; test-first practices; using HTTPUnit for acceptance testing; enhancing testing practices

Out of these, all of which are important, the team votes on three or four Stop, Start or Continue items to focus on for the next iteration. It doesn't mean we'll forget about the lower-priority items, but we want to see a difference in the top few. For example, for the above retrospective, we might vote to do more refactoring, more regression testing, and make sure the team fully understands the customer's requirements before starting development for the next iteration.

As each iteration proceeds, note anything you want to keep in mind before the next iteration starts. We've found that it speeds up the retrospective to solicit ideas before the meeting about how the iteration went.

## Summary

- ✧ Hold a retrospective at the end of each iteration to evaluate the team's progress with Extreme Programming practices.
- ✧ Use a grade card to track progress or have each team member contribute ideas of what to stop doing, what to start doing, and what worked well and should continue. Choose two to four areas for improvement during the next iteration.

## Exercise 20

Here's a retrospective from the first release of XTrack. Which two or three items would you choose to work on for the next iteration?

### Stop

- Having uneven distribution of task ownership
- Starting the iteration with incomplete requirements

### Start

- Pairing more, both to write production code and to test
- Writing the acceptance tests in advance of the iteration
- Having a more regular schedule
- Communicating constantly, have regular standups
- More knowledge sharing

### Continue

- Remote pairing
- Estimating fairly accurately
- Being flexible about changing the requirements when we see things that work better

# Chapter 27

# Keep On Truckin': Completing the XP Road Trip

If your team is just starting out with XP, the first iteration is definitely the hardest. It's like driving in a foreign country. You know how to operate a car and how to read a map, but you can't understand the road signs at first, and everyone else drives much faster than you're used to. The next couple of iterations might not be much easier, but eventually you figure out what the signs mean and get used to the speeds.

The first XP team Lisa worked on completed two or three small projects of two to three iterations each before they started to feel like they knew what the heck they were doing. The retrospective you just completed will give you the starting point for making the next iteration more successful.

Use the short iterations and releases of XP to your advantage. Once your team has tried and gotten good at XP "out of the book," don't be afraid to experiment. Your team can always try something new if an experiment doesn't pan out. Stick with a new idea, tool, technique, or practice for at least three iterations; it may just be that you have to get through a learning curve before you can fairly evaluate the success of a tool or technique. Let the team come to a consensus on how it went and what to try next. Chapter 29 gives an example of how one team experimented with different approaches to test automation.

The second iteration should be pretty much like the first, with a few twists:

⬦ Now we have regression tests to run, in addition to the new tests we have to write and automate. (Aren't we glad we automated all our acceptance tests?)

⬦ Maybe we didn't manage to automate all our acceptance tests, so we have some leftover tasks from the last iteration. This is very bad and not XP, but don't be ashamed. You'll get better each iteration.

⬦ We, or the customer, might find more defects in last iteration's code. How do we handle maintenance?

No magic formula applies, so keep following the principles we've presented in these Part II chapters. Help the customer keep the team focused on the critical areas.

When we did our first release planning session for the XTrack system, our first iteration consisted of stories 1–6 (you can see our stories on www.xptester.org). We created a system to record and track iterations, stories, and tasks by project. The second iteration was stories 7–10: printing the items we tracked, adding problem tracking to our system, providing a history of velocity and test results, and allowing problems to be converted to stories. Because we could build on the technology we developed for the first iteration, both for production code and tests, this iteration could go more smoothly. You aren't starting from scratch to automate your tests. You now have a library of methods or modules that can be reused in new tests.

Automating and executing acceptance tests for a story normally takes the team between 20% and 30% of the time spent on developing that story. If your team spent a lot more time than this, stop and look at your approach. Does your application have too much business logic in the user interface layer? Does it take too long to script automated tests with the tool you're using? Do team members need more training in test automation techniques? Brainstorm ways to reduce the time spent creating and maintaining automated tests.

## Regression Testing

Run all the executable acceptance tests as a regression test on every new build in your test environment. The programmers should follow this practice as well. This will probably be at least once per day. If the tests take a long time to run, brainstorm with the programmers on how they could be made to run faster, or split them up so the most critical ones run in the first batch. Programmers need the feedback of the tests to confidently add and refactor code.

Once an acceptance test passes, it should never be allowed to fail. The only exception to this would be if the customer changed her mind so as to make the test irrelevant. If she just changes her mind enough to make the test incorrect, the test must be refactored, along with the code that implements the change. Only when the change renders the test completely unnecessary should it be allowed to fail, at which point it no longer matters and can be discarded altogether.

If you use one system to integrate the latest code and perform unit testing and another to run acceptance and regression testing, make sure you can run tests and report the results equally well in either environment. You'll already have this if you're using the JUnit (or similar) framework and direct calls to interface to the code.

However, if you're running the tests through the user interface with a test tool, minor differences between the systems can cause tests built to run in one environment to fail in the other. Watch out for programmers writing tests that work only in their development environment, and beware of writing tests yourself that work only in the acceptance test environment. Pairing with programmers when working on automation task will help avoid this and give you the critical ability to run tests as needed in both your integration and system test environments.

## Catching Up

If you ended up dropping acceptance tests during the iteration because you couldn't make them run, your job is to remind the team of the risks posed by those missing tests. You'll need to decide whether they should be added in to the next iteration. The risk of a missing test may be higher in subsequent iterations, as the system evolves and code is refactored to support the next set of stories.

If you or any other team member had problems with the mechanics of test automation, pair yourself or that team member with someone who's good at it in the next iteration. If the whole team struggles with automating the tests, have them work through the test automation exercises in Chapters 16–25.

If the number of executable acceptance tests you got running in the last iteration was much smaller than your goal, you need find out why. Were your estimates too low? Did you spend your time documenting tests instead of automating them? Did you try to automate too close to the user interface? Maybe you didn't divide up the automation tasks enough (e.g., you tried to do it all). Fix whatever is broken, but also pad your story estimates for the next iteration, to allow enough time to get those tests and at least some tests from the previous iteration running as well. You have to catch up, or you'll go into death-spiral mode.

## Maintenance?

We're often asked how XP deals with maintenance. In a way, XP is maintenance all the time. We start with a bit of code to do a bit of functionality and maintain it forever.

In our XP projects, we've seen far fewer defects than in more traditionally managed projects. Many XP teams are able to release code that is virtually defect free. That's our goal, but when you encounter bugs, treat them the same as new functionality. Create a story for fixing the defect, estimate the cost in your point system, and allow customers to choose whether to fix the defect instead of spending that amount of resources on a new story.

In our experience, customers handle this concept well until you get to a release or the last iteration of a project. As long as a new iteration in which to fix a problem is imminent, it seems okay to put off the fix. However, if you're launching new code to production tomorrow and the customer just found a defect that won't be included until the next release a month from now, or he just changed his mind about how a piece of functionality should work, he can have a hard time dealing with it.

The customer has the last word. If you have a showstopper defect, which would be hard to imagine in an XP project, your release date might have to slip. This is bad, and it's not XP, but if you're adapting XP to fit into a larger environment that includes non-XP groups, it could happen.

## The Release

Let's talk about releases. As we approach the downhill drive of each iteration's end, we seem to hit more and more unexpected curves and potholes in the form of defects. An imminent release date is sure to produce some tangled, hard-to-reproduce, ugly bug blocking our way. Evidently we, and the customer, become a lot more cunning in our testing as these milestones approach, and we find defects we somehow missed before.

As we discussed in Chapter 26, you should have spent time preparing your customer for these situations. Anxiety over deadlines makes problems seem bigger. If customers understand the process for dealing with defects, they'll react more calmly if defects are found. The best you can do is continue to log defects and get an estimate for fixing each one. Discuss these with the customer every day. Let her prioritize and decide what she can and can't live with. Remind her that fixing defects at this late date will require extensive retesting and runs the risk of introducing new bugs. That's a concept everyone understands.

This is the time you really have to walk a fine line. Make sure the customer gets what she's paid for. The acceptance test results will show if she did. In XP projects, as in any other software projects, customers often ask for just one more teeny added bit of functionality that wasn't in the stories you started the iteration with. Unless your team has finished all the stories originally chosen, don't let them be tempted to squeeze in more work. Our experience is that programmers are a lot more susceptible to these types of requests than testers are. Of course, your manager or coach should manage this sort of thing, but if he doesn't, do what you can to keep the team on track.

Your team will come through on the absolute necessities. The rest can be included as stories in the next iteration and release. We've lived through some hair-raising releases, but most problems were due to basic problems like development and test environments that didn't match production (yes, this is a mortal sin in the QA world, but Lisa has worked on projects where this was beyond her team's control, and that could happen to you too).

Having scared you with these worst-case scenarios, we should now say that if your team has done their best to use XP practices, you're probably in for a pleasant surprise. Some of the pleasantest production launches we've enjoyed have been in XP projects. Read on for an example of the advantages of XP from a quality perspective.

## When XP Projects End

In theory, an XP project would never end but just continue to evolve. In real life, your project will probably lose funding one day, being deemed either complete or so far from what the customer wants that they're starting again from scratch. If you're producing software for an external customer, you're likely to reach a point where you turn the software over to that customer. Here are some encouraging observations from an early project for an external customer Lisa worked on, which sold her on the value of XP.

> *During the project, programmers from the customer's development team rotated through and paired with our programmers to learn the code. Various members of the customer team had participated in writing and run-*

*ning acceptance tests each iteration. The next-to-last day of the project, nobody worked late. Our tasks were complete!*

*On the last day, various members of the team presented information to the customer team. The programmers described the system's architecture, using the whiteboard and answering questions from the customer development team. I explained our approach to testing and went over the acceptance test suite, how to run it, and how to view the results.*

*We videotaped the whole thing, so the customers could refer to the whiteboard drawings and the question-and-answer sessions in addition to reading the documentation we wrote and burned to CD for them. Our customers satisfied, we knocked off early and went to celebrate over beers.*

Lisa's friend John Sims had the following epiphany when he read *Extreme Programming Explained*: "I saw that software projects didn't have to end in disaster and burnout for everyone and that there was a way of developing that could allow me to do my best, if I'd let go of some of my current understandings of how to develop software. In short, it changed my mind about how to write software."

Well, yeah! This is why we practice XP.

## Summary

- Don't be afraid to experiment. Take advantage of the short iterations of XP to try new ideas, but give them long enough to make a good judgment about how they worked.

- After the first iteration, you'll have regression tests to run, in addition to writing and automating new tests. This is where you'll see the payoff of automation.

- Don't worry if you didn't get all the tests from the previous iteration automated. Make the story estimates for the second iteration bigger and catch up.

- Estimate what it will cost to fix a defect and let the customer choose whether he wants fixes or new features developed.

- Prepare your customer for the potential chaos that can erupt right before a big release. If you're diligent with your XP practices, the release will feel anticlimactic, but prepare for the worst.

## Exercise 21

Given the following three items we chose to work on in Exercise 20 and the fact that our two-person team is split in two distant locations, how might you try to accomplish these?

- ✧ Stop having uneven distribution of task ownership
- ✧ Pair more often
- ✧ Have regular standups

# Part III

# Road Hazard Survival Kit

During our XP test drive, we were working on a more or less ideal XP project. What if you aren't so lucky? Your team's project may be large, with two dozen or more programmers. You might work for a company where XP is being used for only one project or one small subset of a larger project. Let's look at some ways you can cope when your reality doesn't conform to the type of project for which XP was originally intended.

# Chapter 28

# Challenges in "Testability"

We'll start by looking at an important factor in the ability to automate tests. When thinking of the test infrastructure, we testers tend to start by thinking about tools: test tools, configuration management tools, defect tracking tools. We focus on the *hows* of getting our tests automated.

## Designing for Testability

More important than the gadgets in our toolbox is how testable the application is. The most important factor in ease of test automation is the system's design. Correct application of Extreme Programming practices ought to lead you to the simplest, and thus most testable, design. However, teams must often deal with legacy systems that throw up roadblocks to test automation. If you're developing from scratch, take advantage of your opportunity to design a system that provides places where test scripts can easily hook in.

If the application has a user interface, design it so you can test most of the functionality at the layer just under the user interface. For example, if you have a Java Web application that uses Struts and JSPs, test as much as you can at the Struts layer. You'll spend as much time creating the automated tests, but this layer will be much more stable, and you won't spend nearly as much time maintaining the tests. If the JSPs don't contain too much code that has functionality needing testing, such as Javascript, you can get by with testing the user interface less often—perhaps once every iteration. You may even decide to test it manually. Here's advice from Ron Jeffries:

> *Don't write many tests at the GUI level: keep the GUI very thin so that these can be minimized. Use an available GUI-testing tool for the rest. Do not expect this tool to solve other problems. (Ron Jeffries, e-mail)*

## A Real-Life Example

Testability begins with the layout of your data storage. Lisa's team worked on a Web application initially developed by another organization. It had a complex data model already in place, with each content type being maintained having its own set of tables, for a total of over 50 tables. There was no time to change the schema. The resulting object model had 49 classes.

The same operations on different items in the database needed completely different classes and thus completely different tests. Each test was unique code from start to finish. A `SubmitRequest` for content item *A* would not work for submitting a request for content item *B*. Very little code could be shared between test scripts.

The team was next asked to develop a similar application for a different Web site but was allowed to design the database schema. They were able to make this application much more generic, using only four tables. The object model needed only nine classes. Now the `SubmitRequest` test script worked for every type of content. This made test script development go much faster, and the scripts were vastly easier to maintain.

Rethinking the design for all the content management, the team came up with a design needing just two tables, where a single definition of content could be used to represent all types of information. This generic design meant that the test scripts could take advantage of a library of generic test modules: one for editing, one for submitting a request, one for canceling a change, and so on.

Figure 28.1 shows the design for all three projects. The third design was not only easier to test—it was, of course, much easier to write, and code maintenance was also much easier.

Another good example of designing an application for maximum ease of testing is the project described in "One Team's Experience with Direct-Call Test Automation" in Chapter 23. When programmers have worked alongside testers and learned the value of acceptance tests and the importance of automating them, they think about acceptance testing up front. They're especially good

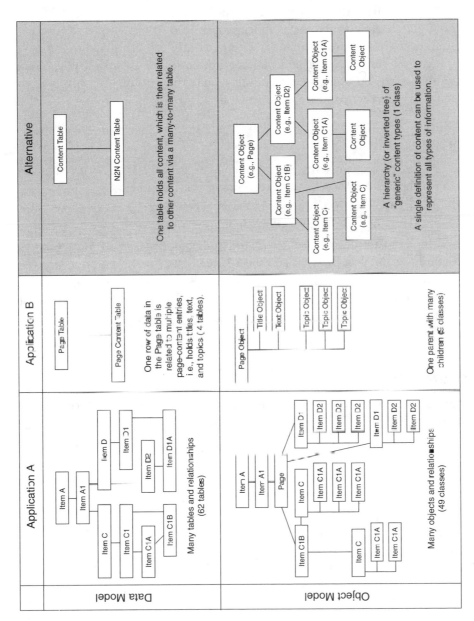

**FIGURE 28.1** The three designs

about doing this when they've suffered the pain of having to automate tests for an application that's test-unfriendly.

If you don't have the luxury of developing a system from the ground up, encourage your team to refactor as much as possible to facilitate test automation. Build time for this into your story estimates. It'll pay off quickly when you spend much less time creating and maintaining automated tests. If your team consistently spends 30% or more of development time doing test automation tasks, see what you can do to improve testability.

## Summary

- ✧ If your project presents special challenges, take a look at our road hazard survival kit for tools and techniques that can help.
- ✧ If your application has a user interface, keep it as thin as possible. Shift business logic to the layers below the user interface.
- ✧ The database design is a key factor in testability. Use XP principles to find the simplest design that could possibly work.
- ✧ Since the team, not just the tester, is responsible for test automation, programmers also feel the pain of automating tests for systems not designed for testability. This provides motivation for better design practices.

## Exercise 22

What are some ways the XTrack application could be redesigned for greater testability?

# Chapter 29

## Selecting and Implementing Tools

Your team may need lots of tools for different purposes, all relating to quality. You need a good way to track bugs. You need practical and trustworthy source code control. You may need a way to run executable tests through a user interface. We can't tell you exactly what path to follow; each situation is unique. Here are some guidelines that have helped us research and select tools.

It might seem obvious, but the first task in choosing a tool is to understand why you need the tool at all. What exactly does it need to do, and what features are critical? If you can't pinpoint these and just have a general requirement that the tool "take care of" a problem area, it's hard separate the wheat from the chaff when evaluating tools. Don't be seduced by bells and whistles that look cool in a demo but don't address what you really need.

Tools are useful, but they're only a start. Don't expect any tool to be a magic bean. A new and improved golf ball won't really make us hit drives like Tiger Woods. No matter how good your tools are, your team's success still comes down to you and your team members.

You need to know what kind of investment you can make in a tool: not just the purchase price but training costs, ramp-up time, time to implement and maintain the tool. If you're investing heavily in a tool, you may have to take the un-XP-like step of anticipating your future needs. If you're about to set off on a two-month car camping trip through the forty-eight states with your family of six, don't buy a two-seater sports car. The nature of XP projects usually dictates the use of low-cost, lightweight tools. However, every project is different, and you'll have to weigh the risk of not having the correct tool for the job against the cost of acquiring and using the tool.

## Evolving Tools

Here's an idea for using XP techniques to grow tools to help your team. First, write a story for what you need. Include features, requirements for ease of use and training, compatibility requirements, what kind of support you need, how much you can spend. The customers, of course, also have a stake in this.

Can you meet the needs for acceptance test automation with an open-source tool such as the following?

- JUnit (www.JUnit.org)
- JUnitPerf (www.clarkware.com/software/JUnitPerf.html)
- HTTPUnit (http://httpunit.sourceforge.net)
- Canoo Web Test (http://webtest.canoo.com/webtest/manual/WebTestHome.html)

These are excellent places to start in any case, and an entire community of XP teams is already involved in adapting and enhancing these tools for specific situations. Someone may already have solved a problem like the one confronting you. If not, enlist help from the rest of the team to evolve the solution in-house.

This could be tricky if you were trying to build something from scratch, but the beauty of open source is, it lets you take up where others have left off. Include a story in the first iteration of the project to make the necessary enhancements, and your problem is solved. Another option is to do a separate project to develop the tool. This can be a great learning experience for a team just starting out with XP. If you assume the customer role in this kind of project, you're going to find out that being a customer isn't all that easy!

## Test Tools

As we discussed in the previous chapter, the testability of your application will have a big impact on your need for test tools. In most cases, investing in the design of the system to allow you to run your tests below the user interface will provide a better return than purchasing a tool to run them through the user interface. Despite all the promises, test automation tools have historically struggled to be worth the effort of using, and probably more shelf space is tied up by test tools no one uses than by any other type of software, including CASE tools (remember those?).

If you do decide to go that route, make your list of necessary and desirable features and avoid being bowled over by vendors who want you to think they have the next test-automation silver bullet. Don't buy anything until *you've* made it work the way *you* want on *your* application.

Let's say you do need to run a lot of tests through a user interface, and your team can't figure out how to evolve a tool to do this or feels it would be too expensive. Commercial capture/playback tools look tempting, but captured scripts are murdered by any change to the application. Look for a tool you can interface your executable tests to, as described in Chapter 23. The more easily this can be done, the better. Ideally, the tool's scripting language would be the same as the one you're using for the system and the executable acceptance tests, or at least one in which you're fluent. At worst, it should have basic program ming constructs for control flow, modularity, and parameter passing.

You can use the tool's capture facility to create the parts of the tests that interact directly with the user interface, but you'll need to program the control structures and interfaces with the executable tests in the tool's scripting lan guage. By combining the tool with the executable tests under the JUnit frame work, we've found it possible to develop, within the timeframe of an XP iteration, reasonably low maintenance tests that run through the user interface.

## Other Tools Related to Quality

You may need other tools to help you deliver quality software. Although there are many ways to report defects, including writing them on story cards or up on the whiteboard, a simple defect-tracking system is a good idea. Issues have a tendency to fall into big, black holes. You can waste a lot of time trying to find out who's supposed to address a particular issue and whether he's done any thing about it. Customers will feel more confident about the project's progress if they can look at defect reports showing defects reported and resolved and find out the status of those in between.

Your retrospective meetings are often the time you'll realize you need a new tool for some purpose. Maybe you're having problems with programmers losing code changes and you need better source-code control. Maybe your user-interface tests are taking too much time to maintain. When these types of prob lems get to the top of your priority list, it's time to search for a new solution.

## Choosing an Off-the-Shelf Tool

Your team isn't able to write a tool you need in-house, for whatever reason. You can't find open-source tools that do the job you need done. So you've decided to look at commercial tools. How do you know if you're selecting an appropriate tool?

In many large, traditional software development organizations, tool selection can take months. First they put together a large, detailed requirements definition. Then they evaluate various tools, spending weeks or months looking at each one. Finally. they compare the pros and cons and choose a tool.

With many projects, when you need a tool for something, you need it right now. You don't have a staff to help you select it. You can't afford "shelfware": fancy tools that sit shrink-wrapped because nobody has time to go to a week-long class to learn them. How do you get something useful quickly?

If open-source tools don't meet your needs and in-house development isn't feasible, do some research to see what off-the-shelf tools may already do what you require. There are lots of quality assurance and testing Web sites that list and even review tools as well as exploring various approaches to automation—for example, Bret Pettichord's hotlist, www.pettichord.com, and Brian Marick's list of agile testing links at www.testing.com/agile and his index of automation techniques at www.testingcraft.com/techniques.html.

Also see our bibliography for books that may guide you on this subject. Ask coworkers and even other vendors you use if they know of anything that might fit the bill. Talk to people in your local quality assurance and testing user group or XP user group. Post a message on related Usenet groups (see www.xptester.org for links) to see what other people might be using for the same purpose.

If you've decided to try a vendor tool and have found one or more candidate products, you need a quick way to separate the winners from the also-rans. Check out the vendor. How easy is it to get a price quote? The ponderousness of a tool seems directly related to the difficulty of getting a straightforward price quote. Lightweight tools usually just have a price, and it's posted on the vendor's Web site. Can the salespeople answer technical questions? Is this tool the specialty of the vendor? This could be an indicator of how good their post-sales support will be.

Get references and see what kinds of businesses the other customers are. Recruit experts from your own organization to join you in calling the references.

If a tool seems to fit, install an evaluation copy and try it out for an iteration or two. Is it easy to install? How long does it take you to ramp up enough to make productive use of it? How good is the tech support? When you're moving at the speed of XP, these issues are critical.

Figure out the cost of the tool, including any training or implementation costs you might incur—not just dollars but time spent. Cost obviously plays a big part in the risk. If you find a tool that seems to do what you want and is inexpensive, you can buy it without much worry. If it turns out to be a dud, you're not out much money, even if you get no further use out of it. Be extremely careful of expensive tools, because if they don't work out, not only will you be out the money, but the big investment will keep you trying to use it way past when you should have abandoned it.

Look past the bells and whistles. Don't fall into the trap of making the "safe" decision. You *can* be criticized for buying the best-selling tool if it adds too much overhead to your testing or doesn't do what you need.

Be careful about anticipating future needs. If you're making a huge investment, you do need to think about what the tool will do for you down the road. Avoid the huge investment if you can. Don't invest heavily in more tool than you need. Always do the simplest thing that could possibly work. The reason your team is using XP is because you can't anticipate what's around the next bend in the road.

Any tool you choose is likely to be used by the entire team. Involve others in the decision-making process. Everyone needs to buy off on the tool, or not everyone will use it.

## Implementing Tools

Once you've picked the tool, hold a brown-bag meeting to give the team an overview on how to use it. If necessary, recruit an expert on the team to demonstrate the tool. Through pairing, the expertise will spread around the team. If no one is an expert, volunteer someone to become one. Get everyone in the habit of using it from the start. It's easy to lose momentum once the thing is installed and people get distracted by other things. You might have to remind the team about it in a daily standup. Let them see how the tool contributes to the team's success.

## Experimenting with Tools

XP's short iterations and frequent releases give you the opportunity to experiment with different solutions for one or more iterations, evaluate the results, and try something new. Just as projects can "fail fast" with XP, so can tools.

A team for which Lisa was the tester used the short and frequent releases in XP as an opportunity to try different tools for acceptance-test automation. Here's Lisa's story:

> When I joined the team, they'd never automated any acceptance tests for the Web applications they were developing. I had been successfully using a vendor tool, WebART, to automate acceptance-test scripts for Web applications in other XP projects. We used this tool for the first release of this new project. We had a dedicated team of testers who learned the tool. We were fairly successful with automation; tests for central functionality were automated. However, the separate-test-team approach had caused a lot of other problems.
>
> For the second release, we applied the XP principle of making the whole development team responsible for acceptance-test automation. The automation tasks were spread amongst programmers who didn't know WebART. We discussed whether we should try using HTTPUnit, which the programmers knew, but the consensus was that HTTPUnit tests took too long to develop.
>
> We decided to try WebART. A couple of team members who had used it tried to pair with others who didn't, to automate the tasks. This was hard, because it was a big team and not enough people were available who had used WebART before. Again, we automated the most critical testing. However, because the programmers didn't know the tool, they felt they spent too much time developing the test scripts—as much as half the time to write the production code.
>
> For the next release, we decided to evaluate each acceptance test. If it were possible to automate it more quickly with HTTPUnit and/or JUnit, we'd use that. If it couldn't be automated with those tools, we'd decide whether it could be automated in a timely manner with WebART. If the automation seemed like too big an investment for the return—for example, it was a complex test but on noncritical functionality and didn't need to be performed often—we'd do the test manually.
>
> This worked well in terms of use of resources, but the acceptance tests automated with JUnit and HTTPUnit didn't really cover the system end to end. They also had a lot of hard-coded inputs and expected outputs and were thus not as flexible and robust as I would have liked. We ended up doing a lot of end-to-end testing manually.
>
> At this point the project ended, but if we'd had another release to experiment with, I would have paired with the programmers to refactor the HTTPUnit and JUnit tests to follow good test-design principles. We would also have used WebART for more tests, because it did a better job of end-to-end testing and found more defects.

If you feel that test automation is taking too long or you're spending too much time maintaining test scripts, try a different approach or a different tool for the next few iterations. As the tester, you can offer your opinion based on experience, but what has worked for you in the past may not be the best choice for the current situation. The team is responsible for quality, and the team should select tools that will help them deliver.

## Summary

- Get the tools you need for achieving the level of quality the customer requires. Develop tools in-house or look to open-source or commercial tools for a solution.
- Test design is more important than the tool you select. Choose a tool that allows you to develop tests according to the test architecture you're using.
- You need more than test tools to deliver quality software. Source-code control, defect tracking, and build tools, among other things, are vital.
- Experiment with different tools and approaches. Try a tool or technique for more than one iteration before deciding whether to continue using it.
- Look for the easy tool, the simplest tool possible, the tool the team is most comfortable with. This minimizes the training costs and improves chances for the tool's quick and painless adoption.

# *Chapter 30*

# Project Tune-Ups

You're three days into your first iteration. What can you do to keep the focus on quality? Everyone on your XP team has a vested interest in quality. XP practices are designed to let you do high-quality work, but only if you practice them with discipline. The retrospectives described in Chapter 26 help you see where you need to fine-tune your practices.

In this chapter, we'll look at parts and labor we've used for our own tune ups. We'll talk about how we enhanced or changed XP practices so we could implement them in a way that worked for our projects. These ideas might work for you (or might not!) At the very least, we hope to inspire you to make your own creative modifications to XP.

Again, none of these things is a tester function. We present them here because you, as a team member focused on quality, can provide some leadership in finding ways to make the team more successful.

First, a caveat: your team must master using all the XP practices together before customizing XP to fit your own needs.

## Office Space

*Extreme Programming Explained* includes a chapter on facilities strategy. In our XP experience, teams generally work in a large room or a pod reconfigured from cubicles to form an open space. Sometimes each team member has her own cube or space somewhere else.

In a lot of traditional development shops, test teams are kept separate from programmers. Everyone has to get over that for XP teams to jell. As a tester, you'll be much happier when you truly feel like part of the development team. It might feel weird at first, if you haven't enjoyed a close working relationship with programmers before. It's weird for the programmers too. They may not know what the heck you're doing there.

Working and pairing with programmers will give you all great mutual understanding. If you have a burning question or have uncovered a showstopper defect, usually someone can free up pretty quickly to help you. If a programmer needs help testing some new code, you're there to help.

Working together as a team requires a place to do that. If you're working onsite for an external customer, devote time to explaining your development strategy to them. Ask for the facilities you need—nothing fancy, just enough room for customers, room to pair-program and hold standups, facilities for good communication.

With large projects, it can be a challenge to accommodate everyone on the team. No matter what size your project, planning is essential. If issues with facilities arise mid-project, they can eat up as much time as a ten-car wreck during rush hour. If possible, assign responsibility to this area to someone outside the development team: an information services administrator or someone in a similar role, who has the time and knowledge to take care of problems that arise.

With XP projects, our customers are supposed to be working side by side with us. Even if you have an onsite customer, he may not wish to work in the team's workspace 100% of the time. He may want to spend some time in his own space, so he can remain productive with his "real" jobs. Although XP works best when the customer is physically always present, you may be forced to be flexible on this issue. If so, make arrangements with the customer so he's always available by cell phone, instant message, or some other means.

## Accessorizing for XP

The XP books describe tools and accessories that facilitate learning and applying XP practices. Below are some suggestions based on our experiences. Your team will come up with more ideas, particularly as a result of your retrospectives after each iteration.

### Whiteboards

The whiteboard is your friend. Not only does it usually contain a lot of helpful information, such as diagrams and pictures left over from planning discussions and lists of tasks and priorities, but you can use it in a variety of ways to facilitate testing-related tasks.

Keep a list on a whiteboard of the highest-priority issues discovered, to remind you to show them to the programmers. The programmers can check them off when they fix them, and you can erase them after verifying the fixes. Be sure to track these in an online defect-tracking system as well, so nothing drops into a black hole and so you have the records in case the defect recurs.

Some teams list tasks on the whiteboard as well as on the story or task cards. This way, everyone can see who's working on what task and know when it's complete. You might list testing tasks on the board, so team members can check off when they've run a particular set of tests.

Questions you think of for a customer or programmer who isn't immediately available can go on a whiteboard, to prompt your own memory or others'.

If your team is spread across more than one location, the whiteboard has obvious limitations. In this case, a **wiki,** where team members can easily update the information on the Web pages (more on the wiki later in this chapter), may be able to perform some of the same functions.

## Celebrating Successes

One team we worked with really liked, and adopted, the suggestion in *Extreme Programming Installed* to ring a bell when a task was completed. It provided the regular sense of accomplishment and completion that distinguishes XP from other methodologies. Ring the bell when you complete an automated acceptance-test script, when the acceptance tests for a story pass, or when a defect has been successfully fixed.

Some teams might find a bell annoying. Just be sure you celebrate successes, such as completed tasks. Finished defining the acceptance tests for this iteration? Reward yourself (and your customers!) with a walk around the block, a quick game of foosball, a coffee break. Pick rewards that are fun for you. The team should celebrate its collective successes too. How about pizza and/or beer after a successful release?

We heard about a group where the testers awarded ribbons to team members who "went the extra mile." The ribbons were silly and corny, but the recipients were proud of them, and the testers enjoyed the fun of choosing the winners. It's a lot of fun to recognize a "quality hero" with a ribbon, toy, or plate of cookies. Celebrating each others' accomplishments helps offset the times when team members have to deliver bad news ("We have to drop a story." "We found a giant defect").

## Timer

Standups are brief (ideally, ten-minute) daily meetings where each team member reports what he's accomplished the previous day, how much time it took, what he's working on today, how much time he needs to complete his current task, and what problems may be in his way. Team members may decide on their pairings for the day.

When the team is anxious to get on with their tasks, an overly long standup can impede progress. A kitchen timer is a great help to limit standup meetings. A modification of this practice is to have the person talking hold the timer. This helps him remember to be concise and helps focus the team's attention on him. One team didn't stand up until the timer went off, which is cheating somewhat, but having to stand when time's up helps conclude the meeting quickly.

Some teams do fine without a timer. One large, multilocation project Lisa worked on easily concluded its standup in fifteen minutes every day without one. Every team member is responsible for staying on track during standups. It takes practice and focus, but most people prefer short meetings!

## Wiki

Whiteboards aren't practical for every documentation need. A project wiki, which is a Web site everyone can easily update on the fly, is a good resource for keeping everybody in sync. (*Wiki-wiki* is an alliterative substitute for *quick,* and we use *wiki* as a shorthand for the official name, *WikiWikiWeb*. See www.c2.com/cgi/wiki?WikiHistory for a history of wiki.) If your team doesn't have one and you can see beneficial applications of using one, suggest it. Here are some of the pages that might be on the project wiki:

- ◇ Customer contact information
- ◇ Iteration planning output: task tracking
- ◇ Status
- ◇ Standup notes
- ◇ Grade cards
- ◇ Customers' schedules, when and where they'll be offsite and onsite
- ◇ Technical resources; how-tos, intranet access account info
- ◇ Install information and access to installation files
- ◇ Metrics
- ◇ Acceptance tests
- ◇ UML diagrams

## Metrics

XP is designed to be lightweight and streamlined, producing fewer expensive artifacts. Producing a lot of metrics seems counterintuitive. However, feedback is crucial in XP. Customers and managers need to have concrete information about how effective and productive the team has been. Your car's gauges (and possibly some funny noises) tell you when it's time for preventive maintenance. Software metrics have been compared to a dashboard, to tell you the state of your vehicle. They provide simple ways to keep tabs on your project's health.

Once again, we're talking about something that isn't a tester function, but we've often found ourselves suggesting practices associated with keeping metrics and found them useful, which is why we include them in this book.

Your team is unlikely to produce high-quality software in a timely manner without someone performing the tracker function. If you're the tester, don't try to take on the tracker role as well. It's a job best done by a technical lead or programmer. Some metrics are more appropriately kept by a project manager or XP coach.

At the very least, your team has to track the progress of the iteration in some way, so you know each day whether you're still on target to complete all the stories by the end of the iteration. Whoever is tracking your project should track each task, the estimate for the task, the amount of time spent so far on the task, and the estimated time to complete the task. Adding up this last number for each task will tell you whether you need to drop one or more stories or ask the customer for more.

Update this information every day in the standup meeting. Tracking is critical to avoid last-minute surprises. You can keep track on a whiteboard if you want, so the whole team can see the progress. If your team is split into multiple geographical locations, as one of Lisa's was, a spreadsheet may be a useful way to do the tracking. See www.xptester.org for a sample tracking spreadsheet.

Some organizations need to gather more formal information. Here are examples of metrics kept by teams we've been on or talked with:

- ✧ Iteration velocity, start and end dates
- ✧ Story estimates, description, association with iterations
- ✧ Task descriptions, estimates, responsible programmer(s), status, actual time spent
- ✧ Daily standup meeting notes

If you've stored this type of data, you can produce whatever reports you or the customer finds useful. For example:

⟡ Tasks assigned to a particular programmer
⟡ Estimated versus actual velocity for an iteration
⟡ Estimated versus actual effort for a story

Find tools that will automatically produce useful metrics. As a means of encouraging the creation of unit tests, programmers on one project Lisa worked on wrote a simple script that traversed their source tree daily and sent email with the details of the unit tests written, organized by package and class. They also used JavaNCSS, a source measurement suite for Java that generates information such as

⟡ Global, class, or function-level metrics
⟡ Non-Commenting Source Statements (NCSS)
⟡ Cyclomatic Complexity Number (McCabe metric)
⟡ Count of packages, classes, functions, and inner classes

JavaNCSS is free software distributed under the GNU general public license from www.kclee.com/clemens/java/javancss.

You can generate these metrics automatically daily and display the results on the project wiki to help the team determine what parts of the code are ripe for refactoring and whether test coverage is adequate.

The most important metrics are the test results. Unit tests should always be 100%, but it's a good idea to keep track of how many new tests are written each day and post this on the "big board" or other prominent location. Acceptance test results, in graphical form if possible, should be posted where all project members can see them (in more than one location if needed).

Janet Gregory passes along this suggestion for metrics:

*I use the tried and true defect find-and-fix rate. I found that the developers really like the way I tracked number of lines covered by JUnit test code. We used JProbe for that. You can run it on every iteration, or in our case, we did it when I first started with the project, and then again at the end of the project. The rate increased, showing that suggested new tests gave better unit test coverage. [The developers] were actually quite proud of the fact that they managed to improve. (Janet Gregory, personal communication)*

## Test Environment

Whether you use XP or some other software development process, you absolutely must have a test environment separate from both the development and production environments. This is not negotiable. You might even have multiple test environments, especially if you work in an organization that has post-development test cycles. You might be able to test on your own personal machine using a local build for the early stages of a release, but you'll need a separate production surrogate for realistic testing.

Don't try to test on the programmers' integration machine. That's theirs to break at will. Trying to use the integration machine as a production surrogate will slow up the whole project and cause all kinds of headaches. Ditto for attempting to test on a demo environment. Testing should happen in its very own happy space. Most important, the software and data in the test environment must be controlled by the people doing the testing. They must have the ability to roll back to a previous version of software if needed.

What if you don't have this separate test environment? You'll have an impossible task. Keep pushing for the test environment until you get it. Keep documenting the time wasted and the defects not caught in time because you didn't have it. The need for a separate test environment isn't rocket science. Everyone knows it in his heart; you just need to keep pointing out the emperor's clothesless state until the people with the means to do something about it acknowledge the problem.

Customers should have their own production surrogate environment for user acceptance testing. Once your team has tested a code base and found it solid enough, you can install it on the customer's test environment. Even so, retain control of the customer's production surrogate. Finished releases will be installed on the actual production environment. Demos, design work, or other tasks should be carried out on a separate, dedicated environment.

This brings up the issue of how software should be delivered for testing. At some point, you're going to have to have some kind of release package, either to promote to production or to hand off to an external customer. The earlier in your project the programmers can start producing this, the better.

At the very least, have them label versions in the source-code control, so you know exactly what you're testing. The team needs to be able to roll back to an earlier version when necessary. It's frustrating to install a new build only to discover something broken that keeps you from testing.

On the other hand, it's good to have the capability to check modules out from the source-code control and build them yourself. This allows you to test individual modules that are ready early or test individual fixes.

## Other Obvious Best Practices

We'd think this patently obvious if we hadn't worked on or known about software development projects that didn't do this: you need adequate source-code control. With ineffective source-code control, or none, you're testing a moving target at all times. You need the ability to build with a known snapshot of code and return to a previous snapshot whenever necessary.

When the team has performed a successful integration, label it and promote it to the acceptance-test environment. Collective code ownership can't work without source-code control anyway, so we'd think all Extreme Programming teams would have it. Still, sometimes one has to state the obvious.

Acceptance test cases, automated test scripts, and test results must also be kept in the source-code control system. The whole team will have collective ownership of these as well as the production software. It's vital that programmers be able to see the most current acceptance tests at all times. It's also essential that anyone who wants to kick off acceptance tests can get the correct version of automated tests to run.

## Additional Tester Duties

*Extreme Programming Explained* assigns the provision of snacks to the coach. A smart tester will bring treats as well. Let's face it, much of the time programmers cringe to see you coming. They're afraid you're going to make them fix a new bug or automate more acceptance tests. Surprise them with brownies, doughnuts, chip and dip, fruit, or other yummy treats. It doesn't hurt to keep a jar of Double-Stuf Oreos in the team area. Okay, that may adversely impact cholesterol levels, so maybe apples are better. Toys are also a vital part of any software-delivery team environment.

## Summary

- ✧ Continually look for new ways to keep the team focused on quality.
- ✧ Do what you can to make sure the workspace is conducive to successful XP teamwork.
- ✧ You can't have too many whiteboards.
- ✧ Celebrate small, and big, successes.
- ✧ Use a timer if standup meetings run too long.

- Use a project wiki to help the team communicate and transfer knowledge.
- Gather only metrics that provide useful feedback for the team and the organization. Keep them simple.
- Your project needs separate development, test, and production environments, all configured the same way and containing the same software components.
- Encourage smart use of good source-code control tools.
- Snacks and toys make every project go better.

# *Chapter 31*

# Introducing XP to
# Your Organization:
# A Tester's Point of View

Does the road hazard survival kit provide enough equipment to help you bring XP into an organization for the first time? Change is hard. XP is hard to master. It requires an incredible amount of discipline and attention. However, we're willing to suffer a little pain in the short run to enjoy the benefits of XP in the long run.

Time for a disclaimer: we, the authors of this book, have not had the experience of working for a large corporation into which we introduced XP. What we *have* done are XP projects for small and large external customers who use traditional software development methodologies. We've helped implement XP in small organizations already committed to practicing XP. We've used other agile development methodologies in large corporations. So some of the things we suggest here are just our opinions of what would work—we haven't tried them in all these scenarios.

We've worked with companies where we had the following situation, and we've talked to several testers who have had similar experiences: a corporation with a large software development organization decides to start using XP. The testing organization is currently separate from development. When the programmers release the code to testers, it usually takes about a month to go through the testing cycle. During this period, the code base is essentially frozen. Some releases have required several passes through the testing cycle before being launched to production.

Extreme Programming asks programmers to release code every two (or one or three) weeks. The code must correctly run acceptance tests, defined by the customer, before the end of each iteration. The testers are part of the XP development team.

We've heard of many cases where the testing/QA organization is wary of XP, worried it will cause important steps to be bypassed, resulting in potential disaster. The testers might also fret about their job security, since many XP publications talk about customers writing and running acceptance tests and programmers automating them—and fail to talk about testers much at all.

How do you successfully roll XP out in a situation like this? Should you keep the separate test organization? Do you need independent testers and quality assurance staff? If your testers and programmers have never worked closely together, how do you get them to start?

Here's an additional scenario: an organization introducing XP has testers, but they're nontechnical testers, who manually perform user acceptance testing. Can these testers be integrated into an XP team?

What if the organization needs to hire new testers? With the fast pace of XP, how do the new testers get up to speed on the domain knowledge and understanding of the project?

In introducing XP, we believe many criteria must be considered when thinking about how to set up the test functions.

- Do the test environments available to the development team exactly mirror production, with all systems installed and running?
- Do the systems needing development require extensive load and performance testing?
- Are the existing test organization and/or senior management fearful that XP schedules won't provide time for adequate testing?
- Is a professional tester, with experience in test automation or programming, available for each development team?
- Is the development organization responsible for all parts of the system under development, or must you integrate code from external development teams?
- What experience do the programmers on the team have? Are they senior programmers, well versed in best practices, or cowboy hackers, or fresh out of school? Do they have experience writing unit tests or other kinds of tests? Have they tried to write unit tests before, only to give up because it took them too long and they had to crank out production code?

❖ Do your teams have strong leadership?

❖ Does the organization have a solid commitment to quality?

## Test Phases and Practices

Writing, automating, and performing acceptance tests during the iteration are fundamental practices of XP. Are you going to throw all your existing testing process away when you start using Extreme Programming? You need to work hard to master all the XP practices as soon as possible, but at the same time, scrapping all your existing testing process may not be the best idea.

Consider each process and the reason for it. If you still need a particular testing phase or practice, keep it. Here are a couple of examples. Your development team should be able to test in an environment that looks just like production, but if the reality is that company resources are limited and several projects must share test machines, you may be forced to test in a more complete environment after the end of development. Or say you're releasing a new version of a retail Web site and you want to allow a group of customers to give the site a dry run, to make sure order fulfillment works correctly. In cases like these, it doesn't make sense to drop additional test phases after development.

Even if you don't have a technical reason to preserve a practice such as post-development testing, if your test organization or upper management is worried about the radical change XP will bring, it might be a good idea to ease gradually into XP from the testing perspective. Do have the development team (which should include a tester) complete acceptance testing before the end of each iteration. Then, if you usually spend two weeks in system test and a week in operational readiness test before each release, keep doing that, at least for the near future.

Post-development test phases are a two-edged sword. They may increase stakeholders' comfort level that the software package is ready for launch. On the other hand, they often become ominous regression spirals, where defects appear every few weeks, get fixed, and reappear later. In XP, we know unit tests must always pass 100%. We believe that acceptance tests, once they pass, must forever after pass 100%. This way, the regression death spiral can't occur. After a few releases, your customers may feel confident enough about the quality of the software as delivered by the development team to drop the extra test phases.

Another reason you might have to maintain some traditional practices, such as extra test cycles, is if your XP project produces software that has to interact with other systems delivered by non-XP teams. If your team's software is closely tied to that of a team using other development practices, establish a good working relationship with this other team at the start of your project.

As the tester, you can contribute lots of value here. Meet with the testers, programmers, and project managers of the other team. Explain your own testing practices and have them explain theirs. Set milestones for each team to produce code needed by the other, test records you may need for their system, and any other deliverables needed for development and testing. Define processes for dealing with defects whose source is hard to identify. Find out in advance what to do about a problem that appears to come from the other team's code.

XP is all about people. Developing personal relationships with the other team, whether they practice XP or not, will increase your project's chances for success and make everyone's life more pleasant.

## Introducing People to the XP Tester Role

Going from working in a separate test group to being a member of the development team is a tricky transition for some testers. If you're a tester who's interested in trying new things and you like the way Extreme Programming practices are designed to promote quality, you're probably excited about taking on the role of XP tester. If you're not confident of your technical skills, you've had bad experiences in the past working with programmers, you like the security of working in a test organization, you feel testing should be independent from development, or for a host of other good reasons, you may not be so keen on becoming an XP tester.

You might be champing at the bit to start working on an XP team, but if you're new to the project and lack domain knowledge, you wonder how you'll begin to understand the stories and help customers write acceptance tests. Maybe you're a programmer or an analyst who's been asked to pitch in and take on the tester role. What's the best way to introduce testers into XP teams so they have the courage to succeed?

## Helping XP Testers Succeed

Strong team leadership will allow even the timid or less enthusiastic tester to be productive on an XP team. The XP coach, project manager, tech lead, or whoever is in a position of authority has to make sure the team follows best XP practices and supports the tester. Some essentials:

- ✧ **Programmers code comprehensive unit tests.** Unit tests are hard to write and automate if you've never tried it before, and programmers who don't know how won't try. As a result, code will be too buggy, and acceptance tests can't be completed during the iteration. Lisa had this experience on her first XP team. Until the team mastered test-first coding, she was so buried in defects that it hampered her ability to automate and run acceptance tests. Her manager worked with the team to help them brainstorm ways to practice test-first coding (while insisting that this be the practice), and the problem disappeared.

- ✧ **Programmers (and other members of the team, as appropriate, such as analysts) willingly take on acceptance testing tasks.** Most programmers, given a choice, would rather not have to do acceptance tests. So don't give them a choice. The leader should make sure the team understands the concept that acceptance-test tasks are part of the story, and the story isn't finished until the acceptance tests pass.

- ✧ **Programmers and other members of the team support testers.** Programmers are willing to pair with the tester, answer the tester's questions, review acceptance tests, explain how the code works or how the unit tests work, provide information about tests, and comply with any reasonable request from the tester in a timely manner. The tester may be required by circumstances to do something un-XPish, such as write a test plan. Everything related to the project is the team's responsibility, so the whole team should help.

- ✧ **Testers feel free to ask questions, lots of questions, of customers, programmers, anyone involved with the project.** Naturally, testers should use good sense and ask questions at an appropriate time, of the appropriate person. Testers must feel free to say, "I don't know this" or "I think we might be making an assumption here" and ask questions to get the necessary information. Sometimes team members are critical of coworkers who ask a lot of questions. No doubt there's a fine line between acquiring needed information and coming off as stupid or lacking in self-esteem, but the culture should promote conversation between all project participants.

## XP Testing with Blended Practices

If your project includes test phases after development for each release, you have the dilemma of needing testers during these additional test phases. At the same time, they need to be involved in the next release, which the programmers are already starting. Speaking from experience, trying to work on two or more releases at once is guaranteed to adversely impact the sanity of any tester and make her feel doomed to doing a mediocre job with all her various testing and quality assurance tasks.

Here are a few of the key practices we've talked about that lead to successful XP projects:

- The team is responsible for quality.
- Programmers automate and execute acceptance tests, with the help of the tester.
- Acceptance tests are written before iteration planning, if possible, and completed by the second day of the iteration.
- Customers and programmers communicate constantly.

As the tester, you remain involved with a release when it goes into additional test phases. At the same time, the team begins development on the next iteration. How can you help write the acceptance tests if you're coordinating a separate team testing the previous release? How can you work with the programmers on test automation when you have to put together test reports for a customer who can't let go of all the old waterfall practices? Even though the team is responsible for acceptance testing, you won't feel able to effectively perform your tester role in this situation.

It's easy to *say* we should just convince the customer to trust XP and throw away the old process he's followed between development and release. Hard to *do*, though—so let's say you're stuck with it for a few releases at least. We worked on a project where the schedule looked something like Table 31.1, requiring a large development team broken into subteams. The customer was an external corporation. Each release also included related software produced by other, non-XP teams.

The ideal approach to solving this dilemma is to have one tester responsible for each release. Testers need to be intimately familiar with the functionality and technology of a project to test it effectively and shepherd it successfully into production. They also need to be intimately familiar with customer needs to be effective. You can't send Tester A out to do all the customer facing work and have Tester B do all the technical work with the development team. Neither tester will have all the information needed to be effective. By performing the complete tester role from start to finish of a release, you can maximize your value to the team.

**TABLE 31.1** Release schedule—the old way

| Release | Aug | Sep | Oct | Nov | Dec | Jan | Feb |
|---|---|---|---|---|---|---|---|
| 1.0 | ========| | -------> | | | | |
| 1.01 | | | ===| | --> | | | |
| 1.1 | | | ====| | -------> | | | |
| 2.0 | | ===============| | --------------> | | | |
| 1.13 | | | =====| | -----> | | | |
| 3.0 | | | | ===================| | -------------> | |

```
===    Development
-----  Testing
```

To handle the schedule shown in Table 31.1, we'll have three different people in the tester role: Lisa, Joe, and Kay. Each release will have a primary tester responsible for the tester role from start to finish. All testers can help on all releases as they have time, but each release will have one devoted tester, and no tester gets stuck with two releases at once.

The testers will still be responsible for releases that overlap, but the overlap is between a major release and a minor release rather than two major releases (see Table 31.2). Lisa, Kay, and Joe will each perform the full range of tester tasks and responsibilities, working with the programmers, customer, and the customer's own programmer and testing organizations.

**TABLE 31.2** Release schedule—the XP way

| Tester | Release | Aug | Sep | Oct | Nov | Dec | Jan | Feb |
|---|---|---|---|---|---|---|---|---|
| Lisa | 1.0 | ========| | -----> | | | | |
| Kay | 1.01 | | | ===| | --> | | | |
| Lisa | 1.1 | | | ====| | ----> | | | |
| Joe | 2.0 | | ============| | --------> | | | |
| Lisa | 1.13 | | | ====| | ---> | | | |
| Kay | 3.0 | | | | ===============| | ----------> | |

```
===    Development
-----  Testing
```

You wouldn't have this problem in a self-contained XP team, which would continuously execute small iterations and release them to production without additional testing phases. XP "outside the box" requires adjustments like this one, and introducing XP into an existing development culture will also require these types of adjustments.

## What If You Don't Have Enough Testers?

The previous example solves a problem with additional testers. What if you don't have more testers or the budget to hire them? This is also a dilemma we've faced, with no really satisfying solution. Here are a few approaches we've tried. We think you need at least one experienced tester, who can mentor the "volunteers," to make any of these work.

- ✧ **Press a programmer into service as a tester for the duration of an iteration or release.** This works okay, but you end up with a programmer who isn't terribly happy and can't wait to get back to writing code. On the plus side, he'll be much more aware of the challenges as well as the value of acceptance testing, and more likely, in the future, to design code with testability in mind. Using a programmer as a tester works best if the programmer "owns" the tester role for that iteration or release. Programmers usually (though not always) want to be more than tester worker bees. If they assume all the tester responsibilities, they're more likely to be enthusiastic about learning more acceptance-testing and quality-assurance skills.

- ✧ **Rotate the tester hat among programmers on a daily basis.** For the purpose of automating acceptance tests, this tactic works fine. It's basically the same as having someone take on a testing task for the day. However, if XP is new to the organization or the project has criteria that take it outside the bounds of standard XP, it doesn't give the continuity needed for tasks, such as working with the customer to define and refine quality criteria throughout the release. You need a tester who's continuously committed to acceptance-testing tasks.

- ✧ **Recruit a nonprogrammer (e.g., analyst, technical writer) into the testing role.** If your organization is trying out XP for the first time, you've probably got people in nonprogrammer jobs who have domain knowledge and an understanding of customer needs. These folks— requirements analysts, technical writers, or project managers, for example—may want to learn the testing role as a way to get involved with XP. A caveat: if the volunteer doesn't have programming experience, she'll need a long time and a lot of help to get up to speed on test automation.

## Summary

✧ When introducing Extreme Programming into a software development organization that has a separate testing and QA group, plan carefully how to overcome potential resistance and fear about XP and how to make the testers successful in an XP project.

✧ Consider the current process, such as testing phases. Decide whether you're ready to drop certain waterfall practices, such as post-development testing phases. An incremental approach may be best.

✧ Help testers succeed by making sure that
  ■ Programmers use the test-first practice effectively.
  ■ Programmers willingly take on acceptance-testing tasks.
  ■ All members of the team support testing and the testers.
  ■ Testers feel free to ask questions and pair with other team members.

✧ Consider ways to maximize tester effectiveness when using non-XP processes, such as post-development testing phases. Multiple testers, each with responsibility for a particular release, may be needed.

✧ When not enough testers are available, be creative in having programmers, analysts, or other team members fill in. Give them the responsibility for an iteration or release—don't just assign tasks to them.

# Chapter 32

# XP for Projects of Unusual Size

XP evolved with teams of a certain size in mind: usually up to eight or twelve programmers. The earlier XP published materials don't go into a lot of detail about testers and don't mention at all other common members of software projects: analysts, project managers, technical writers, graphical designers, product managers.

Using XP practices with larger projects brings a totally different set of challenges. It often means cutting teams and stories into pieces the size XP can handle. This is no easy task:

> *The division of the whole application into its story parts would be like cutting a whole chicken into its familiar pieces. Even though the joints may not be immediately visible, there are places to do the dividing that are more appropriate than others. But if you are cutting the chicken up for the first time . . . you may encounter great difficulty, because you do not know where the joints are. (Gregory Schalliol, "Challenges for Analysts on a Large XP Project")*

## Adjusting XP

We've worked on successful XP projects with up to 20 programmers, plus assorted requirements analysts, project managers, and members wearing various other hats. Customers were not always neatly located together, much less onsite with the project team. Larger projects may have to include customers from several different departments, with completely different viewpoints, which can be a challenge.

Teams of several dozen members are using XP successfully. Perhaps XP purists wouldn't call it XP, but these teams are using XP practices and expanding on them. These projects may use un-XP-like practices as well. For example, it would be difficult to do large software development projects, especially with geographically dispersed teams, without some form of written requirements documentation or a system like our sample XTrack application.

## Advance Planning Pays Off

On one of our projects, a team of programmers and analysts met at length with customers before the start of the project to define preliminary stories. During the project, these stories were used as a basis for release and iteration planning but were also expanded into functional requirements that the traditional customer felt more comfortable having as artifacts.

You can also use this time, before the first iteration starts, to educate the customer on how development will proceed and set his expectations about XP. Maybe you don't even call it Extreme Programming. Just explain how it will work from his point of view. He'll get to write up all the features he wants as stories. He'll get to choose his highest-priority stories every two weeks and see the finished result at the end of the two weeks. Sometimes the team may not complete all the features he wants for an iteration, but he'll be informed. He'll be allowed to make adjustments throughout the life of the project.

As we mentioned earlier in the book, one company created an XP owner's manual for customers, to help them understand their roles and responsibilities on the project. Customers must know they have to drive decisions about how the software will work from the business point of view and that it's most productive if they let programmers make the technical decisions. To steer safely and speedily down the road, they have to understand how to operate with XP.

We've talked in earlier chapters about managing customers' expectations, but this is an area that can't be emphasized too much. With large projects, it may be impossible to deliver, at the end of any particular iteration, functionality the customer can actually use for his business. In the project Schalliol wrote about, he said, "We had to prepare our customer to be patient with partially finished business functions after certain iterations were completed."

## Working with Customers

In large projects, you're likely to have stakeholders scattered through multiple departments, maybe with different agendas with respect to your project. On one of Lisa's large projects, where the customers weren't on site, a subteam of testers, analysts, and tech leads had regular "face time" with the customers. Customers were available via e-mail, phone and instant messaging for ad hoc questions, but most planning and feedback was done in one or two customer meetings per week. A weekly meeting was set up to go over stories and acceptance tests for the iteration. Analysts spent additional time meeting individually with stakeholders as much as possible. A subteam of analysts rotated this duty, so one analyst was always onsite with the development team, to act as a customer proxy.

The weekly meeting was also a time to show the customers the working code produced in each iteration. Their feedback resulted in updated or new stories. Additional meetings were scheduled each week whenever necessary. This limited interaction worked, because several team members were familiar with customer needs, the customers and the rest of the team trusted each other, and the customers were flexible.

In the paper quoted earlier, Gregory Schalliol points out that when your customer has several distinct and different "customers," each with peculiar requirements that aren't always compatible, you can have trouble. We've experienced this ourselves and have met this challenge by going to each customer for the stories that were most important to him and having him invest in the acceptance testing. You can't expect all customers to care about all the stories and tests.

Here's an example from one of Lisa's projects: "Once I went to various stakeholders with a list of issues left over after a release. I asked them to prioritize. Each stakeholder came up with a completely different list of priorities." This is no surprise. The tricky part is getting a consensus: what defects are important enough to take precedence over new functionality in the next iteration/release? What workarounds can we live with? You have to get all the customers together in a room for this type of discussion.

Getting customers to define acceptance tests can be a major challenge. As Gregory Schalliol says in his paper, customer teams

> *Needed not just specify the functionality to build, but also to develop the tests to verify its completion. They eventually did so, but only after having relied on many, many samples from our own analysts for a long time.*

> *. . . There was a clear difference . . . between devising a business sce-*
> *nario and devising a functional test. . . . Our customer team did not need*
> *much coaching to provide us with business scenarios, but the functional test*
> *itself, in all of its detail, required us to do much more training with the cus-*
> *tomer than we had anticipated.*

Having an analyst as intermediary here is no doubt a huge help. You, as the tester, can provide the same function. You can guide the customer team to think of, in Schalliol's words, "the proper functioning of all negative and atypical actions that could occur in the process, widget action on screens, behind-the-scenes dependencies. . . ."

## Satisfying Customer Test Documentation Requirements

Chapters 16 and 17 showed some ways to document acceptance tests for an XP project. A spreadsheet can work well for test cases, but for larger projects, the customer may feel more comfortable with a formal test plan. If you're a consulting company working for an external client, your client may require this. You have to meet your customer's needs, even if they don't seem to fit well with XP. Flexibility is required on both sides to introduce XP into an organization.

If you have to write a test plan, use it as a place to define processes to be used for the project:

- Definition of the scope of the testing
- Procedures for reporting, tracking, fixing, and retesting defects
- Definitions of severity levels for defect reports
- Procedures for doing builds
- Definition of roles and responsibilities of programmers, testers, customers, support staff
- Definition of schedules and milestones
- Definitions of all the test phases included before release
- Communication process
- Plan for deployment

You can find a sample test plan at www.xptester.org. If you're working with large projects, take a look at this sample. It will give you ideas on coordinating work of multiple teams and handling multiple post-development test phases.

If you're a consultant or contractor developing software for an external customer who has their own testing organization, you need someone to work with that organization to agree on test procedures and coordinate the release all the way to launch. The XP team's tester may not have enough bandwidth for these activities, so consider having another tester or a project manager perform this role. For more ideas, read the discussion in Chapter 31 of alternative approaches to a shortage of testers.

## Iteration Planning and Execution for Large or Multilocation Projects

Lisa's large team, which was both large and split into two geographic locations, used the following procedures to successfully complete iteration planning in a timely manner and to complete the tasks during the iteration:

- The teams met in each location and connected via speakerphone. Aids to remote collaboration such as NetMeeting, VNC, or a Webcam trained on a whiteboard were sometimes employed. All members were present, including testers, analysts, project managers, technical writers, anyone who would help deliver the software.

- Analysts, working with the customer, wrote up the narratives of the stories in advance. Analysts and/or testers wrote the high-level acceptance tests for each story before iteration planning. At the meeting, someone (usually the analyst) read the stories for the entire team (both locations).

- Before the meeting, each story was assigned to a programmer, who used the stories and acceptance tests to do an initial task breakdown. Each programmer who had been thus assigned wrote these tasks up on the whiteboard. Each geographic subteam prepared a subset of stories.

- The teams broke into small groups within their geographic locations and did a more detailed task breakdown for their assigned stories.

- The teams got back together by speakerphone and went through the tasks for each story.

- Individual programmers chose stories for estimating.

- Task cards were written up and each location received a set of tasks.

◇ Each day, programmers chose tasks to perform. The programmer who ended up with the task was free to reestimate it if necessary.

◇ Each day at the standup, pairings for that day were decided. Programmers from separate locations paired using VNC or NetMeeting and phone.

◇ Estimates, actual time spent so far, and estimated remaining time were tracked every day during the standup.

Planning the iteration together, having story tasks spread across both locations, and practicing remote pairing allowed both locations to achieve collective code ownership.

## Summary

◇ Large projects lead to adaptations. Often, teams and/or stories need to be subdivided into pieces that are a better size for XP.

◇ Planning meetings with the customer before the first release planning meeting save time and gives you a chance to educate the customer and set expectations.

◇ If the customer isn't onsite, team members need to schedule regular meetings with her in addition to ad hoc meetings and contact with individual stakeholders.

◇ Different stakeholders have different priorities. Work with them individually and together to get them to speak with one voice.

◇ Educate the customer to improve his skill at writing acceptance tests.

◇ Additional documentation, such as a formal test plan, may be necessary in larger projects or where the customer requires a test plan.

◇ Large projects whose teams are in different locations can successfully plan and complete iterations by sharing responsibility for task breakdown and estimation and by remote pair programming.

# Chapter 33

## Extreme Testing without Extreme Programming

"Hmmmph," you say. "It all sounds lovely, but I don't work in an XP shop." If this is the case, are you doomed—hemmed in by traditional software development methodologies? Do you just have to wait for that buggy software to thump over the wall? Must you keep burying yourself in giant test plans and other unwieldy artifacts?

No! Fly and be free! Just because the development team doesn't take advantage of XP practices is no reason you can't. *Why can't testers use XP to transform the test community the way XP is transforming the development community?* We believe that even testing and quality assurance professionals who don't work in XP environments can gain significant benefits by adopting XP practices.

Even when the development team is doing traditional software development, you can still benefit from XP practices in a number of ways. This is a situation Lisa has experienced firsthand. We're not saying it's easy, but the payoff makes this a battle worth fighting.

Let's look at a typical project life cycle using a waterfall development methodology and see where you can apply extreme practices. We'll borrow a term from Bret Pettichord and refer to the "customer" as the **business expert.** When we refer to "business expert" here, this could be the person or persons managing the project, the person who instigated the project, the stakeholders of the application, or the individual or group responsible for determining whether a release goes into production.

## Gathering Requirements

No rule says *you* can't work more closely with the business experts or someone who can act as proxy for the customers. (If there *is* such a "rule" where you work, and customers are off limits to you due to perceived time constraints or political reasons, we'd urge you to explore other career opportunities, if at all possible.) Seek out the parties responsible for producing business requirements. Ask them to tell you how they define quality for this application. Review the requirements document and see if it matches what they tell you. If you help the business experts clearly state what they want, you'll make a huge contribution toward the success of the project.

As the project proceeds, felling rainforests and contributing to global warming as it churns out paper, review ensuing documents, such as functional requirements and user interface design, with the customers. Keep working with them to define and refine their quality criteria and make sure these criteria are reflected in the documentation. Business experts are bound to change their minds on a daily basis, and in a traditional methodology, this is the time when it's okay for them to do so. Challenge them to think ahead, and help them visualize how the application is really going to work. Screen mockups or even drawings on a whiteboard can help them do this.

Prototyping and usability testing are a huge help, particularly for end-user-oriented applications, but few shops make this investment. Push for them anyway. You can be an agent for change. If nothing else, you'll have more fun at work (or possibly more frustration; we can't guarantee anything!).

If there's no formal usability testing, get samples of the application from the requirements and specification documents and show them to anyone who faintly resembles the ultimate user of the application. If you can't do this together with the business experts, give them feedback anyway. You may save them from locking themselves into a function or feature they'd be unhappy with later. Business experts are usually glad to have this kind of feedback. Just as when you report defects to programmers, keep the emotion out of your feedback. Point out your research results and let the marketing professional, product designer, or whoever your business expert is decide how to react.

Once you've gathered some information, do what you can to move the project along. The longer you spend on the requirements and definition phase, the more likely it is that the business expert's requirements will be obsolete by the time the software is delivered. Push whoever is managing the project to get signoff, and proceed to development as quickly as possible. Push for shorter releases and more iterative development. If you get discouraged and think nobody is open for change, talk with the development managers and tell them your ideas. You could be pleasantly surprised.

## System Design

You've spent a lot of time with the business experts, reviewing the specifications, and perhaps even talking with potential end users or end user surrogates. Your input to the system design may be valuable, especially if the business experts don't participate in design meetings.

Depending on your level of interest and expertise in system architecture and design, you may find design meetings tedious and hard to follow. Programmers and architects may go off on obscure tangents. If they're not practicing XP, they may be trying to see way too far into the future. Do what you can to tactfully help keep the meetings focused on what the customers need now. Be alert for developer misunderstanding of the requirements, and clarify the customers' needs. Make sure the business experts' criteria for quality are considered in making design decisions.

Raise the issue of testability in the design meetings. A system that's easy to test will get released faster. Think about how you'll test various parts of the system, and ask for features or hooks that might make it easier for you to write test scripts.

If the programmers didn't participate in creating or reviewing requirements, they might find a feature that would be difficult to implement. You can facilitate a conversation between business experts and programmers to make adjustments. This may produce something close enough to the business experts' needs more quickly than meeting the original requirement. In a traditional development shop, this may be the business experts' last chance to change their collective mind until after the first production release.

## Planning and Defining Tests

Toss out those tree-killing test plans. By test plans, we mean the formal documents that describe the scope of the testing, what functionality will and won't be tested, and a list of the tests to be performed for each bit of functionality: positive, negative, boundary, error, and so on. They're usually in some kind of text format that's impossible to maintain.

Be honest: does anyone but you ever actually read these? Why spend a lot of time writing about what you are and aren't going to test? Why spend days producing a document that will be out of date soon and be a nightmare to maintain? The only reason would be that your project management office or other authority forces you to deliver one. If so, keep it as lightweight and useful as possible.

Focus your energy instead on the test cases themselves. Go ahead and use the same techniques we recommend in Chapters 16 and 17: start writing the automated test scripts themselves. If the business experts are more comfortable, use a lightweight spreadsheet format to document them. Get as much input from the customers as you can. Have the business experts and a programmer and/or architect review your test cases and suggest additions, modifications and deletions. Ask the business experts to identify test cases critical to acceptance.

As for test automation, the principles in Chapters 16–25 apply even to traditional waterfall development. Use XP practices such as pair testing and refactoring to improve your productivity and quality. Turn your testing effort into a sort of self-contained XP project. Impress everyone with how quickly and effectively you and your team can automate tests. They may start wondering how you're getting that done and may be willing to try agile practices for software development.

## Running Tests

Watch for falling objects! Don't let the developers throw code over the wall at the end of the coding phase. You established a relationship with the developers and architects during the system design. Brainstorm with them about how they can deliver bits and pieces to you to test early. Pair with them to do integration testing. Budget time in your schedule for starting testing as early in the cycle as you can.

The advantages of testing early in the cycle will be apparent to everyone. As long as you have control over your own test environment, so changes by programmers can't catch you unawares and potentially slow down your testing, you can test parts of the software that aren't ready for prime time and give the programmers valuable feedback. Programmers know defects are lurking in their code. It's helpful for them to find out if the major features work without blowing up or that the architecture performs as expected under heavy loads.

You might agree to just do "smoke" testing at first and give feedback without opening defect reports. You're not in a competition to see who can find the most bugs; you're trying to ensure that when the programmers think they're finished, they really are.

Do whatever you can to encourage the programmers to write unit tests. The advantages of unit tests and test-first programming, as described in

*Extreme Programming Explained,* apply no matter what methodology you're developing with. Automated unit testing has become a widely accepted practice. It will help the programmers gain courage and go faster. Effective unit testing means that when you start doing functional or system testing, you aren't spending your time finding defects, especially regression bugs, that could have been ferreted out at build time by the unit tests. All software development projects, not just those using XP, will suffer adverse consequences if they fail to write and use effective automated unit tests.

Automated unit testing, especially the concept of test-first design, can be a challenge for the uninitiated. If programmers haven't written automated unit tests before, it's tough to get them to start. You need management on your side for this one. Offer to help the programmers figure out the best way to unit test. Introduce them to XUnit if they're not familiar with it. If you have to, bring in an expert test-first programmer to show how it's done. Document the results of automated unit testing. You'll see a drop in the number of defects you find in post development testing. The defects your acceptance tests find will be a different type, not isolated to one piece of code but produced by a combination of factors.

Ask the business experts to do acceptance testing. They can use the test cases they helped you produce that they identified as crucial to acceptance, or they can just do their own thing. Either way, you'll get valuable feedback, and they'll have a level of confidence and comfort that they're in charge of their own destiny—that what gets put into production isn't something totally different from what they requested

You and the business experts can start planning what changes will be needed as soon as changes are allowed—usually after the production release. You could be really subversive and show the business experts' desired changes to a programmer and get an estimate of how much time will be needed to implement them. Who knows—if the programmers have written automated unit tests to give themselves more courage and confidence to make changes, they might even be willing to make the changes *before* the production release. You don't mind—you have a lightweight, flexible test design, and you can easily modify your automated test scripts.

## Retrospectives

After each iteration and release, get all the players together to look at the good and bad of the project so far and plan the next iteration or release (see Chapter 26 for more about retrospectives). Encourage a shorter release cycle, smaller in scope but with much faster time to production. Don't be afraid to be an agent for change. Show how the agile practices you used, such as pair testing and your flexible test design, helped you be more productive and help create a higher-quality product. Change is hard, and you may not always succeed with your suggestions, but give yourself the satisfaction of being a leader. Meanwhile, you can be more satisfied with your own work because you've used agile practices effectively.

## Let Worry Be Your Guide

The following interchange is from a conversation on the agile-testing mailing list postings in December 2001. The discussion centered around letting the customer decide the level of quality for a software package. XP gives the customer responsibility for influencing quality through acceptance tests. No matter what software development process you're using, the customer is still responsible for defining what quality is for a software package under development.

Mike Clark contributed this scenario:

> *Let's say our product is supported to run on 2 application servers, each having three different versions. Each application server version is supported on three different operating systems. In the interest of time and resources, we've been testing these configurations using a pair-wise strategy in general. We've never shipped a defect related to running the product on application server A.x on any operations system. We're confident in the product's support for these permutations, so we only pair-wise test our product with application server A.1 using operating system A. In other words, the application server version and operating system are arbitrary, and we don't test all the permutations. The customer makes a conscious decision to accept the risk.*
>
> *On the other hand, we know that we've shipped more defects over time related to the running of the product on the combination of application server B.x and operating system C. Perhaps there's something subtle about this combination that we don't understand, so we ensure that we always devote resources to thoroughly testing this specific permutation. The customer makes a conscious decision to reduce the risk.*
>
> *In these cases, the customer knows that she's getting a reduction of risk for her money if she chooses to test a specific permutation. Testing all permutations is ideal, but probably not necessary or feasible. The product may ship sooner by relaxing the quality constraints for some configurations, without deliberately sacrificing quality. Nevertheless, it's a business decision, so I'll let the customer choose the testing level, and thereby influence the quality.*

Brian Marick responds:

*I suggest that the metaphor "setting a quality level" isn't a good one. It makes the process seem precise, quantitative, and product-wide. To me, it seems rough and uncertain, qualitative, and focused on particular risks.*

*(I have no objection to things that are rough, uncertain, or qualitative, by the way.)*

*Here's an alternate slogan: "assigning worry tasks." Because that doesn't mean anything obvious, you'd always be forced to explain it the first time you use it. (I think that's an advantage.) Here's an explanation.*

*There's someone responsible for spending money wisely. In XP, that's the Customer. In a mass-market project, it would be the project manager (or the combination of the project and product manager). I'll call that person Bob.*

*Bob says two things.*

1. *"Make X work." The programmers then spring into action. In XP, they implement a story. In other development styles, they implement some chunk of a specification or list of requirements.*
2. *"I'm worried about Y." The programmers and testers spring into action. The testers check if that worry is justified. The programmers do things to make it not justified. Both of them calibrate their effort by discovering how worried Bob is.*

*How much Bob delegates worry tasks depends on the project and Bob. For example, every time Bob says, "Make X work," he probably worries about whether X really will.*

- *In some XP projects, Bob would create the customer tests that would persuade him to stop worrying.*
- *In others, Bob talks with a tester about X. She creates the tests for him.*
- *In the mass-market projects I've seen, Bob staffs the project with testers, based on his experience of what proportion of testers to code is required to achieve good enough quality, then lets them decide how to test each X. They'll let him know if something comes up that requires he make a business decision.*

## Summary

- Even if your development team isn't using agile practices, you can benefit by applying agile practices to quality assurance and testing.
- Work closely with business experts, a.k.a. customers or customer proxies, in the early stages of the project.

- Help business experts visualize the final product; write acceptance tests and requirements accordingly.
- Have the business experts define what quality is for the software being produced.
- Attend system design meetings and help the programmers stay focused on the immediate needs of the customers.
- Use the test-automation practices outlined in Chapters 16–25. They aren't just for XP projects.
- Use XP practices such as pair testing and refactoring to produce and maintain effective tests.
- Work with programmers to test components as soon as the components are ready. Don't wait and test at the tail end of the project.
- Be a change agent; work to get your team to implement practices such as unit testing.
- Involve the business experts in acceptance testing.
- Hold a retrospective to review what worked and what didn't and select areas for improvement in the next release.

# Chapter 34

## In Closing: May the Road Rise Up to Meet You

*The church is near, but the road is icy; the bar is far away, but I'll walk carefully.*

—*Russian proverb*

*No amount of travel on the wrong road will bring you to the right destination.*

—*Ben Gaye, III*

Are we there yet?

This brings to an end our road hazard survival kit. We hope this section gave you some strategies that will allow you to benefit from XP practices, even if your project doesn't conform to the parameters of an ideal XP project.

This also completes our exploration of the role of testing and testers in Extreme Programming, at least for now. We've seen some interesting sights along the way. (Dinosaur National Monument was a bit out of our way, but just the name reminded us of some projects we've worked on.) We've examined how we think testers add value to Extreme Programming teams. We've considered what's in it for the tester and for the XP project. Our XP test drive took us step by step through the early stages of a typical XP project, and we hope it gave you an idea what to expect, as well as some ways to ensure your success.

Like the faded grins in pictures from family vacations long past, we hope some of our ideas will stick with you as go on to future projects and that you'll take the opportunity to try them out in an XP environment when you get the chance.

Here are some points we hope will guide you as you continue your own journey:

- ◇ Although quality is a team responsibility, as a tester you have a special focus on quality. You can add value to your team in many ways, acting as an agent for continual improvement.
- ◇ Help the customer specify acceptance tests that produce the minimum level of quality he needs and can afford.
- ◇ Tasks related to acceptance tests are part of each story and part of the team's velocity. Include these tasks, and estimate them as accurately as possible, during each release and iteration planning session.
- ◇ Extreme Programming practices maximize your value as a tester, even if you work on a project using some other approach to software development.

We stated at the outset that we believe XP and QA have a lot to gain from each other. In fact, they already have. XP teams are the fruit of seeds planted many years ago by the testing and quality assurance community: test automation, peer review, unit testing, code inspections, test-then-code, the buddy system—the list goes on. Now is the time to cultivate an alliance that will yield the cash crops of the future. It would be ironic indeed to leave them rotting in the field.

In short, XP needs you, and you need XP. We'll all happily ride (or drive) off into the sunset knowing that if we work together, we can produce software that meets our customers' needs for quality and our needs for quality of life. See you on the road. . . . Happy trails!

# Answers to Exercises

## Exercise 1 (Chapter 7)

Identify as many questionable or incorrect assumptions as you can in the following statement:

> *Testers run tests, and running tests requires that the code be written, and no code is available until the end of the first iteration. Therefore, the earliest the tester is needed is the end of iteration 1.*

## Answer

1. **Testers run tests.** In fact, testers perform many other activities, including identifying hidden assumptions (wow, this is recursive), helping the customer write acceptance tests, estimating time for acceptance test tasks, and helping the team accurately estimate each story.

2. **Running tests requires that the code be written.** This may sound like a stretch, but other things besides code require testing. Identifying hidden assumptions in stories is one example of a test on something besides code. Usability testing a user interface is another. It's also a good idea to "test" user documentation.

3. **No code is available until the end of the first iteration.** Programmers will produce working code the first day. It's possible to do testing

that goes beyond unit testing even before all the code for a single story is completed. For example, a programmer may spike a design and want to have it load-tested to make sure it's scalable.

4. **The earliest a tester is needed is the end of iteration 1.** See points 1–3.

## Exercise 2 (Chapter 8)

> **Story:** The user can create, read, and update a story via a Web interface. The data fields in a story are number, name, author, description, estimate, iteration, timestamps, and state.

1. Given the above XTrack story, use the process we describe in this chapter to find hidden assumptions.

### Answer

**Step 1: Customer view**

◇ **I'm the customer. How does this relate to my project?** I can keep track of a story on an index card, but what if my management is in a different location and wants to see this information? What if I'm doing a project for an external customer, and stakeholders at that organization want to see the stories? This tool would allow them to do that.

◇ **What business problem is it solving? How does it solve it?** Index cards work great for small, self-contained projects, where everyone who needs to know the status of a story can simply walk in and look at the index cards and talk to the team. If my team is split across two or more locations, I need some way for everyone to see the stories. If my management or my clients' management wants to track the progress of stories, they could use this system.

◇ **How could the system implement this and not solve the problem?** Someone has to input the data into the system and keep it current. If it's not easy to use or up to date, stakeholders may still wait to find out the information some other way.

✧ **Are there alternate solutions? Are there related problems?** We could put the data into a simple spreadsheet and put it on a shared drive on a LAN or put a link to it on a Web site. It would have the same problems of someone needing to keep it current and would require a little more work for users to find the information.

## Step 2: User view

✧ **I'm a user, searching for information about a story. What are the worst and best things that can happen? What would really irritate me?**

**Worst thing:** I can't locate the story—it's in the system, but I can't find it. I can't figure out how to add a new story. Two stories are similar—I can't tell which is the one I want.

**Best thing:** I can see all the stories for an iteration and all the pertinent information about them online and select the one I want from a list.

**Irritating:** How, exactly, am I locating the story? Can I search by iteration? By name? By number? When I add the story, is the system going to do a lot of picky field validation?

✧ **How can I screw up? How should the system respond?** What if I enter the same story name twice for the same iteration? Does it have to be unique? Do any of the fields have special formats? Do I have to enter the timestamps myself, or are they automatically generated?

✧ **How often will I do this? What will I do before and after?** We'd need to update the information about a story at least twice per iteration: once to create it and once to update the status and any other information that changed before the end of the iteration. I'll probably gather information about the stories from the customer and then enter all the stories for the iteration or for the project so far. If I'm a stakeholder who just wants to find out information about stories, I might do that once or twice per iteration.

## Step 3: Programmer view

✧ **I'm the programmer. What's the simplest implementation that could possibly work?** A form with text input fields for story number, name, author, description, estimate, iteration, timestamps, and state. This information is stored in some kind of repository: a database, an XML file. I need to know what fields are required, the size and format of them, what validation is expected.

**Step 4: Identifying the mismatch**

⬦ **How likely is the implementation to solve the business problem?** Fairly likely, because this system doesn't have to handle a large volume of data or transactions.

⬦ **How likely is the implementation to solve the related problems?** It doesn't really solve the problem of someone needing to keep the data current, regardless of where we store it.

⬦ **How likely is the implementation to avoid irritating the user? Respond appropriately to user mistakes?** Fairly likely, as it's a simple application and users will be familiar with it. The biggest risk is for users outside the project team who want information and don't access the system as often. So we have to satisfy both "expert" and "occasional" users.

**Step 5: The assumptions**

⬦ What information is the customer assuming we know?

1. The system has fairly low transaction volume, used only by members of the project team, managers, and stakeholders outside the team. Team members will input the information; everyone will access the system for tracking and information.

2. The user can find stories by iteration and name. A unique key identifies each story and avoids confusion with other stories.

3. The user can browse and select the story from a list. The system has some way to tell stories apart.

**2.** Identify the questions related to these assumptions that you'd ask in discussion.

## Answer

1. How many people will be using the system at any given time?

2. Will some users have read-only access, while others are able to add and update? If the answer to this is yes, we have other questions:

   ⬦ We must need some sort of login screen. What should this look like? What should happen if the login name or password is invalid? Are there criteria for the login name and password—for example, does the password have to contain a number or special character, are special characters or leading spaces allowed in the login name, and so on?

- ◇ Are there just two levels of users, read-only and access to all features? Should read-only users see only the features they can use and not, for example, an Add button?
- ◇ Where will the login names and passwords be stored?

3. What unique key identifies a particular story? Can two stories have the same name? Can the user select an iteration and see all the stories for that iteration? Can the user then select a story from this list? How can the user tell which story to select?

## Exercise 3 (Chapter 9)

1. Define high-level acceptance tests for the following story from the XTrack application (same project as Exercise 2 in the previous chapter). Don't look for hidden assumptions; just do it based on the bare bones of the story:

> **Story:** The user can provide an estimate for how long it will take to implement a story, prioritize the story, and assign the story to an iteration.

### Answer

Based on the bare bones of the story, we came up with just one test:

Test for Exercise 3.1

| Action | Data | Expected Result |
| --- | --- | --- |
| 1. Update story with estimate, priority, and iteration | A story already added to the repository, estimate, priority and iteration number | Success: story is updated with appropriate information |

**2.** Use the technique from the previous chapter (or your own) to identify problematic hidden assumptions in this story and define additional acceptance tests that make them explicit.

## Answer

### Assumptions

We used the method from Chapter 8 to come up with the following (see below for the details):

1. The system provides a list of stories not already assigned to an iteration.
2. The system provides a list of the stories assigned to a particular iteration.
3. The system provides a running total of estimates for all stories in an iteration.
4. Estimate, priority, and iteration number aren't required fields.
5. The user can list stories and see the current values for estimate, priority, and iteration.
6. The user can select a story for update and update these fields at any time.
7. The system will not validate for duplicate story names. It's up to the user to make sure names are unique.

### Additional Tests

Based on the assumptions, we came up with the following additional tests:

Additional tests for Exercise 3.1

| Action | Data | Expected Result |
|---|---|---|
| 2. | Existing story, no values entered in iteration, priority, or estimate | Success: these aren't required fields |
| 3. | Existing story, exceed maximum values for estimate, priority, and iteration | Failure: should not be able to enter a number that large |

Additional tests for Exercise 3.1 (Continued)

| Action | Data | Expected Result |
|---|---|---|
| 4. Add a new story with estimate, iteration, and priority | New story with valid values for estimate, iteration, and priority | Success: story is added with appropriate information |
| 5. Search for stories not assigned to an iteration and select one to update | Search criteria and existing stories with nothing in the iteration field | Success: stories are listed with current values for estimate, priority, and iteration. When user clicks on story name, story fields appear on update screen and are modifiable. |
| 6. Search for stories assigned to an iteration and select one to update | Search criteria and existing stories for a particular iteration | Success: stories are listed with current values for estimate, priority and iteration. When user clicks on story name, story fields appear on update screen with current values and are modifiable. |

## Details of how we identified assumptions:

### Step 1: Customer view

◇ **I'm the customer. How does this relate to my project?** We need a way to track estimates for stories, to help with choosing stories for an iteration. We need to be able to track the stories included in an iteration and know what progress we're making, based on the estimates. Priority will help us decide which story to start first. We could use the priority field outside iteration if we wanted to prioritize the stories in advance, to make choosing stories for the next iteration go faster. But we may want to change our minds at any time.

◇ **What business problem is it solving? How does it solve it?** Customers need to know how much a story costs before they can choose stories for an iteration. The team needs a way to prioritize and track the stories within the iteration. By storing this information online, it's available to the whole team, even if we're not all in the same room. It's also easily available to management. The online screen can list all the stories available to the iteration, those assigned to the iteration, and totals of the estimates.

⬦ **How could the system implement this and not solve the problem?** As with Exercise 2, this story gives us a way to estimate a story and assign it to an iteration, but someone still has to input and maintain the online data. Some stories may not have estimates yet. That's why it has to be easy to update the priority, iteration, and estimate. None of these fields can be required, because we'll have stories for which we don't know this information yet.

⬦ **Are there alternate solutions? Are there related problems?** We could put the information on a whiteboard, story cards, or a spreadsheet, but that makes it harder to share the information with others who aren't in our location and has the same problem of needing to be kept current.

## Step 2: User view

⬦ **I'm a user, searching for information about a story or release. What are the worst and best things that can happen? What would really irritate me?**

**Worst thing:** I can't locate the story or iteration I want—it's in the system, but I can't find it. I can't figure out how to assign a new story to an iteration. Two stories are similar—I can't tell which one I want.

**Best thing:** I can see all the stories for an iteration and all the pertinent information about them online and select the one I want from a list.

**Irritating:** How, exactly, am I locating the story? Can I search by iteration? By name? By number?

⬦ **How can I screw up? How should the system respond?** Can I accidentally assign the same story to more than one iteration? Assign the same story twice to one iteration? Is it worth having the system prevent me from doing that, or do we think the few people using this system will be able to avoid that kind of mistake?

⬦ **How often will I do this? What will I do before and after?** During release planning, we'll write the stories and estimate them. During iteration planning, we'll choose the stories for that iteration and prioritize them. Or maybe we'll prioritize them outside of iteration, as an aid to choosing stories for future iterations.

## Step 3: Programmer view

- ✧ **I'm the programmer. What's the simplest implementation that could possibly work?** A list of all the stories, with columns for estimate, iteration, and priority. Click on the story to select it to update these fields. We need some way to identify the iteration, probably by number.

## Step 4: Identifying the mismatch

- ✧ **How likely is the implementation to solve the business problem?** Fairly likely.
- ✧ **How likely is the implementation to solve the related problems?** We need to be able to unassign stories from an iteration, in case the customer changes his mind or we can't complete all the stories.
- ✧ **How likely is the implementation to avoid irritating the user? Respond appropriately to user mistakes?** As with Exercise 2, we aren't likely to have a lot of user mistakes, but we want to accommodate our managers who just want to get the high-level information.

## Step 5: The assumptions

See Exercise 3, Step 6.

## Exercise 4 (Chapter 10)

1. Define high-level acceptance tests for the following story from the XTrack application, using the techniques from Chapters 7, 8, and 9, or your own favorite method:

> **Story:** The user can create, update, display, and delete a task. A task has a name, description, assignee, estimate, actual time spent, state, and created/updated timestamps.

### Answer

We came up with the following tests (the details are below):

Tests for Exercise 4.1

| Action | Data | Expected Result |
|---|---|---|
| 1. Add a new task | An existing story, values for the task fields | Success: the task is added |
| 2. | An existing story, values only for task name, description, and state | Success: none of these is a required field |
| 3. | An existing story, no values for task name, description, or state | Failure: these are required fields |
| 4. Select an existing task and update | An existing task, new values for estimate, assignee | Success: task fields are updated |
| 5. | An existing task, empty values for description, status | Failure: these are required fields |
| 6. Select a task and click to delete | An existing task | Success: task is deleted |

## Details

### Step 1: Customer view

- ◇ **I'm the customer. How does this relate to my project?** Tracking tasks is important to the success of the project. I always want to know how close the team is to finishing the iteration and whether it's possible for all the stories to be completed on time.

- ◇ **What business problem is it solving? How does it solve it?** Tasks can be tracked with cards or spreadsheets, but an online system works better if the team is not located in the same place. It will also retain important historical information—for example, to see how accurate estimates are. An online system also allows stakeholders who aren't involved with the team on a daily basis to track the team's progress.

- ◇ **How could the system implement this and not solve the problem?** If the data is not maintained on a daily basis, it won't be useful.

- ◇ **Are there alternate solutions? Are there related problems?** We could put the data into a simple spreadsheet and put it on a shared drive on a LAN or put a link to it on a Web site. It would have the same problem of someone needing to keep it current and would take more work for users to find information.

## Step 2: User view

❖ **I'm a user, searching for information about a story or its tasks or inputting new task data. What are the worst and best things that can happen? What would really irritate me?**

**Worst thing:** I can't locate the story or task—it's in the system, but I can't find it. I can't figure out how to add a new task. I can't tell which is the task I want—two tasks are similar.

**Best thing:** I can see all the tasks for a story and the pertinent information about them online and select the one I want from a list.

**Irritating:** How, exactly, am I locating the task? Can I search by story? By name? By number? When I add the task, is the system going to do a lot of picky field validation?

❖ **How can I screw up? How should the system respond?** What if I enter the same task name twice for the same iteration? Does the name have to be unique? Do any of the fields have special formats? Do I have to enter the timestamps myself, or are they automatically generated?

❖ **How often will I do this? What will I do before and after?** We'd need to update the information about a task on a daily basis. The tracker will get data on time spent per task from each team member and input it. Stakeholders who want to see the team's progress can see up to date information after a certain time each morning.

## Step 3: Programmer view

❖ **I'm the programmer. What's the simplest implementation that could possibly work?** A form with text input fields for name, description, assignee, estimate, actual time spent, and state. Timestamps would be automatically generated. The user would select a story from a list and see a list of tasks. He would be able to click a button to add a new task or select an existing task to update it.

## Step 4: Identifying the mismatch

❖ **How likely is the implementation to solve the business problem?** Fairly likely.

❖ **How likely is the implementation to solve the business problems?** It doesn't really solve the problem of someone needing to keep the data current, wherever we decide to store the data.

- ◇ **How likely is the implementation to avoid irritating the user? Respond appropriately to user mistakes?** Fairly likely, as it's a simple application and users will be familiar with it. The biggest risk is for users outside the project team who want information and don't access the system as often. So we have to satisfy both "expert" and "occasional" users.

**Step 5: The assumptions**

- ◇ The system has fairly low transaction volume, used only by members of the project team, managers, and stakeholders outside the team. Team members will input the information; everyone will access the system for tracking and information.
- ◇ The user can find a task by selecting a story and browsing tasks for the story.
- ◇ The user can select the task from a list for updating or click a link to add a new task.
- ◇ Required fields are name, description, and state.
- ◇ All fields can be updated at any time, except timestamps, which are automatically generated.
- ◇ The system will not validate for duplicate task names within the story; this is up to the user.
- ◇ Name and assignee have a maximum of 50 characters. Description has a maximum of 4,000 characters. Estimate and actual time spent can be up to 3 digits long. State is a select list consisting of Started, Not Started, and Complete.

2. Assume the programmers have estimated that it will take $D$ ideal days to develop this (we're not going to tell you what number $D$ is, so it doesn't influence your answer to question 3). Use the first method in this chapter to estimate the acceptance-test time (hint: your answer will be in terms of $D$).

## Answer

This looks like fairly straightforward Web testing. The test data isn't hard to get. However, we're testing through the user interface, which is more work than testing at a lower level. Our estimate is that we'll spend 30% of the development time creating these automated tests. So the answer is $0.3D$.

**3.** Use the second method in this chapter to estimate the acceptance-test time in ideal days.

## Answer

Test for Exercise 4.3

| Action | Data | Expected Result |
|---|---|---|
| 1. Add a new task | An existing story, values for the task fields | Success: the task is added |

Estimate for Exercise 4.3 (in hours)

| Test | Preparation | | Execution | | Special | Estimate |
|---|---|---|---|---|---|---|
| 3 | Define details | 0.5 | Setup | 0.0 | | |
| | Create test records | 0.3 | Run | 0.1 | | |
| | Automation spike | 0.5 | Evaluate | 0.0 | | |
| | Automation | 0.3 | Report | 0.0 | | |
| | **Total** | 1.6 | Total | 0.1 | **Total** 0.0 | **Total** 1.7 |

All these tests look to be fairly similar, so we can use this same estimate for them, too, except we expect to save on the automation spike on all but the first. Here's the summary:

Summary for Exercise 4.3 (in hours)

| Test | Preparation | Execution | Special | Estimate |
|---|---|---|---|---|
| 1 | 1.6 | .1 | 0.0 | 1.7 |
| 2 | 1.1 | .1 | 0.0 | 1.2 |
| 3 | 1.1 | .1 | 0.0 | 1.2 |
| 4 | 1.1 | .1 | 0.0 | 1.2 |
| 5 | 1.1 | .1 | 0.0 | 1.2 |
| 6 | 1.1 | .1 | 0.0 | 1.2 |
| | | | | **Total: 7.7** |

So the answer is 7.7 ideal hours, or about 1 ideal day.

## Exercise 5 (Chapter 11)

(We're worried if you really needed to look up these answers!)

1. Joan, a programmer new to the team, has provided an estimate for a directory service that you think is way too low. You say:

    a. "You dolt! Where did you learn to program? Wal-Mart?"

    b. "Can I smoke some of what you're smokin'?"

    c. "Not!"

    d. "Wait, let's look at the acceptance tests for that story. I think the validation is pretty complex. What do you think, maybe we need to build in more time just in case?"

2. Jim, the project manager, says, "This is a new client, and we really want to impress him. Let's forget about automating the acceptance tests this iteration, so we have time to squeeze in an extra story." You say:

    a. "Have you lost your #$%@!*&^ mind???"

    b. "Oh, heck, why not just do away with testing? Then maybe we can squeeze in two more stories."

    c. "Let's think about this. We might save a little time this iteration if we skip the test automation tasks, but next iteration it'll take us longer to perform the regression acceptance tests from this iteration. We won't be able to keep up the same velocity, and the customer will be disappointed. If we automate tests for this iteration now, that'll save us time later, and we can provide the customer with consistent, high-quality deliverables."

3. Bob and Tom, both programmers, have come up with widely different estimates for two stories that clearly seem to require about the same effort. Tom is one of the younger team members, recently married, and his estimate is less than half of Bob's, who has over 20 years in the business. You say:

    a. "I don't know which of you is the idiot, but there's no way one of these can take twice as long as the other. Maybe you both are."

b. "Tom, aren't you worried you'll have a mighty short marriage if you're in here all night getting that story right?"

c. "Doesn't it seem like these should take about the same amount of effort? Maybe one of these is too high or too low—what do you think?"

## Exercise 6 (Chapter 12)

For each of the following questions, indicate whether it's more of the "widening" or "narrowing" type:

### Answer

Answers for Exercise 6

| Question | Type |
|---|---|
| "Does the user need to log in to use the system?" | Widening |
| "When a user clicks that link, should the document display in the current browser window or pop up in another?" | Narrowing |
| "How many search forms should the user be able to enter on this page?" | Narrowing |
| "Would a user ever have to change any of this information?" | Widening |
| "What's the maximum length for the customer name?" | Narrowing |

## Exercise 7 (Chapter 13)

Break out and estimate testing tasks for the following story from the Xtrack application. This is the same story for which you defined acceptance tests in Exercise 4, so use those or our answer to that exercise as a starting point:

> **Story:** User can create, update, display, and delete a task. A task has a name, a description, assignee, estimate, actual time spent, state, and created/ updated timestamps.

## Answer

Here are the tests we defined for Exercise 4:

Tests for Exercise 4

| Action | Data | Expected Result |
|---|---|---|
| 1. Add a new task | An existing story, values for the task fields | Success: the task is added |
| 2. | An existing story, values only for task name, description, and state | Success: none of these is a required field |
| 3. | An existing story, no values for task name, description, and state | Failure: these are required fields |
| 4. Select an existing task and update | An existing task, new values for estimate, assignee | Success: task fields are updated |
| 5. | An existing task, empty values for description, status | Failure: these are required fields |
| 6. Select a task and click to delete | An existing task | Success: task is deleted |

## Functional and Acceptance Testing Tasks

1. We need to work with the customer to define detailed acceptance tests that will include all the details not provided in the high-level tests. (This includes defining error messages, verifying look and feel of the input form and display list, defining typical and potentially tricky user scenarios. Because this is an internal application that will be used mainly by trained users, we don't need to worry about this as much as we would for an external product.) We estimate 1 hour.

2. It should be pretty easy to define and load this test data. We just need data for some existing stories and some tasks. Neither has very many fields. We estimate 0.5 hour.

3. We think we're probably going to need to code three automation modules for this: addTask, updateTask, and deleteTask. They're all pretty similar, so we figure an hour to spike the automation and an hour to code and test each. We estimate 4 hours.

- - - - - - - - - - - - - - - - - - - - - - - - - - - - - - - - - - - - - - - - - - - -

4. Setting up and executing tests will be fast, but we'll probably run them at least three times. We estimate 0.5 hour.
5. Same with evaluation and reporting results. We estimate 0.5 hour.

Here are our tasks and estimates:

Tasks and estimates for Exercise 7

| Task | Estimate (hours) |
|---|---|
| Define task story details | 1.0 |
| Define and create test data | 0.5 |
| Code and test addTask module | 2.0 |
| Code and test updateTask module | 1.0 |
| Code and test deleteTask module | 1.0 |
| Test execution | 0.5 |
| Reporting | 0.5 |
| Total | 6.5 |

## Exercise 8 (Chapter 14)

Indicate whether each of the following pertains more to internal quality or external quality:

Answers for Exercise 8

| Item | Type |
|---|---|
| Number of defects in the code | Internal |
| Number of overtime hours spent | Internal |
| Customer satisfaction | External |
| Development team morale | Internal |
| System reliability | External |
| Code readability | Internal |

## Exercise 9 (Chapter 15)

**Story:** The user can display and update information about an iteration. The iteration display shows the iteration start and end dates, the projected team velocity, all stories assigned to the iteration, and the total of the estimates for those stories. For completed iterations, it displays the sum of the actuals for each story and the actual team velocity for that iteration. The user can update the estimated velocity, start date, and end date.

1. For the above story from the XTrack application, identify which of the following details you would a) assume responsibility for defining yourself, b) ask for confirmation on, or c) ask open-ended questions about:

### Answer

Answers for Exercise 9

| Item | Type |
|------|------|
| Constraints on the allowable inputs for start and end dates during update. | b |
| What should happen when invalid data is input during update. | b |
| The units in which to display the velocity, estimates, and actual totals. | c |
| What determines that an iteration is complete. | b |
| Which information will be included about each story. | c |
| What happens when a story is moved from one iteration to another. | a |
| Can completed stories in a completed iteration be moved to another iteration? | a |
| The order in which the stories appear. | b |

2. For the above story, identify some additional details based on

   ✧ The happy path
   ✧ The sad path
   ✧ The bad path

## Answer

### Happy Path

1. Add an iteration with start and end dates and projected team velocity. Select stories and associate them with the iteration. Verify the total estimates.
2. Select an iteration and update both dates and the velocity.
3. Update some stories in the iteration to mark them completed.
4. Update all the stories in the iteration as completed. Verify the total actual time for the iteration.
5. Display the iteration in read-only mode.

Data conditions for happy path:

1. Remove a completed story from the iteration. Verify that total actual time and total actual velocity are updated accordingly.

### Sad Path

1. Add or update an iteration, enter alpha characters in the velocity field.
2. Add or update an iteration, enter alpha characters in the date fields.

### Bad Path

1. User clicks to save an iteration with no data in any fields.
2. User adds an iteration, clicks the Back button in the browser, updates the data to add another iteration, clicks to save again.
3. User who is not authorized to add or update iterations enters the URL for the update or add page.
4. User enters every special character on the keyboard into the data fields.

External events for bad path:

1. Maximum database connections exceeded.
2. Server goes down in the middle of an add or update.

**3.** Based on risk, where would you focus the most attention in designing tests for the following first four XTrack stories?

> **Story 1:** Be able to create, read, and update a story via a Web interface. The data fields in a story are number, name, author, description, estimate, iteration, timestamps, and state

> **Story 2:** The user can provide an estimate for how long it will take to implement a story, prioritize the story, and assign the story to an iteration.

> **Story 3:** The user can create, update, display, and delete a task. A task has a name, a description, assignee, estimate, actual time spent, state, and created/updated timestamps.

> **Story 4:** The user can display and update information about an iteration. The iteration display shows the iteration start and end dates, the projected team velocity, all stories assigned to the iteration, and the total of the estimates for those stories. For completed iterations, it displays the sum of the actuals for each story and the actual team velocity for that iteration. The user can update the estimated velocity, start date, and end date.

## Answer

We've found it best to concentrate on two types of outcomes when identifying the areas of risk: the worst possible outcomes and the most likely (though not necessarily worst) bad outcomes. To do this, we need to look at the system's intended purpose, how it could fail, and the impact of these failures.

The XTrack system has three major purposes:

1. Allow the team to track stories, tasks, and estimates while working on them
2. Provide snapshots of the project's status to management and other interested parties
3. Capture a record of what happened for retrospectives at the ends of iterations, releases, and projects and for "tuning" the XP practices

In our opinion, the first purpose is the least important, because an Extreme team will have simpler mechanisms that work as well or better (story cards, standup meetings, pairing, and so on). Likewise, the second purpose can be handled by judicious involvement of the interested parties in standup meetings, by providing periodic briefings, or by writing status reports. If the XTrack system fails to fulfill the third purpose, however, retrospectives will have to rely only on team members' memories, which will become increasingly unreliable about the earlier iterations as the project continues.

So we think the worst thing that could happen would be for the system to fail to provide historical data for retrospectives and tuning. This leads us to focus on the system's capability to retain whatever data is entered and to reproduce it accurately when needed. Although each of the first four stories involves this kind of function, story 4 addresses data entered in multiple places: the story description, title, and so on from story 1, the estimates and iteration assignment from story 2, and the actuals from story 3.

In terms of the most likely (though not necessarily the most serious) failures, our experience with this type of system is that problems usually arise when validating input fields. Some of these won't matter: who cares if the title contains a misspelling, for instance?

On the other hand, consider the state field in story 1. If this field determines whether the story displays or is counted into the totals of an iteration, then not validating an incorrectly typed state could cause the iteration totals and velocity calculations in story 4 to be wrong. Likewise, failure to validate a numeric input for an estimate or actual (a negative number, for example) could have the same result.

Based on this, we would focus our attention on designing tests for story 4: validating that all the stories assigned to an iteration show up on the display, that the totals are correct for estimates and actuals, and that velocity calculations are correct. Examples might be sad and bad path scenarios where stories are assigned to iterations with bad state values or negative estimates or are moved back and forth from one iteration to another.

## Exercise 10 (Chapter 16)

> **Story:** User can create, update, display, and delete a task. A task has a name (required), a description, assignee, estimate, actual time spent, state (required), and created/updated timestamps (automatically generated).

For the above XTrack story, assume we've defined the following high-level acceptance tests in release planning (we know this isn't complete; it's just enough to illustrate the ideas):

Tests for Exercise 10

| Action | Data | Expected Result |
|---|---|---|
| 1. Add a new task | Valid values for the task fields | Success: the task is added |
| 2. Add a new task | Invalid values for task fields | Failure: invalid fields message |

Also assume we've come up with the following additional information while planning and beginning the first iteration:

- ✧ Users must be logged in to add, update, or delete tasks.
- ✧ The name and description fields are required.
- ✧ State has a fixed list of values: Started, Not Started, Complete.
- ✧ Estimate and actual time spent must be numeric.

Write these as an executable test in the style illustrated in the two examples in this chapter.

### Answer

```
// got to be logged in

login("bob","bobspassword")
```

```
// Add a new task with valid values - it succeeds

assertTrue( addTask( "User Gui",            // name
                     "Create GUI",          // description
                     "Bob",                 // assignee
                     "2",                   // estimate
                     "3",                   // actual
                     "Not Started" ) );     // state



assertTrue( addTask( "User Gui",                 // name
                     "Create GUI",               // description
                     "Bob",                  // assignee
                     "2",                 // estimate
                     "3",                 // actual
                     "Started" ) );              // state

assertTrue( addTask( "User Gui",                 // name
                     "Create GUI",               // description
                     "Bob",                  // assignee
                     "2",                // estimate
                     "3",                // actual
                     "Complete" ) );             // state

// add task with invalid values - it fails

assertFalse( addTask( "",                    // name - missing
                      "",                    // description - missing
                      "Bob",                 // assignee
                      "long time",    // estimate -not numeric
                      "longer",       // actual - not numeric
                      "Ohio" ) );       // state - invalid
```

addTask() adds a task using the specified values and returns true if the task was added and false if it failed.

# Exercise 11 (Chapter 17)

> **Story 4:** The user can display and update information about an iteration. The iteration display shows the iteration start and end dates, the stories assigned to the iteration, and the estimated velocity for the iteration. The user can update the estimated velocity, start date, and end date.

For the above XTrack story:

1. Write an executable test, including the class and method declarations, as illustrated in this chapter. Include at least one test case in each method, but don't worry about completeness. The point is the organization, not the details.

2. Pretend your customer can't stand the executable format. Create or mock up a spreadsheet for him that corresponds to the executable test in question 1.

## Answer

1. The class name is `IterationStoryTest`, and it has two methods: `testDisplay()` and `testUpdate()`:

```
public class IterationStoryTest {

    public void testDisplay() {

        login("bob","bobspassword")

        assertTrue( displayIteration( "1") );
        assertFalse( displayIteration( "-1") );
    }

    public void testUpdate() {

        login("bob","bobspassword");

        assertTrue( UpdateIteration( "10",
                                     "20041201",
```

```
                                              "20041215") );
            assertFalse( UpdateIteration( "non-numeric",
                                          "bad date",
                                          "bad date" ) );
        }
    }
```

2. The spreadsheet would be `IterationTestStory.xls`, and it would have two workbooks:

**testDisplay**

| | Outcome | Iteration |
|---|---|---|
| | success | 1 |
| | fail | -1 |

**testUpdate**

| Outcome | Estimated Velocity | Start Date | End Date |
|---|---|---|---|
| success | 10 | 20021201 | 20021215 |
| fail | non-numeric | bad date | bad date |

## Exercise 12 (Chapter 18)

1. Identify the assumptions about the initial system state in the following tests for XTrack story 1:

```
public class IterationStoryTest {

    public void testDisplay() {

        assertTrue( displayIteration("1") );
        assertFalse( displayIteration("2") );
    }

    public void testUpdate() {

        login("bob,""bobspassword");
```

```
        assertTrue( UpdateIteration( "1,"
                                     "10,"
                                     "20041201,"
                                     "20041215") );
        assertFalse( UpdateIteration( "2,"
                                      "non-numeric,"
                                      "bad date,"
                                      "bad date" ) );

    }
}
```

2. Are these tests rerunnable without resetting the system?

## Answer

1. The display test assumes iteration 1 has been defined and iteration 2 has not. The update test also assumes iteration 1 has been defined.

2. Yes, because executing the tests has no effect on the truth of the assumptions.

## *Exercise 13 (Chapter 19)*

1. What about manual tests?

## Answer

1. No manual tests.

## *Exercise 14 (Chapter 20)*

Assume that the following four stories are in the first iteration of the XTrack project:

**Story 1:** User can create, update, and display a story.

**Story 2:** User can estimate a story and assign it to an iteration.

**Story 3:** User can create, update, and display a task.

**Story 4:** User can update and display information about an iteration.

1. How many acceptance tests should be run manually?

2. What about the tests you can't automate?

### Answer

1. None.

2. Don't run them.

## Exercise 15 (Chapter 21)

Given the following two Xtrack stories, identify as many modules and their parameters as you can:

**Story 1:** A user can create, read, and update a story via a Web interface. The data fields in a story are number, name, author, description, estimate, iteration, timestamps, and state.

**Story 2:** The user can provide an estimate for how long it will take to implement a story, prioritize the story, and assign the story to an iteration.

## Answer

```
createStory(number,name,author,description,
            estimate,iteration,state)
```

Attempts to create a story with the specified fields. If they're valid and the story is successfully added, it returns `true`; otherwise, `false`.

```
displayStory(number)
```

Returns a display of the specified story.

```
updateStory(number,name,author,description,
            estimate,iteration,state)
```

Attempts to update the story specified by `number` with the specified values. If they're valid and the specified story exists and is updated successfully, it returns `true`; otherwise, `false`.

```
prioritizeStory(number,priority)
```

Attempts to update the story specified by `number` with the specified priority. If the story exists, the specified priority is valid, and the story is successfully updated, it returns `true`; otherwise, `false`.

```
assignIteration(storyNumber,iterationNumber)
```

Attempts to update the story specified by `storyNumber` to the specified iteration. If the specified story exists, the specified iteration number is valid, and the story is successfully updated, it returns `true`; otherwise, `false`.

## Exercise 16 (Chapter 22)

1. Assume you've written the following test for creating tasks in the XTrack system:

```
public class TaskStoryTest {
    public void testCreate() {
        login("bob,""bobspassword");
        assertTrue( addTask( "User Gui,"
                             "Create GUI,"
                             "Bob,"
                             "2,"
```

```
                                                    "3,"
                                                    "Not Started" ) );
              }
          }
```

Indicate the modifications required to TaskStoryTest to make it run.

2. Assume you've already gotten LoginStoryTest and UserIdStoryTest to run, as illustrated in this chapter. Assume that the code in the XTrack system that creates tasks works as follows:

> *An* XTrackTask *class in the XTrack system represents a task. An* XTrack-Task *has an* add *method that sets the task's name, description, assignee, estimate, actual, and status fields to values specified as parameters. If the specified values are all valid, it then attempts to add the task to the database. If the addition is successful, it returns* true; *otherwise, if the add fails or if any of the specified values is invalid, it returns* false.

Show what you'd have to add to XTrackTest to call this code and make the TaskStoryTest run.

## Answer

### 1. TaskStoryTest.java

```java
public class TaskStoryTest extends XTrackTest {
    public TaskStoryTest(String name) { super(name); }
    public void testCreate() {
        login("bob","bobspassword");
        assertTrue( addTask( "User Gui",
                             "Create GUI",
                             "Bob",
                             "2",
                             "3",
                             "Not Started" ) );
    }
}
```

### 2. XTrackTest.java

```java
import junit.framework.*;
```

```java
import xtrack.*;

public class XTrackTest extends TestCase {
    public XTrackTest(String name) { super(name); }

    public void assertFalse( boolean b) {
        assertTrue(!b);
    }

    public boolean login( String id,String psw) {
        XTrackSession session = new XTrackSession();
        return session.login(id,psw);
    }

    public boolean createUserId( String id, String psw,
                                 String email) {
        XTrackUser user = new XTrackUser();
        return user.create(id,psw,email);
    }

    public boolean deleteUserId( String id) {
        XTrackUser user = new XTrackUser(id);
        return user.delete();
    }

    public boolean createTask( String name,
                               String description,
                               String assignee,
                               String estimate,
                               String actual,
                               String state) {
        XTrackTask task = new XTrackTask();
        return task.add(name,
                        description,
                        assignee,
                        estimate,
                        actual,
                        state);
    }

}
```

## Exercise 17 (Chapter 23)

Assume you've made the changes to XTrackTest and created the additional classes, as illustrated in this chapter. Assume you're now going to add a third interface that will run the tests through a GUI tool called GUITAR.

1. Indicate the changes required to LoginStoryTest (warning: this is a trick question):

```
public class LoginStoryTest {
    public void testLogin() {
        assertTrue( login("bob,""bobspassword") );
        assertTrue( login("BOB,""bobspassword") );
        assertFalse(login("bob,"""));
        assertFalse(login("bob,""BOBSPASSWORD") );
    }
}
```

2. Indicate the changes required to the setInterface method of XTrackTest:

```
public void setTestInterface(String interfaceType){
            if (interfaceType.equals("direct"))
            testInf - new TrackDirectInterface();
            else if (interfaceType.equals("webart"))
                testInf = new TrackWebARTInterface();
            else
                fail("Undefined interface " +
                 interfaceType);
        }
```

3. Are other changes required to XTrackTest or any other existing class?

## Answers

1. No changes are required to LoginStoryTest or any other executable test.

2. You need to test for guitar and create the appropriate interface:

```
public void setTestInterface(String interfaceType){
            if (interfaceType.equals("direct"))
            testInf = new TrackDirectInterface();
            else if (interfaceType.equals("webart"))
                testInf = new TrackWebARTInterface();
        else if (interfaceType.equals("guitar"))
```

```
                    testInf = new TrackGUITARInterface();

                else
                    fail("Undefined interface " +
                        interfaceType);
    }
```

**3.** No other changes are required to any existing class.

## Exercise 18 (Chapter 24)

**1.** Assume you've done everything on the Java side to make the following executable test run through WebART:

```
public class TaskStoryTest {
    public void testCreate() {
        login("bob,""bobspassword");
        assertTrue( addTask( "User Gui,"
                             "Create GUI,"
                             "Bob,"
                             "2,"
                             "3,"
                             "Not Started" ) );
    }
}
```

Indicate the changes that would be necessary to the WebART XTRACKIF.

### Answer

Add an include statement for the addTask subscript:

```
!script xtrackif
!param cfile = ""
!param gTestCaseFile(Test Cases)="xtrackif.testcase"
!include zdutil
!include login
!include createuserid
!include deleteuserid
!include addtask
!include jwebart
! {
  init();
  getTestCase();
  getTestCaseName(gtTestCase1);
```

```
    jWebartInterface();
    log ( script, gOutCome);
    }
!end
```

2. Assume you obtained the following statements by capturing the process of adding a task to XTrack manually:

```
>0>$get(pPage,
        "http://${zzorghostzz}/.../createtask.htm")[];

    form.pPage.0.name.tb.0[0] = "User Gui";
    form.pPage.0.description.tb.1[0] = "Create GUI";
    form.pPage.0.assignee.tb.2[0] = "Bob";
    form.pPage.0.estimate.tb.3[0] = "2";
    form.pPage.0.actual.tb.4[0] = "3";
    form.pPage.0.status.tb.5[0] = "Not Started";
    form.pPage.0.Submit.su.0[0] = "Create";
    >7>$submit(pPage,pPage,0)[];
```

Using login in this chapter as a model, write the complete addTask subscript module.

## Answer

```
!subscript addTask *pOut pIn tData vLevel *outCome
                    vCrit
!declare zzName zzDesc zzAssignee zzEst zzActual
!declare zzStatus pPage
!declare myOutCome
! {
    trace (login, interface, pOut, pIn, tData, vLevel);
    myOutCome=UnKn;

    getField(zzName,name,tData);
    getField(zzDesc,desc,tData);
    getField(zzAssignee,assignee,tData);
    getField(zzEst,est,tData);
    getField(zzActual,actual,tData);
    getField(zzStatus,status,tData);
    getField(zzDesc,desc,tData);

    >0>$get(pPage,
        "http://${zzorghostzz}/.../createtask.htm")[];

    form.pPage.0.name.tb.0[0] = "zzName";
```

```
form.pPage.0.description.tb.1[0] = "zzDesc";
form.pPage.0.assignee.tb.2[0] = "zzAsignee";
form.pPage.0.estimate.tb.3[0] = "zzEst";
form.pPage.0.actual.tb.4[0] = "zzActual";
form.pPage.0.status.tb.5[0] = "zzStatus";
form.pPage.0.Submit.su.0[0] = "Create";
>7>$submit(pOut,pPage,0)[];


doValidation(outCome, myOutCome, tData, vCrit,
             vLevel, pOut);
}
!end
```

## Exercise 19 (Chapter 25)

Run the executable acceptance tests for the LoginStoryTest and UserId-
StoryTests for the XTrack system, which you can download from www.
xptester.org/framework/examples/xtrack/downld.htm. What defects do the
test results show?

### Answer

No defects should appear. The test results should look like this:

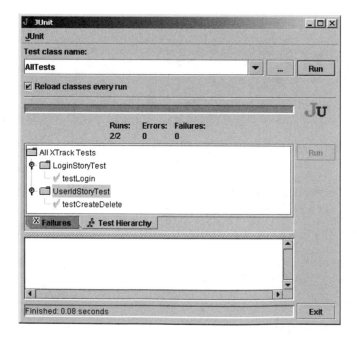

## Exercise 20 (Chapter 26)

Here's a retrospective from the first release of XTrack. Which two or three items would you choose to work on for the next iteration?

**Stop**

- Having uneven distribution of task ownership
- Starting the iteration with incomplete requirements

**Start**

- Pairing more, both to write production code and to test
- Writing the acceptance tests in advance of the iteration
- Having a more regular schedule
- Communicating constantly, have regular standups
- More knowledge sharing

**Continue**

- Remote pairing
- Estimating fairly accurately
- Being flexible about changing the requirements when we see things that work better

### Answer

This is totally subjective, of course. Our top three would be to stop having uneven distribution of task ownership (this could be reworded as start allocating tasks more evenly), pair more, and have regular standups. We're in two locations, which makes pairing and communication a special challenge.

## Exercise 21 (Chapter 27)

Given the following three items we chose to work on in Exercise 20 and the fact that our two-person team is split in two distant locations, how might you try to accomplish these?

- ✧ Stop having uneven distribution of task ownership
- ✧ Pair more often
- ✧ Have regular standups

## Answer

Please contact us with your answers! We'd like to know! This question has no specific answer, but here are some ideas:

- ✧ Research software packages that could be used for pairing. We've been using NetMeeting, but it's a bit slow, and the audio slows it even more.
- ✧ Set a time to meet via an instant message chat each day.
- ✧ Have the team member whose task ownership load has been lighter take on tasks she's not knowledgeable about, and let the other team member coach her, so she gets more expertise. This will slow the team down in the short run but speed it up in the long run.
- ✧ Be more diligent in setting and keeping appointments for remote pairing.

## Exercise 22 (Chapter 28)

What are some ways the XTrack application could be redesigned for greater testability?

## Answer

This is really hard to answer, since as a reader of this book, you don't know the underlying architecture of XTrack. If you tried any of the exercises, though, you may have a feel for what would make it easier to test. If so, we want to hear from you!

One obvious feature that would help with the automated tests is a `delete` function for users, stories, and so on. We have `add`, `update`, and `display`, but no `delete`. The tests that test the `add` functions can't clean up after themselves; we need a separate mechanism for putting the data back into the state in which we started.

XTrack is written in C, and it's perfectly possible to automate the tests below the user interface, if desired. We did Exercise 19 through the user interface, because we felt the UI was fairly stable and our test framework enables us to automate quickly.

# Bibliography

Calvin Austin and Monica Pawlan, *Advanced Programming for the Java Platform*, Addison-Wesley, 2000; ISBN 0201715015.

Joseph Jean Baptiste Laurent Arban, *Complete Conservatory Method for Cornet*, Carl Fischer, 1982 (1894); ISBN 0825803853.

Kent Beck, *Extreme Programming Explained: Embrace Change*, Addison-Wesley, 2000; ISBN 0201616416.

Kent Beck and Martin Fowler, *Planning Extreme Programming*, Addison-Wesley, 2001; ISBN 0201710919.

Kent Beck and Erich Gamma, "Test Infected: Programmers Love Writing Tests," in *Java Report*, July 1998, vol. 3, no. 7, pp. 37–50.

Kent Beck and Erich Gamma, *JUnit Cookbook*, http://junit.sourceforge.net/doc/cookbook/cookbook.htm.

Mary Campione and Kathy Walrath, *The Java™ Tutorial: Object-Oriented Programming for the Internet*, Addison-Wesley, 1996; ISBN 0201634546.

Canoo Engineering AG, "Canoo Web Test White Paper," http://webtest.canoo.com/webtest/manual/whitepaper.html.

Mike Clark, "JUnit Primer," www.clarkware.com/articles/JUnitPrimer.html.

Alistair Cockburn, *Agile Software Development,* Addison-Wesley, 2002; ISBN 0201699699.

Alistair Cockburn, "Characterizing People as Non-Linear, First-Order Components in Software Development," http://alistair.cockburn.us.

Martin Fowler, *Refactoring: Improving the Design of Existing Code,* Addison-Wesley, 1999; ISBN 0201485672.

Garth House, *More Litanies for All Occasions,* Judson Press, 2000; ISBN 0817013547.

Marilyn G. House, *Ice Skating Fundamentals,* Kendall/Hunt, 1996; ISBN 0787209945.

Verl Lee House, "The Interaction of Three Mutants Affecting the Vein Pattern in *Drosophila melanogaster,*" Ph.D. diss., University of California at Berkeley, 1950.

Ron Jeffries, Ann Anderson, and Chet Hendrickson, *Extreme Programming Installed,* Addison-Wesley, 2001; ISBN 0201708426.

Andrew Hunt and David Thomas, *The Practical Programmer: From Journeyman to Master,* Addison-Wesley, 2000; ISBN 020161622X.

Cem Kaner, James Bach, and Bret Pettichord, *Lessons Learned in Software Testing,* John Wiley & Sons, 2001; ISBN 0471081124.

Cem Kaner, Hung Quoc Nguyen, and Jack Falk, *Testing Computer Software,* 2nd ed., John Wiley & Sons, 1999; ISBN 0471358460.

Natraj Kini and Steve Collins, "Steering the Car: Lessons Learned from an Outsourced XP Project," paper presented at 2001 XP Universe, Raleigh, NC, July 2001, www.xpuniverse.com/2001/pdfs/XPU03.pdf.

James W. Newkirk and Robert C. Martin, *Extreme Programming in Practice,* Addison-Wesley, 2001; ISBN 0201709376.

Gregory Schalliol, "Challenges for Analysts on a Large XP Project," paper presented at 2001 XP Universe, Raleigh, NC, July 2001, www.xpuniverse.com/2001/pdfs/EP205.pdf.

Steven Splaine, Stefan P. Jaskiel, and Alberto Savoia, *The Web Testing Handbook,* Software Quality Engineering, 2001; ISBN 0970436300.

Giancarlo Succi, Michele Marchesi, James Donovan Wells, and Laurie Williams, *Extreme Programming Perspectives,* Addison-Wesley, 2003; ISBN 0201770059.

James Thurber, *The Wonderful O,* Simon and Schuster, 1957.

William Wake, *Extreme Programming Explored,* Addison-Wesley, 2002; ISBN 0201733978.

Don Wells, *Extreme Programming: A Gentle Introduction,* http://www.extremeprogramming.org.

# Afterword

Well, in spite of all the obstacles I set in their path, Lisa and Tip have put together an excellent book on testing in the Extreme Programming context, and I'm happy to recommend it.

If you're a tester, the book will help you understand your role on an XP project. That role is different from what you're used to: it will take you closer to the "front" of the project and will give you responsibility for things you may not have done before, including working closely with the customer and participating in automating the tests.

If you're setting up an XP project, this book will help you decide whether to have dedicated testers—and how to apply them if you do. Equally important, even if you don't add the testing role to your team, the things Lisa and Tip describe here are things your team needs to understand and do.

If, for some reason, you've started with the afterword instead of working your way through the book, you now know what you need to know: buy this book.

If you've completed reading the book, I'd invite you to take away two key messages:

First: Test. Test with automated tests. Test relentlessly, test automatically, test without fail. No matter what else, test. And don't forget automated tests!

Second: How to test. The book is filled with good advice on how to figure out what to test, how to test it, how to interact with the rest of the team and with management, how to document your tests, and every other important aspect of XP testing from the customer viewpoint.

Congratulations, Lisa and Tip. You've survived all my advice and, in spite of it, have produced a valuable contribution to the XP and agile literature. Well done!

Ron Jeffries
Pinckney, Michigan
June 2002
www.Xprogramming.com
www.ObjectMentor.com

# Index

Acceptance tests, *continued*
  unit tests versus, 19–21
  in user stories, 43–44
  version control for, 119–120
  writing, 100, 108–117, 230
Accessories, 216–218
Accountants, 18, 38
addTask() method, 273
addTask module, 266–267,
    282–283
Agile-testing mailing list, 246–247
Air Force (United States), 27
Algorithms, 56, 106
AllTests class, 154–155
AllTests.java, 154–155
Application
  program interfaces (APIs), 84
  test classes, 148–149, 160–166
Arguments, passing, 165
assertEquals() method, 112
assertFalse() method, 110–111,
    148–150, 163
assertTrue() method, 110–113, 144,
    148[150
Assumptions
  examples of, 49–54
  identifying, 43–45, 47–54,
    251–258, 262
  iteration planning and, 80
  XTrack application and, 53–54
Automation
  acceptance tests and, 64, 67, 84,
    90–91, 133–137, 194, 208
  accessories and, 216–218
  baseline comparison method and,
    142–144, 145
  basic description of, 133–137,
    139–145
  capture/replay, 140, 170

data-independent tests and,
    142–143
design spike, 86
direct-call testing and, 166–167
evolving tools and, 208
legacy systems and, 203
mastering, 133–134
metrics and, 219–220
modular tests and, 141–142
self-verifying tests and, 143–144
test infrastructure and, 86
time estimates for, 44
tools for, 211–212
unit testing and, 7, 9, 18, 245

## B

Back button, 101
Bad path, 101–102, 104–108,
    268–270
Baseline comparison method,
    142–144, 145, 170
Beck, Kent
  on the comparison between XP and
    driving a car, 20
  core values of XP and, 4
  on feedback, 26
  on internal and external quality, 95
  introduction of XP by, 3
  on the Programmer's Bill of Rights,
    31
  on simplicity, 25
  on teamwork, 23
  on testers, 43
Bells, ringing, 217
Best practices, 30, 222
"Big-bang" integration, 120
Bill of Rights
  for programmers, 31
  for testers, 31–32, 78–79

Blended practices, 229–232
BoldTech Systems, 159, 166–167
Bootstrap time, 85
Brainstorming, 182–183, 194, 244
Bug(s). *See also* Defects
  testing resources wasted on, 7
  tracking systems, 182, 209
Build scripts, 84
Business
  experts, 241–245
  logic, 194
  problems, solving, 49–54, 252,
    257–260
"Button push" action, 166

## C

Canoo Web Test, 208
Capture/replay-style automation,
  140, 170. *See also* Automation
CASE tools, 209
Celebrating success, 185, 217
CGI (Common Gateway Interface)
  scripts, 159. *See also* Scripts
"Challenges for Analysts on a Large
  XP Project" (Schalliol), 235,
  236, 237–238
Checks and balances, 18–19
Clark, Mike, 246–247
Classes
  application test-interface, 148–149,
    160–166
  refactoring, 162–163
  tool-specific, 164–166
Coaches
  provision of snacks by, 222
  support of testers by, 228
  tester and, similarities between, 20
Cockburn, Alistair, 23
Code. *See also* Scripts (listed by name)

collective ownership of, 6, 135,
  222
compiling, 90, 148, 149, 151
standards, basic description of, 5
Collins, Steve, 42
Communication. *See also* Feedback;
  Meetings
  basic description of, 4–5, 24–25
  with customers, 4–5, 24–25,
    100–101
  grade cards and, 186
  iteration planning and, 80–81
  as one of the four core values of XP,
    4–5
  with programmers, 100–101
  test infrastructure and, 88
  tools, educating the customer
    about, 181
Compilers, 90, 148, 149, 151
Concurrent users
  acceptance tests and, 62, 67
  hidden assumptions and, 52
  number of, 52, 96
  quality assurance and, 52, 96
Constructors, 148, 152, 163
Continuous integration, 5, 7
Contractors, 12–13, 18. *See also*
  Remodeling project
Core values. *See also* Communication
  basic description of, 4, 23–28
  courage, 4, 6, 25, 27–28, 30–31
  feedback, 4–5, 26–29, 219–220
    242, 244
  simplicity, 4–6, 25, 186
Coupling, between tests, 128–129
Courage
  basic description of, 6, 27–28
  embracing simplicity and, 25
  fears held by testers and, 30–31

Courage, *continued*
  as one of the four core values of XP, 4
  tester role and, 30
Crashes, 37, 96
create() method, 129, 153
createUserID() method, 127–128, 153, 160, 163, 165
createUserID module, 170–171, 173–175
Creativity, in writing tests, 105
Customer(s)
  acceptance tests run by, 178–179, 246
  as business experts, 241–245
  communication with, 4–5, 24–25, 100–101
  defect reports and, 209
  educating, 180–181, 183
  expectations of, grade cards and, 186
  hidden assumptions and, 47–54
  interviews with, 100–101
  iteration planning and, 78
  non-critical tests and, 104–105
  "picking the brains" of, 100
  quality assurance and, 94–95
  role of, in XP, 29–30, 36
  test environments and, 221
  turning software over to, 197–198
  weekly meetings with, 237
  working with, overview of, 237–238
Cyclomatic Complexity Number, 220

**D**

Databases, 56–59, 89, 101, 159
  system state and, 126
  testability and, 204–205

Data-independent tests, 142–143
Deadlocks, 36
Debugging tests, time estimates for, 44
Defects. *See also* Bugs
  acceptance criteria and, 181
  code missed by direct calls and, 158
  educating the customer about, 180
  issues that look like, but are outside the scope of iterations, 181
  logging, 196
  maintenance and, 196
  management of, 181–182
  reporting, 86, 179–180, 209
  tracking systems, 182, 209
delete() method, 129, 153
deleteTask module, 266–267
deleteUserID() method, 128, 153, 160, 163, 165
deleteUserID module, 171–175
Development
  infrastructure, iteration planning and, 79
  separating acceptance testing from, 87–91
  test phases after, 227–228
  waterfall, 106, 230, 241
Direct call(s)
  code missed by, 157, 158
  interface, refactoring, 161–162
  test automation, 166–167
Discipline, importance of, 225
Documentation
  grade cards and, 186
  quality assurance and, 38
  requirements, 238–239, 242
  retrospectives and, 186, 190
  test plans, 238–239, 243–244

Gregory, Janet, 220
gTestCaseFile parameter, 171
GUI (graphical user interface), 101,
    151–152, 159, 168, 204, 281.
    *See also* User interface
GUITAR tool, 168, 281–282

## H

Hacker attacks, planning for, 102
Handoffs, 186
Happy path, 101, 103, 107–108,
    268, 269
HTML (HyperText Markup
    Language), 166
HTTP (HyperText Transfer
    Protocol), 65, 159–160, 171,
    173, 208, 212
HTTPUnit, 208, 212

## I

IDE (integrated development
    environment), 79, 188
import jWebART.*; statement,
    165
import xtrack.*; statement, 162, 163
Individuals, characteristics of,
    importance of, 23–24
init() method, 171
Integration tests
    lack of adequate, 8
    road-trip metaphor and, 40
    using short, 193
invoke() method, 165
Iteration(s). *See also* Iteration
    planning
    display/update information about,
        107
    feedback and, 26–27
    grade cards and, 186

retrospectives at the end of,
    185–186
testing at the end of, 179
Iteration planning. *See also* Planning
    acceptance tests and, 62, 93, 230
    basic description of, 77–81
    development infrastructure and, 79
    educating the customer about, 180
    enhancing communication and,
        80–81
    identifying tasks during, 79–80
    for large or multi-location projects,
        239–240
    release planning and, 78
    road-trip metaphor and, 40
    role of testers in, 78–81
    test infrastructure and, 80, 83–92
IterationTestStory.xsl, 275–276

## J

Java. *See also* .java scripts
    acceptance tests and, 110–113,
        120–121, 148–152
    advantages of, 110
    compilers, 148, 149, 151
    interpreter, 151
    Native Interface (JNI), 157
    packages, 164, 170, 171
    release planning and, 42
    server pages (JSP), 166, 203
    testability and, 293
    use of, for examples in this book,
        110
JavaNCSS, 220
JavaScript
    testability and, 293
    WebArt and, 160
.java scripts
    AllTests.java, 154–155

search() method, 112, 143
search module, 142–143
Search screens, 102–104
Self-verifying tests, 143–144
Servers, 96, 159, 246
setInterface() method, 168, 281
setTestInterface() method, 163,
    165–166
Shell scripts, 89
Simplicity, 4–6, 25, 186
Sims, John, 198
"Smoke" testing, 244
Source code control, 79, 189, 204,
    207, 209, 213, 221, 222, 223
Spreadsheets, 121–123, 275–276
    for metrics, 219–220
    test documentation, 238–239
Standup meetings
    grade cards and, 186
    notes, 218, 219
    restricting the time taken up by,
        218
    retrospectives and, 186, 188, 190,
        191
"Steering the Car: Lessons Learned
    from an Outsourced XP Project"
    (Collins and Kini), 42
Stories. See also Story cards
    acceptance tests and, 43–44, 55,
        56–59, 61–69, 113–115
    assumptions in, identifying, 43–44,
        48
    basic description of, 41–45
    creation of, 41–45, 276–277
    release planning and, 73
    road-trip metaphor and, 40
    selection of, educating the
        customer about, 180
Story cards, 179–180, 209

Struts framework, 166, 203
Submit button, 101, 166
SubmitRequest script, 204–205
Success
    celebrating, 217
    of XP testers, supporting, 228–229
Sustainable pace, importance of, 6
Syntax rules, 110
System state
    assumptions about, identifying,
        130, 275–276
    establishing, 125–126
    left unchanged by tests, 126–128

## T

Tasks
    categories of, 79–80
    creating, 116–117, 259–267,
        272–273, 278–280
    deleting, 116–117, 121, 259–267,
        272–273
    estimating, 80–81, 83–92
    identifying, 79–80
    retrospectives and, 190, 191
    updating, 116–117, 121, 259–267,
        272–273
TaskStoryTest class, 122, 156
TaskStoryTest.java, 279
TaskStoryTest.xsl, 122
tdata, 172, 173
Teams
    acceptance tests and, 99
    celebrating success and, 185
    defect management and, 182
    insuring that XP practices are really
        implemented by, 9
    iteration planning and, 78, 80–81
    organization of office space for,
        215–216

Test tools
  basic description of, 169–176,
      208–209
  cost of, 211
  evaluation copies of, 210–211
  evolving, 208
  experimenting with, 211–213
  implementing, 207–213
  interfacing to, 159–160
  off-the-shelf, 210–211
  selecting, 207–213
testUpdate worksheet, 122
Timestamps, 116, 270
Tools. *See also* Test tools
building, 208, 213
  implementing, 207–208, 211
  selecting, 207–208, 210–211, 213
Transactions, concurrent, support for,
      36. *See also* Concurrent users

**U**

UML (Unified Modeling Language),
      218
Unit tests
  acceptance tests and, 19–21, 55–56
  advantages of, 244–245
  automation of, 7, 9, 18, 245
  check and balances and, 18–19
  creation of, before generating code,
      6
  effective, 245
  feedback and, 5, 26
  grade cards and, 186
  lack of adequate, 8
  metrics and, 220
  poorly written, problems caused by,
      229
  quality assurance and, 96
  road-trip metaphor and, 40

rules for, 120
updateTask module, 266–267
Usability testing, 242
Usenet newsgroups, 210
User groups, 210
User IDs, 111, 113–115
  creating, 126–128
  deleting, 126–128
  executable tests and, 150, 152–153
  login module and, 172
UserIDStoryTest class, 154–156,
      279, 284
UserIDStoryTest.java, 152–153
User interface. *See also* GUI (graphical
      user interface)
  direct-call test automation and, 166
  testing, 135–136
  testing, below, 167
Users, concurrent
  acceptance tests and, 62, 67
  hidden assumptions and, 52
  number of, 52, 96
  quality assurance and, 52, 96
User stories. *See also* Story cards
  acceptance tests and, 43–44, 55,
      56–59, 61–69, 113–115
  assumptions in, identifying, 43–44,
      48
  basic description of, 41–45
  creation of, 41–45, 276–277
  release planning and, 73
  road-trip metaphor and, 40
  selection of, educating the
      customer about, 180

**V**

Validation
  criteria, 173–175
  direct-call test automation and, 166

# The XP Series

Kent Beck, Series Advisor

**The XP manifesto**

0201616416

**Planning projects with XP**

0201710919

**Insights and practical wisdom from leaders in the XP community**

0201770059

**Get XP up and running in your organization**

0201708426

**Best XP practices**

0201710404

**Is XP right for your organization?**

0201844575

**Learn from the chronicle of an XP project**

0201709376

**Best XP practices for developers**

0201733978

**Master the intricacies of XP testing**

0321113551

**Practical advice from experienced practitioners on how to get started with XP**

0201616408

**Apply XP to web projects**

0201794276

# Register
## Your Book

at www.awprofessional.com/register

You may be eligible to receive:

- Advance notice of forthcoming editions of the book
- Related book recommendations
- Chapter excerpts and supplements of forthcoming titles
- Information about special contests and promotions throughout the year
- Notices and reminders about author appearances, tradeshows, and online chats with special guests

## Contact us

If you are interested in writing a book or reviewing manuscripts prior to publication, please write to us at:

Editorial Department
Addison-Wesley Professional
75 Arlington Street, Suite 300
Boston, MA 02116 USA
Email: AWPro@aw.com

**Addison-Wesley**

Visit us on the Web: http://www.awprofessional.com

U.W.E.L. LEARNING RESOURCES